New Hampshire

Crosscurrents in Its Development

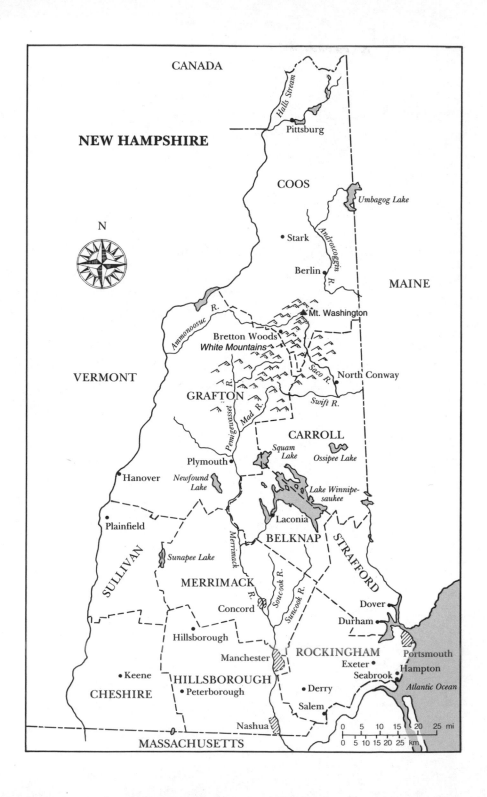

New Hampshire

Crosscurrents in Its Development

UPDATED EDITION

Nancy Coffey Heffernan

Ann Page Stecker

University Press of New England
Hanover and London

University Press of New England, Hanover, NH 03755
© 1986, 1996 by Nancy Coffey Heffernan
and Ann Page Stecker
First published 1986 by Tompson & Rutter Inc.,
Grantham, New Hampshire 03753-0297
Printed in the United States of America   5 4 3 2 1
CIP data appear at the end of the book

*The selection on page 84 from Donald Hall's "The Ox Cart Man" is reprinted
with permission from* Kicking the Leaves *(Harper & Row). © 1977 The
New Yorker Magazine, Inc.*

To Rick, Hardy, Jim,
Virginia, and Andrew

Contents

Illustrations

Acknowledgments

OUR BOOK relates the major trends and crosscurrents in New Hampshire as they emerge in published histories of particular times and events and in the biographies of important people in the state. Thus we wish particularly to acknowledge our debt to historians and biographers who have written detailed accounts of special aspects of the state's history which have made the writing of this book possible and to refer the reader to the notes at the end of this book for references to these specific works.

We are indebted to numerous people for guidance and advice. R. Stuart Wallace and Joan Esch at the New Hampshire Historical Society, Professors Jere Daniell and Richard Winters of Dartmouth College, Edgar Mead, Mildred Crockett Tunis, Dudley Dudley and Frederick Kocher have been most generous with their time and resources. The state library in Concord, Baker Library and the Hood Museum at Dartmouth College, Colby-Sawyer College Library and Tracy Memorial Library in New London, the Ezekiel W. Dimond Library of the University of New Hampshire, the library at the State Historical Association, and Howe Library in Hanover have all provided material for our work, and their staffs have been most helpful. Most of all we would like to thank our families for their patience and understanding.

Chronology

1607   English found their first permanent settlement at
        Jamestown, Virginia.
1610(?) English fishermen remain year-round on Monhegan
        Island.
1620   Puritan separatists found colony at Plymouth.
1622   Council for New England grants charters for land to Sir
        Ferdinando Gorges and Captain John Mason.
1623   David Thomson begins the first English settlement at
        Pannaway (now Rye, New Hampshire).
1634   First pine masts leave New Hampshire for British ports.
1635   Captain John Mason dies.
1638   Sawmill built at Exeter.
1640   By this time four towns settled—Strawbery Banke
        (Portsmouth), Exeter, Hampton, and Hilton's Point
        (Dover).
1646   Darby Field and two guides ascend Mount Washington.
1675   A succession of wars between settlers and an alliance of
        French and Indians begins.
1679   Crown first declares New Hampshire a royal colony.
1697   Hannah Duston escapes from her Indian captors.
1708   Privy Council declares Richard Waldron's land claims
        valid.
1717   John Wentworth appointed lieutenant governor of New
        Hampshire.

1730	John Wentworth dies.
1740	Southern boundary between New Hampshire and Massachusetts settled.
1741	Benning Wentworth becomes Royal Governor of New Hampshire.
1742	Five hundred pine masts shipped from Portsmouth, the province's largest shipment on record.
1753	Richard Waldron II dies.
1763	Peace treaty ends nearly one hundred years of wars between settlers and the French and the Indians.
1765	By this time 60 percent of the 240 townships in present-day New Hampshire are settled.
1767	Benning Wentworth retires from governorship; John Wentworth II, his nephew, is appointed governor.
1769	Dartmouth College is founded by Eleazar Wheelock.
1774	In October Governor John Wentworth hires New Hampshire carpenters to build barracks for General Gage's troops in Boston.
1774	In December four hundred men under the leadership of Langdon and Sullivan sack Castle William and Mary in Portsmouth Harbor.
1775	Governor Wentworth departs from New Hampshire.
1775	Portsmouth shipwrights begin building the *Raleigh, Ranger,* and *America* for the Continental Navy.
1776	In January New Hampshire adopts a Revolutionary constitution.
1776	In July Declaration of Independence is signed in Philadelphia.
1777	John Stark leads American troops in Battle of Bennington.
1782	Secessionist movement in western towns ends.
1784	State constitution is adopted; bridge is built from Newington to Durham.
1789	President George Washington visits New Hampshire.
1792	Jeremy Belknap's *History of New Hampshire* is completed in Boston.
1814	Middlesex Canal from Boston to Lowell and Concord is completed.
1815	William Plumer proposes to turn Dartmouth College into a state university.

1818	Daniel Webster argues the Dartmouth College case before the Supreme Court of the United States.
1819	General Court passes Toleration Act.
1820	Census lists 52,384 people engaged in farming; 8,699 in manufacturing; 1,068 in commerce.
1836	Governor Isaac Hill notes to General Court that sections of New Hampshire, particularly the Merrimack River Valley, are no longer self-sufficient in food production.
1836	First railroad line runs from Lowell, Massachusetts, to Manchester, New Hampshire.
1838	Construction of Amoskeag mills begins.
1848	John Parker Hale nominated for the presidency by the Liberty Party.
1851	Amoskeag textiles winning prizes in London.
1852	Franklin Pierce elected president of the United States.
1853	Amos Tuck holds meeting in Exeter of factions which would form the Republican Party.
1867	State sells 172,000 acres of public land in the White Mountains for twenty-five thousand dollars.
1869	Franklin Pierce dies.
1881	William Chandler proposes three bills in General Court to curb powers of the railroads.
1885	General Court appoints commission to investigate condition of state forests.
1895	Boston & Maine Railroad gains monopoly in state.
1903	Devastating forest fires in north country burn twelve thousand acres.
1906	Reformers challenge political domination of the Boston & Maine.
1911	Weeks Act leads to establishment of White Mountains National Forest.
1911	Robert P. Bass elected governor.
1922	Strikes close Amoskeag mills.
1922	Democrats dominate state government electing Fred Brown governor, the first popularly elected Democratic governor in sixty-eight years.
1924	John G. Winant elected governor for the first time.
1926	Mary Hill Coolidge opens craft shop that begins the League of New Hampshire Craftsmen.

1931   John Winant elected governor.
1944   Meeting of economists and financiers at Bretton Woods.
1946   William Loeb buys *Manchester Union Leader*.
1949   Sherman Adams elected governor.
1950   Governor Sherman Adams institutes reorganization of
        state bureaucracy.
1952   New Hampshire's presidential primary widely acclaimed
        as first in the nation.
1953   Beginning of massive advertising campaign to promote
        New Hampshire throughout the nation.
1956   Federal Highway Act leads to expansion of state road
        system.
1961   Commander Alan B. Shepard, Jr. of East Derry mans first
        U.S. space flight.
1963   Governor John King establishes sweepstakes lottery.
1970   From 1970 to 1980 the state gains 181,000 people.
1973   Meldrim Thomson elected governor.
1974   Durham town meeting rejects proposed oil refinery.
1975   Construction of Seabrook Nuclear Power Plant begins.
1980   Approximately twenty-seven hundred farms still operate
        in the state.
1981   William Loeb dies.
1986   Christa McAuliffe, science teacher at Concord High School,
        to be the first civilian in space, dies in Challenger space
        shuttle accident at Cape Canaveral.
1991   Seabrook Nuclear Power Plant goes on line.

Prologue

As the seasons of New Hampshire vary from the breathless beauty of the first snow or the spectacular color of leaves in autumn to the grimness of a November day or the dreariness of mud season, so the political seasons seem to follow the patterns of nature. New Hampshire's politics have been caught in a variety of crosscurrents from the fiercely independent democracy of the town meeting or the wholesale representation in the General Court to the colony's embarrassing dependence on Massachusetts during its infancy or its truckling to the rule of the Boston & Maine Railroad during the latter years of the nineteenth century. The politics of New Hampshire tend to high plateaus and deep dark holes. So, too, the economic development of the state has swung from the early lucrative trade in timber to the back-breaking solitary farming in the granite hills to the boom and bust of the textile mills to the cushion provided by the tourism trade and the current growth in high-tech industries. The story of the political and economic development of the state is like the story of a New Hampshire day in February when the temperature can swing from minus ten degrees to thirty degrees in a few hours. Only the uninitiated are surprised, and even they take a certain pleasure in the sheer contrariness of it.

Unlike most of the original colonies, New Hampshire had no original charter or strong-willed proprietor to shape the destiny of the settlement. Instead it began with fishermen, merchants, adventurers, and opportunists seeking wealth that might lie in the sea and in the virgin wilderness. Very soon these worldly fortune hunters encountered the stern and ambitious Puritans of Massachusetts Bay

Colony and learned that in government and politics revelling and avarice were no match for self-righteous ambition. In only a few years the British Crown, eager for pine masts and suspicious of the imperialism of Massachusetts, entered the fray. Thus New Hampshire began in the kind of political and economic free-for-all that makes the history of the state colorful and gritty and provocative.

1

Fish, Ports, Politics, and the Masting Trade

THE SETTLERS OF New Hampshire encountered a stern climate, inhospitable land, and a short growing season—a wilderness challenge unlike their counterparts in Virginia and the Carolinas. And unlike their neighbors in Massachusetts Bay Colony, the settlers in New Hampshire were not inspired by religious convictions nor were they armed with a clear compact for orderly governance. Nonetheless, by the late 1600s New Hampshire settlers had built a brisk international maritime economy that made the province very attractive to both her Puritan neighbors in Massachusetts and the British Crown. But the path to economic and political independence was as rocky as the state's granite hills.

Had they read accounts of the region written by explorers in the early seventeenth century, the settlers might have predicted their fortunes. In 1632 a tract by the explorer and publicist of America's coast, Captain John Smith, described the northeast coast with a mixture of awe and enthusiasm which characterized the attitude of English adventurers, speculators, and Massachusetts Bay Colony Puritans who settled the region which became New Hampshire. Reflecting on his coastal explorations of 1614, Smith wrote:

"How to describe a more plaine spectacle of desolation, or more barren, I know not, yet are those rocky Iles so furnished with good Woods, Springs, Fruits, Fish and Fowle, and the Sea, the strangest Fish-pond I ever saw."[1]

Coming as they did from British and European landscapes largely deforested by the sixteenth century, these early visitors were all dazzled by the virgin forest that greeted them and quickly grasped the new economic possibilities of the woods and reported their discoveries to investors at home.

On the face of it, this new world and the New England region in particular offered abundant resources and unlimited opportunity to countries hungry for building materials and for foodstuffs from the sea. Verrazano, exploring along the northeastern coast for France in 1524, reported on one hand seeing forested islands as far as Narragansett Bay and on the other hand remarked on open coastal areas large enough to drive an army through. To this mixed picture he also added observations concerning northern Indian populations subsisting as hunter-gatherers in this land of abundance, forced away, he thought, from traditional European habits of cultivation of land by rigors of climate and sterility of soil.

Martin Pring's expedition considerably later in 1603 provided a good deal more specific information to English merchants and other gentlemen of towns in western England. They had fitted-out Pring's fifty-ton ship the *Speedwell* and William Brown's twenty-ton *Discover*, "being encouraged by the report of divers mariners that come to make fishing voyages on that coast."[2] Outfitted with attractive tradable items ranging from "hats of divers colours" to more useful axes, shovels, and fishhooks, the *Speedwell* sailed for the northeast secure from fears of the native population because of the presence of "two excellent Mastives, of whom the Indians were more afraid, than twenty of our men."[3] Pring, then twenty-three, and his adventurous crew were motivated not so much by a search for fish or Indians, however, as they were for a share of the lucrative English market for sassafras, a plant whose bark, wood, buds, and roots were said to cure swellings, fevers, colds, headaches, toothaches, kidney stones, stomachaches, lameness, gout, and infertility—an attractive panacea to a country accustomed to repeated plagues and chronic diseases. Finding no sassafras along the Maine and New Hampshire coast, the expedition headed south toward present-day Provincetown, Massachusetts, where their efforts were richly rewarded. Pring's reports of a tree-covered landscape made an immediate impression on wood-starved merchants. So too did his accounts of "sundry sorts of beasts, Stags, Deere, Beares, Wolves, Foxes, Lusornes, and Dogges with sharp noses," as well as reports of signs of Indians living in the Piscataqua area, noting with special interest and admiration their birchbark canoes.[4] Within the next ten years

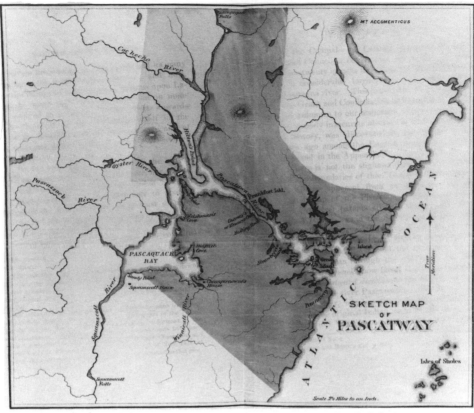

A detail of the Piscataqua region. New Hampshire Historical Society.

both Captain John Smith and Samuel de Champlain provided further glowing advertisements of the economic potential of the spectacular northeast coast of "high craggy clifty Rocks and stony Iles."

Before English settlers reached the port of Piscataqua, which Smith and others had enthusiastically promoted by 1614, there were active fishing communities on the abutting off-shore islands, particularly the Isles of Shoals. Here on this cluster of islands ten miles out of the Piscataqua harbor, English west-country fishermen set up temporary bases while they fished the rich coastal waters, taking advantage of the two fishing seasons, spring and fall, which the region provided.

While English merchants risked money to fortify and expand their fishing outposts in the 1620s and 1630s, the fishermen whom they employed faced risks of their own, learning quickly to adapt to the vagaries of weather and the Indian presence, living a rough communal life dominated by rigorous work and marked by the absence of women and other normal family connections. Unlike their soberminded Puritan neighbors to the south whose main end was to subdue and plant the wilderness, the raucous fishermen of the offshore islands lived to fish and trade. As New Hampshire historian Charles E. Clark notes, once when gathered together by a young Massachusetts clergyman eager to evangelize and convert them to husbandry and sobriety, one fisherman blurted out in the middle of a sermon: "Sir, you are mistaken, you think you are Preaching to the People at Bay; our main End was to catch Fish."[5]

While the fishermen enjoyed their rough living, another group of men recognized the attractions of the deep-water harbor of the Piscataqua with its five-fingered river system which created a twenty-four square mile, port-filled basin, navigable year around. Here they planned settlements designed to be more permanent and just as profitable as fishing. Thus the age of discovery and exploration yielded to the age of settlement in this region now widely regarded as rich in timber and fish — "attractives" at this point in England's history as "powerful" as gold, silver, or a shortcut to the East. Sir Ferdinando Gorges in 1622 initiated the next important step in the settlement of what is now Maine and New Hampshire: he brought men, money and land together.

Unlike Massachusetts where the settlers drew up a government before they even had land to govern, the settlers of New Hampshire were sent to establish plantations by entrepreneurs like Gorges' partner, Captain John Mason, who never governed the land and who seemed to have little interest in doing so; nor did he provide the settlers with any organizing principles on which to establish a government of their own. The outcome of this casual approach to government left the early plantations and towns vulnerable to anarchy or annexation.

The political organization of the settlements, then, begins with land grants, which were often based on misinformation and false assumptions about the geography of the land. For example, the patents granted to Captain John Mason and Sir Ferdinando Gorges, the bedrock of the definition of New Hampshire as a geographical entity, established the Merrimack River as the southern boundary of the grant on the mistaken belief that the river ran due west rather than turning sharply north as it does a few miles inland. Out of this error grew claims and counter claims and boundary disputes that plagued New Hampshire until 1740. Confusion between the Connecticut River and Lake Champlain left the western border in dispute until the Revolutionary War. Sometimes these disputes became so violent that they threatened to destroy the very existence of the state as a political and geographical unit.

The ambitious neighbors on New Hampshire's southern border, the Massachusetts Bay Colony, scented opportunity in the confusion created by the ambiguous boundaries and the haphazard political structure of the struggling settlements. By annexing the settlements of New Hampshire, the General Court of Massachusetts could provide their often dissolute northern neighbors with sober and religious government and, not incidentally, increase the size of their own colony by half again. How New Hampshire managed to avoid being swallowed up by Massachusetts at the same time it established its geographical boundaries and a stable and remarkably successful colonial government is the story of politics in New Hampshire before the Revolutionary War.

Acting for the Crown, a group of men headed by Gorges formed the Council for New England which distributed patents or grants of land in what would become New Hampshire. One David Thomson, who had done some work for the Council, was rewarded with six thousand acres, and in 1623 he made the first English settlement in the region on the Piscataqua River at Pannaway. There he remained for four years.

Though Thomson's plantation failed, a second one at Hilton's Point (which later became Dover) grew out of the first. Two brothers, Edward and William Hilton, London merchants and fishmongers who had joined Thomson at Pannaway in the mid-1620s, moved north to form a colony of their own seven miles up river where they farmed, fished, and traded with the natives. They gained a legal patent for their settlement, but when they realized the powerful Massachusetts Bay Colony might claim the whole Piscataqua region, they sold the patent to a group of English Puritans who might find the rule of the Bay Colony more tolerable than they would.

More important than the Thomson and Hilton grants were those issued to Sir Ferdinando Gorges and Captain John Mason. The men received several overlapping grants, but Mason's charter included an arc of land sixty miles inland between the Merrimack and the Piscataqua River. He founded the Laconia Company which sent settlers to New Hampshire to establish trade, build a plantation, and engage in the fur trade. This province Mason named "New Hampshire" after his family seat located in Hampshire, England.

The settlement proved disappointing. Trade with the Indians was erratic; border disputes with Massachusetts, which claimed the land in and around the Piscataqua, delayed the building of a center for fishing on the Isles of Shoals. By the time the border dispute was settled in favor of Mason's claims, New Hampshire had proved an expensive investment which did not turn a profit quickly enough to suit the London investors. While the owners of the company complained about the lack of profits, the settlers complained about lack of supplies. Ultimately, when the Laconia Company went bankrupt, it left behind in the settlements sixty-six men and twenty-two women who had been sent to New Hampshire during the first two years of the company's operation.

Though the rest of the investors quit, Mason did not. He took over his partners' share of the unprofitable company and poured more money into the settlements, writing at one point, "I have disbursed a great deal of money in the plantation, and never received one penny; but hope, . . . I should, in some reasonable time, be reimbursed again."[6] In fact his plantations were well established, and prospects were good that he would soon be rewarded by his employees' fishing and lumbering enterprises. However, in 1635, at age forty-nine Mason suddenly died.

DIVISION OF THE SPOILS AND THE INCURSION OF MASSACHUSETTS

Since Mason had never governed his plantation himself nor had the settlers established any form of government for themselves, the hundred or so people that Mason employed, left to their own devices, grabbed whatever they could of Mason's property. The man sent by Anne Mason, John Mason's widow, to help Thomas Warnerton, who was responsible for Mason's settlement at Strawberry Bank,* rustled a hundred yellow Danish cattle which Mason had

---

*The restoration in Portsmouth uses the old spelling, "Strawbery Banke."

sent there, herded them to Boston where he sold them for twenty-five hundred pounds and retired to Cambridge. Warnerton, himself, grabbed as many weapons and stores as he could and sold them to the French. Warnerton's successor connived with the Waldrons of Dover, soon to be one of the leading families in the colony, allowing them possession of the "great house" Mason had had built for himself and a thousand acres of prime river front property. They took Mason's valuable brass cannons from Great Island. Lumbermen and millhands and other settlers divided up the land and used or sold the rest of Mason's property. Where greed stopped and the need to survive began in this plunder of the dead man's property is hard to say. Clearly, however, in the wilderness there was no leadership strong enough to maintain order and protect property.

While these settlers in the Piscataqua demonstrated little respect for law and order, the Massachusetts Bay Colony worried about them a great deal. The Puritan settlers had such a high regard for their government that they itched to spread the advantages north to the Piscataqua. From the time of Hilton's settlement when the Bay Colony's claim caused him to sell his grant, to the time that colony intimidated Mason's employees with their claims so that they failed to establish fishing stations, the Bay colony had looked covetously on land clearly part of the grants made to Mason and Gorges. The groundwork for conflict between the Mason heirs and Massachusetts was already laid.

By the middle of the seventeenth century when those heirs came to New Hampshire to claim their inheritance, they discovered that Massachusetts had established itself as a political force in New Hampshire. Puritans who had bought Hiltons' patent and settled in what is now Dover had developed it under the protection of Massachusetts Bay. Furthermore, though some Anglicans had emigrated from England to the Piscataqua, far more people had moved north from the Bay Colony either because they sought economic opportunity or because they dissented from the strict rules of the Puritan government in Massachusetts. By 1640 over half the nearly thousand English residents of the New Hampshire coast and the border between the two colonies came from Massachusetts. This influx of people from Massachusetts intensified the religious conflict in the colony between the Anglicans and the Puritans, particularly since most of the immigrants, even religious dissenters, brought with them an image of the kind of community life that existed in Massachusetts — sober, religious, orderly.

They saw in the leaders left at Strawberry Bank none of the qualities of the leaders they had left behind. Thomas Warnerton was observed by the lofty Governor Winthrop to live "very wickedly in whoredom, drunkenness and quarrelling, so as he . . . kept the Piscataquack men under awe of him divers years."[7] The righteous governor no doubt saw it his duty to save these lost souls, but the fact that Massachusetts could expand its political influence by relieving Warnerton of his was not incidental. The few remaining profligates left at Strawberry Bank and other Masonian settlements were quite overwhelmed by the Puritanism that the immigrants imported from Massachusetts.

The last stand of these settlers Mason had sent against the tidal wave of Puritans disguised itself as a religious dispute between Thomas Larkham, a wealthy and popular Anglican clergyman, and Puritans Captain John Underhill and Hansard Knollys, an evangelical preacher. Both Underhill and Knollys were dissenters from the church in Massachusetts. They had moved to Hilton's Point where they gained control of the settlement by promising the citizens that, under their protection, the settlement would be safe from both Massachusetts and the Crown. However, when the church in the Bay Colony forgave them, both Knollys and Underhill decided that it would be wise to cooperate with the Puritan fathers. Reaffirming his religious orthodoxy, Knollys publicly accused the Anglican Thomas Larkham of "heresy" and "worldliness" and excommunicated him. Larkham responded by indignantly knocking off Knollys' hat.

With this Gilbert-and-Sullivan opening the battle began. The Puritans marched into the fray led by a man flourishing a halberd with a Bible attached. Knollys followed brandishing a pistol. Larkham and his men retreated and sent to Strawberry Bank for help. Francis Williams, a friend of Warnerton and an old employee of the Laconia Company, dashed to the rescue with a troop of armed men. They arrested Knollys and Underhill and took them to court the next day. Williams, donning his judge's hat, found them both guilty of riot and ordered Underhill and several others to return to Massachusetts (which was probably like throwing the rabbit in the briar patch.)

In a fit of general remorse Knollys rescinded Larkham's excommunication, and Williams dropped the banishment order and fines. It appears, however, that Knollys himself was not immune to worldly temptations, for he soon returned to England in disgrace for "dalliance" with his housemaids.

But religious disputes in Massachusetts drove more people into New Hampshire. In 1638, a minister named John Wheelwright, kinsman of Anne Hutchinson, moved with part of his congregation from Mount Wollaston to the falls at Squamscott on a plantation that became Exeter. A careful man, Wheelwright had chosen a site outside the Bay Colony's charter but far enough away from Strawberry Bank so that his flock would not be contaminated by the riotous living indulged in by Warnerton and his friends. He took the final precaution of paying local Indians for the land. None of these measures protected his colony from the intrusion of the Puritans, as they later expanded their settlements northward. The Bay Colony granted approval to a group of their brethren under Stephen Batchelor to found a town at Winnacunnet on part of the land Wheelwright had bought. This settlement, which became Hampton, flourished, and Wheelwright could only struggle to keep control of his own plantation and fume at the Bay Colony for trespassing on his land.

Thus by 1640 there were four towns in the colony: Strawberry Bank (Portsmouth) under the domain of the old, free-wheeling adventurers; Exeter and Hampton under the sober rule of the Puritans; and Hilton's Point (Dover) under uncertain authority since the fishermen fluctuated in their loyalty. The name "New Hampshire," which Mason had dubbed the colony, meant almost nothing to any of these settlers who identified themselves with the four separate towns not as one political unit.

CLAIMANTS TO THE LAND

Out of the scramble for Mason's property after his death in 1635 there emerged an oligarchy of Puritan merchants and landowners — the Cutts, Vaughans, and Waldrons — who dominated the political and economic life of the province from 1640 to 1715. However, the claims of these families to the land they held was always

tenuous, for John Mason's heirs, particularly grandson Robert Tufton Mason and his cousin Edward Randolph, returned again and
again to challenge them with their title to the Mason grants. The Indians, too, began to challenge the settlers's possession of the land,
raiding the outlying settlements, often driving those colonists back to
the comparative safety of the towns.

The Puritan oligarchy understandably allied itself with the Puritans who lived in the Massachusetts Bay Colony. Not only did
these families share common religious tenets with the Boston leaders, they turned to the strong militia from Massachusetts for help
protecting the struggling frontiers of the New Hampshire towns
from Indian raids. Furthermore, since the Bay Colony had always
cast an imperialistic eye on the Piscataqua settlements, the oligarchy
could depend on their southern neighbor to help them resist the
claims of the importunate Masonian heirs. So close did this alliance
become that the leaders in the Piscataqua tried time and time again
to merge the two colonies into one.

The Mason heirs, on the other hand, instituted lawsuits and appealed to the Crown to help them establish their title to the land now
held largely by the oligarchy. And the Crown, wary of the ambitions
of Massachusetts, often assisted Mason by sending commissions to
investigate affairs in the province, sometimes even appointing Edward Randolph, Mason's cousin, to head these investigations. Mason also instituted lawsuits in the courts in the New Hampshire
towns and in London trying to establish his right to the land in
which his grandfather had invested so much time and money.

But those stubborn Puritan families held on to the land in the
Piscataqua, meeting the Crown's commissions with outright defi-
ance and fighting the court battles with every wile they could conceive, from destroying evidence to forging deeds and always striving
to merge New Hampshire with Massachusetts. The Mason heirs
struggled just as persistently to reclaim John Mason's property, bribing the Crown's commissioners, preparing false reports about conditions in the colony, and whenever possible packing the courts which
heard their case, striving to separate the province from Massachusetts and put it under the Crown.

Fed up with the New Hampshire towns and suspicious of Massachusetts, in 1679 the Crown finally declared the two colonies separate, establishing a royal governor, an appointed council, and an

elected assembly to govern the colony—each one of which has a counterpart in the government of the state today. John Cutt was appointed governor, and it was his final illness that prompted the colonists to fast and pray for his recovery, the beginning of New Hampshire's special holiday, Fast Day, long celebrated on April 27. John Cutt did not survive, but Richard Waldron, who succeeded him, led the colonists in a policy of arrogance and noncooperation with the English Crown and clung tenaciously to the land they occupied.

On the other hand, as kings came and went and the political climate varied in England, the Crown wavered in its colonial policy. James II, a Roman Catholic, who admired the viceroyalty system by which the Spanish governed their colonies, abolished the separate governments of Massachusetts, Maine, and New Hampshire and established a central royally appointed government in Boston to govern all three. This Dominion of New England lasted from 1686 to 1689 when James was replaced by William of Orange. Massachusetts Bay took that opportunity to get rid of the Dominion authorities and replace them with their own theocracy, and the four towns of New Hampshire likewise took the opportunity to rejoin Massachusetts Bay Colony.

This happy arrangement lasted only as long as William was too occupied by war in Europe to turn his attention to New Hampshire. But Protestant William had no more intention than Catholic James had of allowing his authority to be eroded by Massachusetts. At the urging of the Mason claimants he appointed as governor of both Massachusetts and New Hampshire the newest owner of those claims, Samuel Allen. As lieutenant governor he appointed one who was in Allen's employ to serve in New Hampshire.

Even as royal governor, however, Allen failed to budge the oligarchy from the land or to establish a significant claim to any land in New Hampshire. He won a few lawsuits in the colony but lost the major ones against big landowners like Waldron. When he appealed the case to London, the records of those early victories had disappeared and the evidence suggested that the culprit might be William Vaughan. Caught in such flagrant disregard of the court, the oligarchy was forced to negotiate, and agreed to a settlement that would have been a bonanza for Allen. They agreed he was entitled to all land outside of the settled towns and five thousand acres within the towns plus payment of money in exchange for a quitclaim on all

other lands. By a quirk of fortune, Allen died before he could sign
the agreement, and the oligarchy decided to test its luck a bit further
before renewing the offer to his son, Thomas.

Impatient, Thomas began legal proceedings against Waldron,
and the Council and Assembly hired William Vaughan's son,
George, to defend Waldron. Instead of destroying evidence as his father had, George Vaughan with the help of Waldron concocted a
false deed supposedly signed by the Indians and the residents of the
Piscataqua that gave the residents title to all the land covered by the
Masonian grants. Needless to say the forged deed antedated the title
Allen had purchased. The English courts never questioned this false
deed; in fact, this famous forgery was not detected for nearly two
hundred years. Discounting the testimony of Allen's lieutenant governor who had a personal stake in the matter, the Privy Council relied on the forged deed and recognized Waldron's claim to the land.

By the end of the seventeenth century, the Crown had established a government for the colony which consisted of an elected Assembly which served at the discretion of the governor or lieutenant
governor, a Council which was appointed to consult with the lieutenant governor, and the lieutenant governor who served in New
Hampshire under the authority of the governor of Massachusetts
Bay and New Hampshire. Piscataqua merchants had learned something about how to work around royal authority, and they were appointed to fill the Council and most important government posts.
Because it was better organized and had the advantage of drafting
legislation, the Council generally dominated the elected Assembly; it
often consulted privately with Assemblymen instead of dealing with
the Assembly as a whole, and it simply abandoned any joint session
that proved troublesome.

However, the Assembly had one power the Council could not
ignore. On revenue bills the Assembly acted as a full partner with
the Council, and by the turn of the century the Assembly was learning to flex its muscle through this authority. By 1699 the Assembly
had organized itself more efficiently through a set of formal rules. It
held separate sessions, developed its own leadership, and kept its
own "House Journal." From these struggles for autonomy, the Assembly of New Hampshire has an uninterrupted history as a body
that steered the colony in the first uncertain days of independence
and grew into one of the largest representative bodies in the western
world.

FUR, FISH, AND LUMBER

While much of the colony's energy in the seventeenth century was still being directed toward achieving permanent, stable, and governable settlements, the natural advantages and attractions of the Piscataqua region began to be developed and exploited—first in trade in fur and fish and later in trade in timber.

Fur trading never met the early settlers expectations. Both Edward Hilton and later settlers at Newichwannock Falls had responded to the Laconia Company's desire for fur pelts, as had other early settlers who saw fur trading as an adjunct to fishing. Unfortunately, hopes of abundant fur-bearing and of Indian populations eager to trade furs were soon disappointed by the realities of the decline in both populations by over-hunting and disease. The trade in fur was equally affected by a fluctuating European market for beaver resulting from changing fashions. By 1700 the fur trade and the popularity of beaver hats had all but disappeared as components in the province's emerging economy.

On the other hand, the ecological importance of the exploitation of the beaver population gives an interesting early indication of how settlement and use of resources have multiple environmental consequences. Jeremy Belknap, the state's first historian, gave considerable attention to the beaver, "one of the most useful as well as sagacious animals," noting that their clever dam-building techniques produced results such that "the best artist could neither mend its position or figure, nor add to its stability."[8] When, however, the equally sagacious hunter had all but eliminated these clever architects and engineers, the land was unalterably and—from the settlers' point of view—profitably changed: abandoned beaver dams made good bridges, became preferred mill sites, and adjacent ponds spawned shad and salmon. Most importantly, however, when the old dams finally collapsed exposing treeless, rich black soil, the wise farmer accustomed to back-breaking land clearing might quickly claim as many as two hundred acres of land ready for cultivation.

Captain John Smith's "strangest Fish-pond" continued to play an important role in New Hampshire's early economic growth, particularly as Portsmouth merchants began to direct and control the offshore fishing stations established early in the seventeenth century. The three families dominant in politics—the Cutts, the Waldrons, and the Vaughans—also began the serious development of the Pis-

cataqua trade in the 1640s. Four Cutt brothers emigrated from
Bath; William Vaughan, a Welshman, came from London, and
Richard Waldron from Warwickshire. Well-trained at home to recognize trade in fish as an easily accessible source of fluid capital,
these first Piscataqua merchants and others with longstanding ties
with the region organized trading activity with promising markets in
Barbados, Bilboa, Madeira, the Canary Islands, Virginia, and Boston, marketing the rich catches from the fishing communities on the
Isles of Shoals and becoming very wealthy themselves.

Piscataqua merchants continued the fishing trade well into the
early decades of the 1700s, despite growing vulnerability to Indian
attack, aggressive competition from Massachusetts and Newfoundland, and fluctuating foreign markets. In sum, though the amount of
fish exported in the trader's heyday never quite rivaled Massachusetts' catches, the fishing trade in New Hampshire was for nearly one
hundred years the backbone of the emerging trade patterns in the region's principal resource — timber. Even as Belknap lamented at the
turn of the eighteenth century that fishing had not "of late years been
prosecuted with the same spirit as formerly,"[9] he knew as well as
merchants like Vaughan, Cutt, and Waldron that New Hampshire's
most promising mercantile opportunities lay in the exploitation of its
forest resources. The forest would be king.

RICHES FROM THE WOODS

In the age of plastic, steel, electricity, and petroleum, it takes
imagination to comprehend the importance of wood products to the
seventeenth- and eighteenth-century colonial and European culture.
Next to food, wood products — for fuel, building materials, contain-
ers for preserving and shipping foodstuffs, household tools — were
the commodities in greatest demand. Today there may still be a visible link with the age of wood, for it is almost impossible to travel
from any small town in New Hampshire to one of its larger cities
without passing a sawmill, large lumberyard, or mammoth truck
carrying timber from the forests.

The giant "sticks" which early explorers of the New Hampshire
coastline had admired ultimately provided the economic tender
which propelled the young colony from dependent provincial begin-

nings to an independent political and economic unit in an emerging national government. Just as earlier the extractive ventures in fur trading and fishing had had their profits and perils, so too did the lumber trade. Taking the forest had multiple internal and external ramifications.

Early settlers, of course, cut trees to clear land for agriculture, to build houses, barns, and fences, canoes and small fishing vessels, and to provide fuel for warmth against New England's long winters. Quite soon the settlers also saw that the wilderness could turn a profit as well. As early as the 1630s at both Mason's Piscataqua plantation and at Laconia Company settlements colonists sawed boards by hand, exporting these and barrel staves right along with their fish. John Wheelwright is reported to have built a sawmill at Exeter as early as 1638. Between 1640 and 1653 court records report as many as twenty-six lumber traders exporting clapboards and pipestaves to Boston. And the figures escalate. Fifty new sawmills were built by 1705. Twice as many Piscataqua ships were loaded with timber for coastal trade in 1681 as forty years earlier and more than twice that number again by 1695. In addition twenty-nine vessels sailed for foreign ports with timber.

The growing number of sawmills attests to the beginning of an organized economic effort in the Piscataqua region and to the importance of Boston, the region's principal market, but the cutting edge in the development of what was to become an immensely profitable lumbering trade lay with plying the Caribbean and English markets and to a lesser extent the so-called Wine Islands and southern European ports. Along with the other New England colonies, New Hampshire profited by the lucrative trans-Atlantic triangular trade.

Why the Caribbean and south European markets? These lucrative markets, as Boston merchants had already discovered, needed wood and wood products and could in turn supply commodities the young colony needed. The case of Barbados is instructive. The most important colony in the British West Indies in the seventeenth century, Barbados by the early 1640s had more settlers in its 166 square miles than in all the New England colonies. Its leading products in the 1630s and early 1640s were tobacco, corn, indigo, tropical fruits and nuts, and cotton. By the 1660s, however, the Barbadian colonists had shifted 80 percent of their land use to the production of sugar cane and in the process became not only one large sugar factory, but by some accounts the most fully developed, populous, and profitable colony in English America.

The consequences of the transformation of this one external market gave New Englanders a prime market for their foodstuffs, but particularly for their timber products. The Barbadians needed clapboards and shingles for domestic and commercial building, fuel for sugar processing, and oak barrels for shipping rum, molasses and sugar. At the same time the Wine Ports of Spain—the Canary Islands, Madeira, and the Azores—required casks and staves to ship their popular products. Besides the New England colonies needed sugar and molasses and, as Belknap lamented, had become quite fond of rum.

This brisk ocean trade, of course, had multiple effects on the emerging provincial society of the Piscataqua region. In a few years merchants made fortunes, and whether by design or necessity their children tended to marry each other, thus consolidating the wealth of the colony in the hands of a few families. This profitable trade provided bills of credit which encouraged the importation of commodities not manufactured at home such as firearms, ironware, and household luxuries. As the continued demand for timber products exhausted coastal timber, interior forests became more attractive, and land speculation flourished. Finally, the economy became more diversified as occupations such as cooper, carpenter, sawyer, lumberer, cordwainer, jointer, blockmaker, shipwright, sailmaker, and mariner evolved to meet the trader's demands for merchantable goods.

MAST PINES ARE KING

The story of the English need for ship's masts, ship's timber, and naval stores and young New Hampshire's ability to provide these commodities is a tale of market dynamics, imperial politics, ecological shortsightedness, and crafty survival tactics—a tale of both fortune and frustration. Furthermore, it is a tale dominated by the Piscataqua ports, particularly Portsmouth, which never again in the state's or region's history regained the influence they attained during the nearly one hundred and twenty-five year history of the masting trade.

By the sixteenth century England had been largely deforested. As recognition of that fact became commonplace so too came recognition of the importance of naval strength in the country's political destiny. In an era of wooden sailing ships (which required more timber than the largest country manor house), there would be an intimate connection between the timber supply and seapower. It is chilling to note that in 1926 in his classic study, *Forests and Seapower*, Robert H. Albion remarked upon the close resemblance between the British timber problem and the modern-day oil situation. At that time, he wrote, since timber, like oil, was a natural product abundant at the outset, but certain to be exhausted, nations sought colonies and exerted diplomatic pressures for shiptimber as they do now for oil. So England and her maritime rivals — France, Spain, and Holland — cast eager eyes on potential timber sources in regions where they either had or might expect to establish political control. Long dependent on timber and naval stores from the unstable Baltic region, the English navy soon relied more and more on abundant North American timber. While the powers-to-be considered American oak for shipbuilding inferior to European varieties, the appeal of the giant and abundant *Pinus strobus* (white pine) began to be acknowledged. No ships, after all, could catch the wind without as many as twenty-three masts, yards, and spars varying in length and diameter from the bulky mainmast to its subordinate parts.

From contemporary to present accounts, it is hard to imagine that any tree, save perhaps California's redwood, has inspired such inflated descriptions as the sort Jeremy Belknap first concocted in the late 1700s, when he wrote of the white pine:

> Notwithstanding the gloomy appearance of an American forest, yet a contemplative mind may find in it many subjects of entertainment. The most obvious remark, is the silence which reigns through it. . . . Another thing, worthy of observation, is the aged and majestic appearance of the trees, of which the most noble is the mast pine. This tree often grows to the height of one hundred and fifty, and sometimes two hundred feet. It is straight as an arrow, and has no branches but very near the top. It is from twenty to forty inches in diameter at its base, and appears like a stately pillar, adorned with a verdant capital, in form of a cone.[10]

The height and circumference of the New Hampshire white pine became the deciding factors in an emerging economic and political
contest for their harvest. While the white pine's wood was softer and
less durable than say its Norwegian counterparts, the white pine was
lighter in weight and retained its natural juices longer so that it had a
useful nautical life of about twenty years.

By 1634 the first pine masts left New Hampshire for British
ports, meeting the urgent demand for timber from a country whose
own country of Hampshire had coincidentally once been heavily forested. The last cargo of masts to leave the Portsmouth harbor pre-
ceded the American Revolution by a year or two. In the meantime,
although trade statistics from this period are sketchy at best, the figures are impressive. In 1695, fifty-six masts were exported; by 1718
nearly two hundred were shipped to England. The most active year
in trading seems to have been 1742 when records indicate the shipment of over five hundred giant white pine masts.

Like each phase of the province's emerging economy, the masting trade was as full of risk as it was full of opportunity. There was
the constant danger in the woods of Indian attack, and Winthrop
Hilton's death in 1710 while prospecting for masts fourteen miles
from Portsmouth attests to the danger. Felling trees weighing fifteen
to twenty tons required careful preparation so as to avoid damaging
the valuable length of the giant. The colonial solution resembles the
nineteenth- and twentieth-century practice of clear-cutting a forest.
The 150- to 200-foot sticks required straight passage to riverbeds
where they were either "twitched" into the river, carried along in the
country's first river-runs, or slipped onto the ice to be carried
downstream in the spring's ice breakup. Taking care not to damage
these cumbersome giants along the way, men drove teams of seventy
or eighty oxen bearing the valuable cargo. In the meantime the
woods were alive with the sounds of clanking chains and colorful
language. As a final step before being loaded on mast ships in Portsmouth's harbor, mastwrights hewed the spars into sixteen sides.

The mast ships, called the ocean-liners of their day, were designed with large stern ports to facilitate the loading of commonly
forty or fifty masts. Like every other component of the larger-than-
life masting trade, these ships took a terrible beating and had very
short lives. Yet none of these risks hampered the growth of the mast
trade between England and her colony in New Hampshire, since

there were clearly profits to be made on both sides of the ocean. However, in the end it was precisely the relationship between the source of demand and the source of supply, an uneasy marriage of conflicting motivation, which not only ended New Hampshire's masting trade, but also contained grounds for eventual divorce and the province's participation in the American Revolution. This part of the tale is dominated by men as much as trees. Competition for this tree became intense. A long, slender pine in New Hampshire awaiting the mast fleet from England, was more than just another colonial export: it had a political and economic significance. One powerful group, the merchants, wanted to saw it into pine boards for shipment to a lucrative West Indies market, while another was equally determined that it would soon become a mast on an English ship of the line. And the settlers knew yet another need: thirty to forty cords of wood were required each year to heat a home.

The English had learned hard lessons from the timber shortage faced in the 1600s; among the most important was the need to devise a system for obtaining timber, which at the same time would conserve woodland resources to assure a continued supply. On the other hand the English colonists had forgotten the lessons they might have learned from seeing their homeland stripped of trees. Confronted with a vast virgin wilderness, they began hasty timber cutting for agricultural purposes; they sought to reap the profits which lumber sales could bring; and they developed a strict sense of the value of land and of the sanctity of private ownership. The two party's goals were not always compatible.

England's Navy Board conducted its acquisition of ship's timber by granting contracts to a small group (as few as four sometimes) of contractors at home, who in turn contracted with a small number of colonial agents, who in turn contracted with the mastmen who delivered the timber to port. These contracts also included a demand for naval stores—pitch, tar, hemp, and turpentine—though cultivation of colonial manufacture of these maritime supplies ever fell below British expectations. To ensure the administration of its contracts for timber, especially masts, the Navy Board as early as 1691 inserted clauses in colonial charters restricting the cutting of pine and as early as 1685 appointed Surveyors of His Majesty's Woods and Forests.

The Crown levied a law in New Hampshire which supplemented earlier provisions by forbidding the cutting of all pines not on private property. The Crown's unpopular surveyors and their deputies, men acting as a combination policeman-forest ranger, were commissioned by the British authorities to cut a "Broad Arrow," the old sign of naval property, in trees to be reserved for the Crown's purchase. Shaped like a crow's track and made by three blows of a hatchet, this sign often had the force of a gauntlet thrown in challenge to New Hampshire millmen. Violations were frequent and flagrant.

In the end, English timber imperialism and the colonial settlers' desire to turn a profit from what seemed an endless forest resouce affected nearly every level of the social, political, and economic life of the Piscataqua frontier. A small and powerful group of Portsmouth lumber merchants sought domination of the mast trade and through it obtained wealth and social and political status. They did so, of course, by obeying both their own desires for profit and their mixed sense of loyalty to their British rulers. In the meantime, though most settlers continued to fish and farm to subsist, their principal energies were expended in cutting, hauling, or milling timber. But the merchant princes of Portsmouth had also built their pre-Revolutionary prosperity on a wooden foundation, which would eventually force them to look to interior regions to replenish their own exhausted timber resources.

2

New Family, New Politics

THE WENTWORTH FAMILY, who dominated both the economic and political life of New Hampshire from 1715 to the Revolutionary War, was the most remarkable family in colonial New Hampshire and one of the most remarkable in the colonies before the war. They made fortunes in the masting trade and produced one lieutenant governor and two royal governors of New Hampshire. Unlike the Waldrons and the Vaughans, who controlled the fishing and timber trade and the politics of the colony before them, the Wentworths rose to political power through the auspices of the Crown and courted the powers in London, not Massachusetts. They established in Portsmouth an elegant and charming society that years later prompted dour John Adams to remark on the "pomps and vanities and ceremonies of the little world of Portsmouth."[11]

The Wentworth dynasty, which dominated the colony for sixty years, began its rise to power with John Wentworth, who moved with his widowed mother and his six brothers and sisters to Portsmouth where his mother kept the old Daniell Tavern, a favorite place for political meetings. As was typical of successful men of that time in New Hampshire, he began his career with a promising first step — marriage into a prosperous family. In 1693 he married Sarah Hunking, daughter of wealthy and influential Captain Mark Hunking.

After John spent two years at sea in deference to the maritime tradition of his wife's family, Sarah and John bought the plain old Daniell Tavern. They lined the walls of the public rooms with elabo-

Warner-MacPhaedris house in Portsmouth. New Hampshire Historical Society.

rate wainscoating, installed a fancy staircase with spiral balusters of oak, a hint that this newcomer to local society liked style and the good life. In fact as early as 1690 the province of New Hampshire was known for its hospitality and polite manners, more like colonies to the south dominated by the Anglicans than its Puritan neighbors. However, since Portsmouth did not have a library until 1750, we might judge that the intellectual life of the city did not keep pace with its gaity and charm. As the Wentworths prospered, they revived on a more respectable level some of the love of pleasure that had marked the early days of the scandalous Warnerton and that had almost been obliterated by the powerful Puritan families. The Wentworths loved balls and fine homes and carriages almost as much as wealth and power.

John joined his father-in-law, Mark Hunking, on the Council and quickly acquired other political appointments. Meantime Sarah and John were producing fourteen children, all of whom took a page from the book of the Vaughans and Waldrons and allied themselves by marriage to the oldest and most influential families in the province. In the days before nepotism and conflict of interest got a bad reputation, it was an efficient system for quickly establishing a political dynasty. The Wentworths polished the system to a fine art with surprisingly agreeable results not only for themselves but for the progress, stability, and prosperity of the whole colony.

Younger than the Vaughans and Waldrons, the Wentworths competed with the old oligarchy for overseas trade as well as political power. They took opposites sides in a bitter religious controversy which had split the Portsmouth church; their center of power was Portsmouth and Newcastle and extended little into the colony. The fact that they managed to placate most of the Puritan settlers in the colony is testimony to their genius for diplomacy.

This new political clan changed the alliance of the colony. While the old guard saw the Bay Colony as a bulwark against the Crown, the Mason grants, the white pine laws, and the navigation acts, John Wentworth perceived dominance by Massachusetts as more threatening than any of these. The realliance began when George Vaughan returned to New Hampshire as the king's appointed lieutenant governor and arrogantly defied the governor, who soon replaced him with John Wentworth. Wentworth took care to impress the Crown with his loyalty and to appear to enforce the regulations that emanated from London—a far cry from the old guard's refusal to cooperate with royal officials.

Needless to say, the Wentworths were not universally beloved. The powerful Waldron family, under the stalwart guidance of Richard Waldron II, made common cause with factions in Massachusetts against the rising tide of Wentworths and never reconciled themselves to the new dynasty. When George Vaughan returned from England with his commission as lieutenant governor, he also contended with the newcomers. But many of the old families were subsumed into the Wentworth dynasty; unlike the Vaughan-Waldron coalition, John Wentworth knew how to compromise, consolidate, and make peace. To the relief of the whole colony, he found a compromise to end a bitter rankling that had split the church in Portsmouth. He tried to accommodate his rivals by retaining young Waldron on the Council and his father as clerk of the Council as well as allowing old William Vaughan to remain as recorder of deeds though he was no longer on the Council. Significantly, when Allen pressed his claims to the Mason grants, Wentworth stood firmly with the Assembly against the unpopular former governor's claims, thus proving that royal governors need not support the old grants.

Besides resolving political conflicts diplomatically, Wentworth administered the colony efficiently. He reorganized many of the political institutions of the colony and encouraged the growth of the Assembly by insisting that new towns send representatives and that all towns pay their Assemblymen. He helped establish a dress code and stricter internal regulations which raised the morale and prestige of the Assembly. When the Assembly proposed the Triannual Act under which the representatives would be elected every three years, Wentworth lobbied for it in England. He also helped establish clear qualifications for voters and candidates.

Lieutenant Governor Wentworth strengthened the legal system persuading the Assembly to repeal all laws not contained in the codification of New Hampshire laws which had been printed shortly before he took office and to continue publishing all new laws. Wentworth and his Council also worked hard to resolve differences and establish firm and fair guidelines for taxation in a society which encompassed the wealthy Vaughans and Wentworths and the poor frontier farmer. Thus the legal system and the system of taxation became fairer, clearer, and more predictable.

However, while making these admirable improvements in the government of the colony, Wentworth distributed the political plums at his disposal much to the advantage of his friends and family. Politics and prosperity went hand in hand: members of the Governor's Council were exempt from provincial taxes, judges collected fees, and military officers had many opportunities to make money through their positions. In the long run every member of Wentworth's family profited one way or another from his appointments.

NEW TOWNS AND THE SOUTHERN BOUNDARY

During the years when New Hampshire was annexed periodically to Massachusetts and the old oligarchy strove to merge the two colonies, the uncertainty of the southern boundary line separating the two colonies seemed unimportant. Now, however, as Wentworth identified the interests of New Hampshire with England rather than Massachusetts Bay, confusion over the line between them erupted into a quarrel between the two colonies. That quarrel precipitated the final separation of New Hampshire from Massachusetts and initiated the settlement of many of the towns that now exist in the southern third of the state.

Massachusetts, refusing to recognize the 1664 ruling of a royal commission that the boundary ran east and west from a point three miles north of the mouth of the Merrimack River, continued to claim according to the first charter that Massachusetts included all land three miles south (and west) of the Merrimack and three miles north of its headwaters (at Lake Winnipesaukee) in a line running northwest. In New Hampshire many of the old guard favored no line at all, secretly hoping to be reunited with Massachusetts while openly supporting the settlement of the boundary through negotiations between the two colonies. But John Wentworth was determined to settle the matter as quickly and advantageously as possible. Thus when efforts to compromise with Massachusetts stalled, Wentworth devised a different strategy. With the backing of the Assembly and the Council, he employed an agent in London to represent New Hampshire's boundary claims to the Crown.

The agent, Captain John Thomlinson, a merchant deeply involved in the masting trade and well-known in New Hampshire, "was a gentleman of great penetration industry and address; and having fully entered into the views of Belcher's opponents [the Wentworths], prosecuted the affair of the line, with ardor and diligence. . . ."[12] Thomlinson and his nimble solicitor, Paris, were key figures in major developments from the 1720s to the 1760s.

When negotiations in London were stalled, Wentworth took other measures to strengthen New Hampshire's claim to the disputed land. As lieutenant governor, Wentworth was empowered to charter towns, and he began granting towns in the disputed territory. Since Governor Belcher could also charter towns, he quickly adopted the same strategy. The race began in the 1720s when New Hampshire incorporated Londonderry right in the middle of land claimed by both provinces. Soon Massachusetts erected the town of Rumford north of Londonderry in what is now Concord. A rash of charters followed — Chester, Barrington, Nottingham, and Rochester — over thirty in all more than half of which were inspired by the quarrel over the boundary line.

The new towns' grants also served Wentworth as political patronage with which to reward old friends and make new ones. And Wentworth, himself, reserved one square mile of land and distributed the rest to proprietors, among them several Councilors and most of the Assemblymen. Every member of the Assembly was a proprietor of the five towns granted in 1727!

Of course, some people criticized Wentworth for shamelessly dividing the land among his wealthy friends, but the lieutenant governor argued with some justification that developing a town required substantial capital, and thus it benefitted the town to have wealthy proprietors. Even so, some towns floundered for long periods because proprietors lacked capital to build roads and a mill and other necessities to prepare the town for settlers. All in all, so long as he spread the patronage around, few people objected to Wentworth's methods.

Predictably, Waldron and Vaughan hated the Wentworths and often quarrelled with the lieutenant governor. One of these quarrels provoked the story that was told of Governor Burnet, newly appointed to govern New Hampshire and Massachusetts, and his trip from Rhode Island to New Hampshire. "One of the committee, who went from Boston, to meet him on the borders of Rhode-Island, and conduct him to the seat of government, was the facetious Col. Tailer. Burnet complained of the long graces which were said [before meals] by clergymen [they met on their journey], and asked Tailer when they would shorten. He answered, 'the graces will increase in length till you come to Boston; after that they will shorten till you come to your government of New-Hampshire, where your Excellency will find no grace at all.' "[13]

Grace or no grace, things boded well for Lieutenant Governor Wentworth under the governorship of Burnet, who arrived with a good reputation from service as governor of New York but unfortunately for Wentworth, Burnet died within a few months.

Diplomatically, John Wentworth sent his compliments and best wishes to both of the two candidates vying to replace Burnet, former Governor Shute and a Boston merchant, Jonathan Belcher. The appointment went to "lofty and aspiring" Jonathan Belcher who was furious when he learned that Wentworth had courted both candidates. The letters aside, Wentworth could hardly have counted on a warm collaboration with the new governor, for Belcher was a relative of

George Vaughan and a long-standing friend of Richard Waldron II. However, before he came to grips with Belcher, John Wentworth died.

SETTLEMENT OF THE SOUTHERN BORDER

With John Wentworth's death in 1730 the battle lines were drawn for the next ten years. The old oligarchy led by Richard Waldron II conspired with Governor Belcher, trying to control the Council (which they often did) and secretly considering how to reannex New Hampshire to Massachustts. The army of Wentworths that John left behind, being out of favor with Governor Belcher, were not often appointed to the Council, and so they employed their political savvy in the Assembly and conspired with John Wentworth's successor, Lieutenant Governor David Dunbar who was also Surveyor of the King's Wood. They worked to expand the colony and to further disassociate it from Massachusetts by persuading the Crown to appoint a separate governor for New Hampshire and by drawing a boundary line between the two provinces, pressing the case through Thomlinson, who represented them and the Assembly in London.

Meantime the situation in the border towns was becoming more and more pressing as the population of the towns grew and nobody knew whether they were governed by Portsmouth or Boston. The governments of both colonies harassed the settlers for taxes; the settlers, themselves, quarrelled and were jailed by one colony or the other. Even Governor Belcher admitted to the Lords of Trade that some action must be taken: "The borderers on the lines live like toads under a barrow, being run into gaols on the one side and the other as often as they please to quarrel. . . . They pull down one another's houses, often wound each other, and I fear it will end in bloodshed."[14]

The Assembly of New Hampshire was fed up with Governor Belcher, who favored Massachusetts, and with the delays in the border negotiations. It sent to London a letter of complaints against Belcher and pleas to settle the controversy between Massachusetts and New Hampshire over their boundaries by recognizing the enlarged boundary of New Hampshire laid out in 1664.

In 1738 Thomlinson learned that a descendant of Mason, John

Tufton Mason, had managed to reclaim the Mason grants through some legal flaw in the transfer of title to Allen and that Mason was quietly negotiating to sell his claim to Massachusetts. Wasting no time, Thomlinson offered the young Mason one thousand pounds to release his claim to the Assembly of New Hampshire. Though the offer was not concluded until after the line between Massachusetts and New Hampshire had been drawn, "Thomlinson was much applauded for his dexterity."[15]

Thomlinson had Solicitor Paris draw up a petition of appeal to the Crown from New Hampshire against Massachusetts. Playing on the Crown's apprehension about the growing power of the Bay Colony, he described Massachusetts as "vast, opulent, overgrown" and New Hampshire as "ready to be devoured, and the king's own property and possessions swallowed up by the boundless rapacity of the charter government" of Massachusetts.[16]

Thomlinson executed a scheme of breathtaking proportions. He proposed to the Privy Council that the southern boundaries be drawn due west from the most southerly curve of the river at Lowell. And on March 8, 1740, the Privy Council, jittery over the boundless rapacity of the Bay Colony, passed the measure making New Hampshire thirty-five hundred square miles larger than it would have been if Massachusetts had been willing to settle the matter as New Hampshire had first proposed.

But Thomlinson didn't stop there. Since no one wanted the ineffectual Dunbar back as lieutenant governor, he proposed that Benning Wentworth, John's son, be appointed as a separate, independent governor to compensate that worthy merchant for the loss of an expensive cargo of timber caused by diplomatic conflicts between England and Portugal.

He then convinced his friend, Dunbar, to sell his other office as Surveyor of the King's Wood to Benning Wentworth. Thomlinson enlisted the aid of Benning's creditors who, no doubt, realized this was an opportunity to make the bankrupt Wentworth solvent and thereby recoup some of their losses. Enlisting their aid, Thomlinson sold the whole package to the Privy Council. With phenomenal efficiency he established an advantageous southern boundary and a governor independent from Massachusetts, settling these matters so much to the colony's advantage that the Wentworths celebrated with a lavish party that was the subject of local gossip for years after.

But not everybody in the colony celebrated. No doubt many of the old Puritans agreed with the sentiments expressed by the mournful Nicholas Gilman in his diary: "It seems now on all hands expected that the Line will soon be settled between Massachusetts and New Hampshire and that this will be a separate Government. May all be in Mercy to this poor divided province."[17] However, the old Puritans could only fight a rearguard action against the new independence of the colony now governed by the second generation of Wentworths.

GOVERNOR BENNING WENTWORTH

Despite his spurious airs of a Spanish grandee, his royalist sympathies, and his concern for his own fortune, Benning Wentworth, who governed New Hampshire from 1741 to 1766, proved to be one of the ablest royal governors to serve in the colonies. His personal commitment to the Crown aside, he pragmatically allied New Hampshire with Massachusetts to defend the colony against attacks during the French and Indian War. By refusing to enforce the Crown's navigation and customs laws, Benning encouraged the development of the lumber industry to benefit the colony (and himself) rather than England. He facilitated settlement of the interior and worked to expand the western borders of the colony by granting towns on both sides of the Connecticut River from which he also profited.

His opening address to the Assembly did not promise such a satisfactory tenure. During the preceding ten years, the Wentworth clan had identified itself with the Assembly which represented the people. Benning, grandson of a Puritan merchant from Boston, had embraced the Anglican religion and now assured his fellow countrymen that he would "in all faithfulness to the Trust committed to me strictly support the Honorable interest and Perogative of the Crown."[18] From now on the Wentworths would fight their political battles from the governor's chair and the Council, and their opposition would fight in the Assembly. And fight they did until the stubborn Richard Waldron II died in 1753.

By making New Hampshire a royalist colony, drawing the line

Benning Wentworth. Painted by Joseph Blackburn. New Hampshire Historical Society.

between Massachusetts and New Hampshire, and appointing an independent governor, the Crown clarified its determination to make New Hampshire a bulwark against expansionist or anti-royalist tendencies of the Bay Colony and to protect its source of masts for the British navy. But the Assembly dominated by the old Puritan oligarchy would have none of it. The Assembly used the most powerful weapon in its command — the control of appropriations — to curb Wentworth. Wentworth countered with repeated attempts to pack the Assembly with sympathetic representatives at the same time he worked to keep disputes from erupting into outright rebellion, sometimes asserting his authority, but often compromising or bribing assemblymen with appointments or land grants. Mostly Wentworth's diplomacy succeeded, and he got his own way.

The Assembly's most serious challenge to his authority came during threats of Indian raids in 1744 when it refused to appropriate money to maintain Fort Dummer which the Crown considered vital to the defenses of the colony. Wentworth dissolved the body and called for new elections inviting five new towns to send representatives whom he thought would support his demands. When the Assembly met again, it approved the military appropriations but balked at seating the new delegates, denying that the governor had the authority to extend the privilege of representation to the new towns. Desperate for money to fight the war, Wentworth let the issue of representation slide.

The second phase of the confrontation between Wentworth and the Assembly took place between 1748 and 1752 when the colony was temporarily at peace and the governor was no longer pressed for money for the military. Recognizing that Waldron persistently conspired against him, in 1742 Wentworth suspended him from the Council and fired him from his civil and military posts. In return, Waldron and others contrived a plan to oust Wentworth and replace him with the popular Sir William Pepperell, who had led the troops in the Battle of Louisbourg, if that gentlemen could be persuaded to accept the post.

But when Wentworth got a King's writ in which the Lords Justice declared he could, " . . . extend the Privilege of sending Representative to such New Towns as His Majesty shall judge to be worthy thereof,"[19] and Pepperell wisely refused to step into the hornets' nest of New Hampshire politics, the plan to replace Wentworth collapsed. Finally in 1752 the Assembly's term expired. When Wentworth summoned a new Assembly eight months later, the body was much chastened. Financial affairs of the colony were in desperate shape, for only the Assembly could straighten them out. Within twenty days the Assembly had capitulated to the governor and elected Meshech Weare as speaker, increased the governor's salary, and seated the delegates from the new towns.

At the same time Wentworth was toughing it out with the Assembly, he secured the good graces of English officials. Through Thomlinson, Wentworth learned how to please imperial officials. He kept Thomlinson up to date on affairs in the colony while Thomlinson cultivated every official in Whitehall who could conceivably help the colony or his employer. Wentworth presented himself as a model of fealty both to the Crown and to the Church of England and flattered useful noblemen by naming towns after them—Grafton, Strafford, Boscawen acquired their names from men whom Wentworth sought to please.

With Richard Waldron's death in 1753 died any will on the part of the Assembly to cross the Governor. One of Benning's opponents admitted that "the House would make no complaints at the Governor, do what he will,"[20] a situation that lasted through most of the last fifteen years of Wentworth's term.

THE LAST WARS WITH THE FRENCH AND THE INDIANS

Until 1763, when Canada fell to the English, New Hampshire was under constant threat of raids from the Indians encouraged or led by the French. The story of those years is one of repeated kidnappings, attacks, burnings, killings as the colony took the brunt of this lingering war of attrition between the French colonies in Canada and the English colonies in New England. In the early years of his term as governor, Wentworth quietly made friends with Governor Shirley of Massachusetts with whom he cooperated in defending the colony. In 1745 the two men collaborated on a scheme to send troops to attack the well-fortified Louisburg on Cape Breton Island. Since such daring offensive tactics were unusual in New Hampshire and Massachusetts, they could not find an experienced leader for the expedition. The best they could do was to settle on William Pepperrell of Kittery, colonel of a regiment of militia, whose unblemished reputation and engaging manners they hoped might command the loyalty of the raw troops under his command.

So enthusiastic was the governor that when Shirley wrote a flattering letter to the gouty Wentworth saying, "It would have been an infinite satisfaction to me, and done great honor to the expedition, if your limbs would have permitted you to take the chief command," that portly gentleman dismissed his gouty condition and offered to dash into the fray at the head of the expedition. At this point Shirley hastily retracted his satisfaction saying that "prudent" gentlemen had assured him "that any alteration of the present command would be attended with great risk." In any event the successful attack on Louisburg "filled America with joy, and Europe with astonishment," and the enterprise confirmed Wentworth's value to the Crown.[21]

Though portly Governor Wentworth never led soldiers in battle against the French and Indians, two other famous Indian fighters emerged from New Hampshire during these years—John Stark and Robert Rogers. With Stark as his lieutenant, Rogers formed the famous "Rogers' Rangers" in 1756 and trained them to fight like Indians, destroying property, taking prisoners and scalps, and scouting the enemy. Rogers's unorthodox tactics caused endless problems with the regular British military, but he had learned from years of hard experience on the frontier that these tactics worked in the wilderness. Ironically, Rogers accepted a commission from the British during the Revolutionary War while his lieutenant, John Stark, fought for the Americans. Though this hero of the French and Indian War was finally defeated by a weakness for rum, Rogers at his best pursued the enemy with cunning, ruthlessness, and endurance; in the kind of war the settlers had been fighting for years, these qualities added up to the kind of military leader the colony needed.

By the time of the official French and Indian War (1755-1763), the settlers had learned how to defend themselves. They had built forts, and they knew how to fight the French and the Indians whom they had been battling for over a century. This experience and the creditable job Governor Wentworth did in organizing the defenses of the colony meant few settlements had to be abandoned, and fewer people were killed or taken captive than in previous wars. Even so, in 1759, nearly a thousand men were enlisted to serve in the army outside the province—a great drain on the manpower of New

Hampshire. Only when the Treaty of Paris was signed in 1763 and Canada became a British possession did New Hampshire breathe easier. Neither the Revolutionary War nor the Civil War took such a direct and devastating toll on the state as the century-long struggle with the Indians and the French.

After the raids on the frontier ended, the prospect of new settlements in the interior brightened. Since some land grants confused Lake Champlain with the Connecticut River, Governor Benning Wentworth chose to believe that New Hampshire extended west of the Connecticut to Lake Champlain and Lake George. To lend credence to this claim, he chartered a number of towns on both sides of the Connecticut River, importing settlers up the river from Connecticut to farm that rich valley. "So rapidly did this work go on, that during the year of 1761, not less than sixty townships were granted on the west, and eighteen on the east side of the river."[22] In fact, Wentworth encouraged immigration generally so that the population rose from 25,000 in the mid-1730s to about 53,000 in 1767 even excluding those towns west of the Connecticut River.

THE SPOILS OF OFFICE

Benning Wentworth did not neglect his own fortune while directing the military and political affairs of the colony; but like his father took full advantage of his position. Chief among the proprietors of new towns were the governor's family and friends, and Wentworth required them to reserve five to eight hundred acres in each town for the royal governor. During Benning's tenure the Mason grants which Thomlinson had purchased in the name of the Assembly predictably fell into the hands of the Wentworth family if not the governor himself and enriched the family coffers.

As Surveyor General of the King's Wood, Wentworth had jurisdiction over all phases of the masting trade from cutting to shipping. Despite wholesale smuggling for which the Piscataqua was famous, Wentworth wrote careful accounts of the occasional case that he prosecuted and blandly assured English officials that "no illegal commerce existed in New Hampshire."[23] Meantime Thomlinson, who had obtained the contract for selling masts to the British navy, appointed the governor's brother, Mark Hunking Wentworth, his agent in New Hampshire. Benning blinked at timber violations by lumbermen who provided Mark with good quality masts. Mark Wentworth and John Thomlinson grew enormously rich; the lumbermen appreciated the freedom the arrangement gave them to pursue their own profits from other sources; and the governor received substantial gifts of appreciation from both sides.

But fortune-hunting and nepotism were nothing new in the colony, and some of Wentworth's self-interested schemes benefited New Hampshire. Though his constituents disapproved of his royalist sympathies, Wentworth's ties to the Crown hastened the process of separating New Hampshire from Massachusetts. His disregard for the navigation and white pine laws allowed the colony to use its resources for its own benefit rather than for Britain's. His vigorous policy of establishing new towns helped settle the interior, encouraged population growth, and stretched the boundaries of the colony. In his last days in power, he even tried to resist the unpopular Stamp Act which would become the rallying cry of the Revolutionary War.

When Benning Wentworth fell out of favor with the powers at Court and relinquished the governorship in 1767, New Hampshire had grown far bigger, stronger, more prosperous, and more secure than it had been when he had become governor twenty-five years before. The Mason grants were in the control of local citizens and no longer posed a worry to the landholders; political and geographical boundaries between Massachusetts and New Hampshire had been established; and the threat from the French and Indians was over.

THE LAST WENTWORTH GOVERNOR

By 1761 Thomlinson had retired, and with the accession of George III to the throne many other friends of the Wentworths lost their influence on the Crown. Realizing the family's political clout was slipping away, the Wentworths sent young John Wentworth II, a nephew of Benning and son of Mark Hunking Wentworth, to London to court new patrons among the favorites of George III. John was not a Wentworth for nothing. He returned to New Hampshire with new patronage and a commission to replace his uncle as governor, and the third Wentworth became chief executive of the colony.

Though John Wentworth II succeeded to the governorship as planned, his patronage in London proved ephemeral.

In New Hampshire as well as in London the new Wentworth governor courted popular opinion. He rejected his uncle's imperiousness for an "easy and polite . . . address," and unlike the rest of his family which huddled on the coast in Portsmouth and plied their trade with England, he had a plantation in Wolfeboro and encouraged farming. In 1769 he chartered Dartmouth College (named for his English patron, Lord Dartmouth) to supply clergy for vacant pulpits in New England. Most important, he helped establish a county system of courts so the people in the west and north did not have to travel over rough roads and paths, through snow and wilderness, to register deeds or have their cases heard in Portsmouth by judges and juries unsympathetic to the farming settlements.

Though as Surveyor Wentworth tried to understand the lumbermen's views and emphasized surveying over policing, he was losing his grip on the province. Without Thomlinson to cover for him in London, Wentworth could not risk ignoring breaches of the white pine regulations, and prosecution of the regulations brought him under attack from the lumbermen. When he failed to establish the colony's claim to land west of the Connecticut, he lost land and pine trees that he could have used to buy support. Besides, when peace broke out in Europe, the British navy stopped getting its masts shot off and demand for pine trees slipped.

Beginnings of the Revolution

Finally, of course, none of these factors proved important in the conclusion of the Wentworth saga, for by the time the last Wentworth governor took his seat the Revolution hovered on the horizon and no royal governor, however popular and skillful, would survive in office.

Not that New Hampshire led the pack in revolutionary fervor. When in February of 1768 Speaker of the House Peter Gilman laid before the Assembly a letter circulated by Massachusetts protesting the import duties imposed by the Townshend Acts and asserting that taxation without representation was contrary to the constitutional rights of Englishmen, Wentworth persuaded the Assembly not to act. By August of that year, however, revolutionary fever was catching on in the colony, and the governor could not persuade the Assembly to ignore Patrick Henry's famous Virginia Resolves protesting the Stamp Act. Though the Assembly drew up a petition asserting that it "heartily concurred" with those resolves,[24] Wentworth convinced Speaker Peter Gilman not to send the petition; he promised Gilman a seat on the Council and pleaded to key Assemblymen that such a petition would endanger the much-desired division of the colony into counties. But in 1770, the House demanded that Gilman forward the petition.

In 1773 when the Assembly received another invitation from Virginia and Rhode Island to appoint a Committee of Correspondence to spread news of interest among the colonies, Wentworth tried to forestall the appointment. Like all royal governors, Wentworth viewed with suspicion efforts of the colonies to establish closer ties with each other, judging rightly that these bonds would strengthen the colonies against the Crown. But the Assembly and the people were disgruntled by the taxes levied through the Stamp and Townshend Acts, and they appointed the Committee of Correspondence over his objections. The governor dissolved the House.

The Tea Act, following the Stamp and Townshend Acts, provoked such violent reactions and radical rhetoric that some of the more conservative citizens drew back from the revolutionary fomentation, and Wentworth took heart. He reconvened the Assembly in January of 1774 in hopes of passing laws which might control the "infectious and pestilential disorders being spread among the inhabitants."[25] But the conservative backlash was not strong enough to affect the Assembly which ignored the governor's request and dealt with routine business before writing to other colonial Assemblies expressing support for their resistance. Again Wentworth adjourned the meeting, dissolved the Assembly, and called for new elections.

Political control of the province was sliding out of the hands of the royal governor and into the hands of the Assembly. Spring elections were called for 1774. When the governor contrived to request delegates from only the third of New Hampshire's towns in which his friends lived, people were so outraged they elected an Assembly that contained more radicals than the Assembly he had dismissed.

Twice the delegates voted to continue the Committee of Correspondence; after conferring with the Council, on June 8 Wentworth dissolved the Assembly once more. This time the Assembly simply continued to meet in a nearby tavern as did the Committee of Correspondence. A Committee of Safety was formed to provide for the security of the colony. In July the Committee asked each town to elect representatives to a provincial congress which would coordinate resistance in New Hampshire. From among these delegates two men, John Sullivan of Durham and Nathaniel Folsom of Exeter, were chosen to represent New Hampshire at the Continental Congress in Philadelphia. These extralegal bodies assumed more and more the authority of the government, and John Wentworth II could not prevent their establishment or influence their decisions. He watched helplessly as extralegal conventions of revolutionaries met through 1775.

In October Governor Wentworth was caught once more between his obligations to the Crown and his need to placate his restless constituents. General Gage, whose British troops were occupying Boston, needed barracks against the winter, but no Boston carpenters would work for him. He appealed to Wentworth for help. Wentworth realized that New Hampshire carpenters were no more willing to build barracks for Gage's occupying forces than were Boston carpenters, and even if he could find carpenters willing to do the work, public opinion would be outraged. Under the flimsiest pretext, he asked some men near his country plantation in Wolfeboro to work on an unspecified job in Boston. Of course, the ruse was soon exposed, and Wentworth was excoriated by a furious citizenery including his uncle, Hunking Wentworth.

The coup de grace to Wentworth's authority came two months after the episode of the carpenters. Paul Revere brought a message to Portsmouth from Boston that the British had banned export of military stores to America and that troops were on their way to occupy Castle William and Mary, the fort at Newcastle that protected Portsmouth and Kittery, Maine. On December 14, four hundred men led by Captain Thomas Pickering and Major John Langdon stormed the fort against its five defenders, carried off all the powder in small boats, and sent it to nearby communities. The next night under the leadership of Major John Sullivan they invaded the fort again and brought away sixteen cannons, about sixty muskets, and other military stores. Wentworth was helpless. The militia ignored his orders; Council members and local authorities refused to get involved; the crew of his personal barge even refused to row him out to the fort.

These raids so eroded royal authority that Wentworth lost control of the military in the colony. When the governor dismissed the officers who had refused to obey his orders to stop the looting of Castle William and Mary, the militia fell into the hands of the radicals. John Sullivan urged his fellow officers to resign as officers under the royal government but to continue to train their men in weekly drills. After one officer refused, the men elected a new leader and continued to drill. When fighting broke out at Lexington and Concord in April 1775, hundreds of these militiamen flocked to the aid of their neighbors.

Two more efforts by the governor to regain control of the Assembly failed miserably, and the last one percipitated the governor's flight from New Hampshire. One of the governor's friends, John Fenton, who had been excluded from the Assembly, tried to speak in defense of the governor and was shouted down. The governor adjourned the meeting once again.

In a long and touching letter found by historian Jere Daniell, Frances Wentworth, the governor's wife, describes for a friend in England her version of the events of the following evening, June 26, 1775, when Fenton visited the governor's house. A crowd appeared and demanded to see Fenton. The governor refused, and the mob "stove at the house with clubs, brought a large cannon and placed it before the door, and swore to fire through the house. They were so cruel as to affirm no one person, man, woman, or child should escape with life; and when we found resistance was vain, Colonel Fenton surrendered himself and was made to walk 15 miles from Portsmouth to Exeter on foot (tho' very unwell) which he did not accomplish till daybreak. It was directly intimated to the governor a design to make him prisoner, and as the house had been besieged, and violent threats out, he was advised immediately to quit the town, which we did with great haste."[26]

On June 12 the governor and his wife and their five-month-old baby retreated to Castle William and Mary and from there to Nova Scotia where he eventually became the royal governor. They never returned to New Hampshire.

The departure of the royal governor marked the end of the po-

Map of New Hampshire, 1761. New Hampshire Historical Society.

litical system that had ruled New Hampshire since 1679, a system
that had done better by this province that it had by many others in
the American colonies. Certainly the Wentworths were unique
among royal governors. They were natives of the colony they governed, and to a large extent the prosperity and growth of the colony
proved to be in their own best interests as much as it was the settlers.
For three generations they fought for power, made their fortunes,
and enjoyed their privileges as they oversaw the development of the

province. They separated New Hampshire from Massachusetts politically, drew the southern boundary, and stretched the western one; they chartered towns, encouraged inland settlements, laid out a rudimentary system of county courts, and organized the Assembly which took over the reins of government from them.

During the 160 years of New Hampshire's development in the colonial period, the citizens of the province clustered around the eighteen mile coastline and concentrated on exploiting the region's natural resources of fish and timber for which there were rich markets in England, Europe, and the West Indies. In manner, outward appearance, political loyalties, and religious inclinations the early settlers ran the gamut from the raucous fishermen to the puritanical and wily Waldrons, from the royalist and pragmatic Wentworths to the anarchistic planters, but their goals were the same — to make their fortunes from the resources of the complex of inland waterways of the Piscataqua. Even the chartering of inland towns was motivated largely by the desire to claim the timber that stood in the new townships. Farming, of necessity, occupied the attention of most settlers for some of the year, but their ambitions focused on the profits to be made from harvesting the wilderness.

To this end, the province consolidated its economic and political power in Portsmouth where the timber and fish could be most readily shipped abroad. There on the edge of the wilderness evolved an attractive and worldly society and a stable government inextricably intertwined with the province's timber trade. From here the province first declared its independence from the Massachusetts Bay Colony and finally its independence from England.

3

"A State of Nature"

"A STATE OF NATURE" aptly describes the fluid condition not only of the western geographical boundaries of the state, but also of the political and economic conditions in New Hampshire during the Revolutionary War — a time of upheavel and opportunity during which the state drastically modified its economy and redefined itself as a political and geographical entity.

The unsettling departure of the royal governor in 1775 both reflected and precipitated this period of change. Most obviously, of course, the people had to fight a war as they organized a new government, but Wentworth governors were as important in the masting trade, the economic backbone of the state, as they were in the government. For some time that trade had been declining and with the departure of Wentworth and the beginning of the war with England, the masting trade virtually ceased. For the immediate future the people of the new state would have to look inland for new economic opportunities instead of outward toward international trade. Furthermore, since the Wentworth governors had granted most of the towns outside of the Masonian grants, particularly in the Connecticut Valley, the departure of John Wentworth cast doubt on the legitimacy of those grants. Thus the boundaries of the territory claimed by New Hampshire became unclear, and violent border disputes broke out along the Connecticut River.

With determination and resourcefulness the people of the state resolved these primary issues during the next ten years. They drew up a temporary, and then a permanent, constitution for the state and instituted a new government; they developed shipbuilding and privateering to substitute for the masting trade at Portsmouth; and they thrashed through the problem of the western boundary of the state at the same time they were engaged in fighting the Revolutionary War and coping with all the problems attendant on that war.

A New Government, Creation and First Trials

In 1775 the people of New Hampshire faced the immediate problem of creating a government of their own without the advice of either Massachusetts or England. The rebellious Assembly which had held its unofficial sessions in Exeter away from the watchful eye of the royal governor now moved the center of the government there, and assemblymen continued to meet to decide what steps they should take in the immediate crisis. Of course, the Committee of Correspondence and the Committee of Safety also stood ready to assume responsibility for governing the province. Meantime the towns, as always, managed their own affairs. Local officials appointed by the royal government were usually solid and prosperous citizens, whose position made them natural leaders in their towns. And those who were willing continued to perform their duties in the name of "the People" instead of "the King."

Though the transition from royal government to government by the people went surprisingly smoothly, the government once again felt the lack of a charter because the whole of the government had rested on the authority of the royal governor. In his absence, were the laws made by him still valid? What about land grants? What about boundaries established by the Crown? And more to the point, what about the Assembly which, although elected by the people, had been established by the royal governor and did not have representatives from a majority of the towns?

The Assembly took several steps toward legitimizing its authority. First, it augmented its membership with representatives from the Connecticut and Merrimack valleys which had been sorely underrepresented under the royal governor. The next step was more dramatic and more complicated.

Both John Langdon and John Sullivan had attended the session of the Continental Congress early in June when John Adams had

John Langdon.
New Hampshire Historical Society.

urged individual provinces to establish governments of their own, and both men had been impressed by that radical idea. When they returned to New Hampshire, they urged the province to apply to the Continental Congress for permission to draw up a constitution that would define a legitimate government for the province. In taking this dramatic step the state set two important historical precedents. Since it was the first state to write its own constitution, New Hampshire pointed the way for other colonies to formalize their independence. Equally important, however, was the process of appealing to the Continental Congress for permission to draw up the constitution. In making this appeal New Hampshire established the pattern for future relationships between the individual states and the federal government.

Since Sullivan meantime had joined the Continental Army, Josiah Bartlett joined Langdon and the two of them returned to Philadelphia seeking permission to form a state government. With the permission granted, the fourth and fifth provincial Assemblies under President Matthew Thornton moved quickly to draw up the first constitution in the nation.

The Continental Congress had made an important reservation—the constitution should be designed to last only for the duration of the war, a reservation regretted by Langdon, Bartlett, and

Sullivan. Sullivan wished the provincial Assembly "to write a formal constitution [that would] create as ideal a form of government as possible,"[1] one in which the people retained power through direct elections at frequent intervals. He thought the governor should have no absolute veto; the house should not only exercise all the powers of the colonial assembly, it should also participate in appointing public officials. Sullivan's ideal of a grass roots republic is recognizable in New Hampshire's state government today.

However, the short document produced so hastily in the winter of 1775-1776 was far from "ideal," reflecting as it did the circumstances under which it was composed. As critics in Portsmouth were quick to note, times were dangerous and not even the large and powerful colonies like Virginia or New York had yet dared establish independent governments. If the rest of the colonies decided to settle their differences with England and the royal governor returned, this document could hang small New Hampshire, or at least those who wrote it and ratified it. Thus the long preamble was cautiously worded. Like the Declaration of Independence a few months later, it lists the colony's grievances and points to the royal governor's departure which made it necessary to establish a government for New Hampshire. The tone is conciliatory, declaring the document temporary and expressing hope that the colonies could quickly settle their differences with England, restore their allegiance, and live in peace.

The body of the constitution provided that all power lay in the hands of the two bodies of the legislature, the House of Representatives (sometimes called the General Court or the Assembly) and the Council. The Assembly which drew up the constitution was to resolve itself into the House of Representatives, a provision that critics argued undermined the authority of the document. Futhermore, the Assembly was to choose twelve persons to serve as Councilors — henceforth to be elected — besides being empowered to appoint nearly every other public official in the province.

With neither a bill of rights nor any other branch of government to check it, with authority to appoint almost all public officials, the Assembly wielded a staggering amount of power; and the system of representation insured that that power remained in the hands of the older towns. The new state constitution put the Exeter government firmly in control for the duration of the war and sometime after, left the western towns disaffected because they felt underrepresented,

In CONGRESS at Exeter,

January 5th, 1776.

WE the Members of the CONGRESS of the Colony of New-Hampshire, chosen and appointed by the free Suffrages of the PEOPLE of said Colony, and authorized and impowered by them, to meet together, and use such Means, and pursue such Measures, as we shall judge best for the public Good ; and in particular to establish some FORM of GOVERNMENT, provided that Measure should be recommended by the Continental CONGRESS : And a Recommendation to that Purpose having been transmitted to us, from the said CONGRESS ; Have taken into our serious Consideration the unhappy Circumstances into which this Colony is involved by Means of many grievous and oppressive Acts of the British Parliament ; depriving us of our native and constitutional Rights and Priviledges ; to enforce Obedience to which Acts, a powerful Fleet and Army have been sent into this Country, by the Ministry of Great-Britain, who have exercised a wanton and cruel Abuse of their Power, in destroying the Lives and Properties of the Colonists, in many Places ; with Fire and Sword, taking the Ships and Lading from many of the honest and industrious Inhabitants of this Colony, employed in Commerce, agreable to the Laws and Customs, a long Time used here.

The sudden and abrupt Departure of his Excellency JOHN WENTWORTH, Esq; our late Governor, and several of the Council, leaving us destitute of Legislation ; and no Executive Courts being open to punish criminal Offenders, whereby the Lives and Properties of the honest People of this Colony, are liable to the Machinations and evil Designs of wicked Men :

Therefore, for the Preservation of Peace and good Order, and for the Security of the Lives and Properties of the Inhabitants of this Colony, we conceive ourselves reduced to the Necessity, of establishing a Form of Government, to continue during the present unhappy and unnatural Contest with Great-Britain ; Protesting and declaring that we never sought to throw off our Dependance upon Great-Britain, but felt ourselves happy under her Protection, while we could enjoy our constitutional Rights and Privileges---and that we shall rejoice if such a Reconciliation between us, and our Parent State, can be effected as shall be approved by the Continental Congress, in whose Prudence and Wisdom we confide.

Accordingly, pursuant to the Trust reposed in us, we do Resolve, that this Congress, assume the Name, Power and Authority of a House of Representatives, or Assembly, for the Colony of New-Hampshire. And that said House, then proceed to choose Twelve Persons, being reputable Freeholders, and Inhabitants within this Colony, in the following Manner, viz. Five in the County of Rockingham, Two in the County of Strafford, Two in the County of Hillsborough, Two in the County of Cheshire, and one in the County of Grafton, to be a distinct and separate Branch of the Legislature, by the Name of a COUNCIL for this Colony, to continue as such until the Third Wednesday in December next ; Any Seven of whom to be a Quorum, to do Business.

That such Council appoint their President ; and in his Absence that the Senior Councellor preside.

That a Secretary be appointed by both Branches, who may be a Counsellor, or otherwise as they shall choose.

That no Act, or Resolve be valid, and put into Execution, unless agreed to and passed by both Branches of the Legislature.

That all Public Officers for the said Colony, and each County, for the current Year, be appointed by the Council and Assembly, except the several Clerks of the Executive Courts, who shall be appointed by the Justices of the respective Courts.

That all Bills, Resolves or Votes for raising, levying and collecting Money, originate in the House of Representatives.

That

(Facing pages). Facsimile of first State Constitution. New Hampshire Historical Society.

(2)

That at any Seſſions of the Council and Aſſembly, neither Branch ſhall adjourn for any longer time than from Saturday till the next Monday, without Conſent of the other.

And it is further Reſolved, that if the preſent unhappy Diſpute with Great-Britain, ſhould continue longer than this preſent Year, and the Continental Congreſs give no Inſtructions, or Directions to the contrary, the Council be choſen by the People of each reſpective County, in ſuch Manner as the Council & Houſe of Repreſentatives ſhall order.

That General and Field Officers of the Militia, on any Vacancy be appointed, by the Two Houſes, and all Inferior Officers be choſen by the reſpective Companies.

That all Officers of the Army be appointed by the Two Houſes, except they ſhould direct otherwiſe in Caſe of any Emergency.

That all civil Officers for the Colony, and for each County be appointed, and the Time of their Continuance in Office be determined, by the Two Houſes, except Clerks of Courts, and County Treaſurers, and Recorders of Deeds.

That a Treaſurer, and a Recorder of Deeds, for each County be Annually choſen by the People of each County reſpectively ; the Votes for ſuch Officers to. be returned to the Reſpective Courts of General Seſſions of the Peace, in the County, there to be aſcertained as the Council, and Aſſembly ſhall hereafter direct.

That Precepts in the Name of the Council, and Aſſembly, ſigned by the Preſident of the Council, and the Speaker of the Houſe of Repreſentatives, ſhall iſſue annually, at or before the firſt Day of November, for the Choice of a Council, and Houſe of Repreſentatives, to be returned by the third Wedneſday in December then next enſuing, in ſuch Manner as the Council, and Aſſembly ſhall hereafter preſcribe.

In the Houſe of Repreſentatives, September 19. 1776.

Voted and THAT as any new Towns or Settlements in this State, ſhall Reſolved, increaſe in their Number of Inhabitants from Year to Year, or from Time to Time, Precepts ſhall iſſue for their ſending Delegates to Council and Aſſembly, ſo as to be fully Repreſented, according to their Numbers, proportionable with other Parts of the State.

Sent up for Concurrence,

P. WHITE, Speaker.

In Council, Eodem Die, Read and concurred,

E. THOMPSON, Secretary.

Copy Examined pr E. THOMPSON, Secretary.

PORTSMOUTH, Printed by DANIEL FOWLE.

and Portsmouth disgruntled at no longer being the seat of government.

If the system of government itself proved controversial, the day-to-day actions of the Assembly were disappointing. The new revolutionary government followed the example of the old royalist government and consolidated its power by appointing the friends and relatives of the Assemblymen to all the most lucrative and powerful positions in the government—justices of the peace, officers of the militia and the army, and county officials. Other than that, John Langdon observed in disgust to Josiah Bartlett, "The most that is done is punning. Laughing, appointing officers one day, reconsidering the next; not a single act yet passed of any importance."[2] Business which required the approval of both branches was delayed for months. Special committees often never completed their work.

But if the Assembly did not exert itself to govern the province efficiently, several members of the Council readily assumed the responsibility for governing the state. The most outstanding of these was Council President Meshech Weare, master administrator, who headed the Committee of Safety during the whole of the war. Weare enlisted the aid of John Dudley of Raymond and Dr. Josiah Bartlett to turn the Committee into a government for the whole state. Other members came and went on the Committee, but these three stalwarts with Weare at the head remained steadfastly at the helm, prompting one Tory to comment that "New Hampshire had never had a more energetic government, nor a more honest executive."[3] Thus even when the Assembly delegated sweeping powers to the Committee to provide for the safety of the state in almost any way it saw fit, Weare wielded the authority so judiciously that, though the people complained of the constitution and the Assembly, they seldom complained of the Committee of Safety.

Besides Weare, other leaders emerged to replace the departed Wentworths in positions of authority. Of course, John Langdon and John Sullivan who had led the raids on Castle William and Mary remained ardent revolutionaries and served in various posts in the state government including that of governor. Sullivan became a general in the Revolutionary Army. After the war when the rivalry of these two men became disruptive, the voters elected the level-headed Josiah Bartlett governor. William Whipple, a Portsmouth business man, served in the Assembly and also commanded one of the two brigades of state militia (John Stark, who had served with distinction in the French and Indian War, commanded the other). After the war Whipple served as judge of the superior court. Matthew Thornton, a physician, was nearly as active in the state government as Meshech Weare. Besides serving in the Continental Congress, he accepted major judicial appointments and served on the Committee of Safety. Most important, it was under his leadership as president that the fourth and fifth provincial congresses enacted the first constitution.

These men, along with others like John Taylor Gilman, who was later governor for several terms, Samuel Livermore, who worked on the problem of secession in the western towns, and Woodbury Langdon, brother of John, who was later appointed judge, were molding themselves into a new political power structure which dominated New Hampshire from the beginning of the Revolution through the formative years under the presidencies of Washington, Adams, and Jefferson. Significantly, none of these men was Anglican. All were either Congregationalists or Presbyterians. Only Whipple and Langdon had been overseas traders, and they were not involved in masting. Both Thornton and Bartlett were physicians; Samuel Livermore was a lawyer; Weare was a farmer. Some of the new leaders lived in Portsmouth, but not most. They were prosperous, solid citizens (hardly revolutionary rabble) who had served with local governments.

Armed only with a flimsy constitution and revolutionary zeal these men were not adequately equipped to cope with the enormous problems facing the state: the threat of subversion and sabotage from the Loyalists, the threat of invasion by the British, the demands for support both with men and money from the Continental Army, the recurrent financial crises and rampant inflation, and worst of all, the threat by the western towns to secede from the state. The complexity of these problems combined with the instability of the entire political situation would have taxed the acumen of the most sophisticated statesmen, but somehow the political leaders guided the rudimentary government through these dilemmas.

First, of course, the state had to be secured against threats both internal and external. As the Declaration of Independence dissolved ties with Britain, Loyalists and all who worked against the revolutionary cause were outlawed in New Hampshire. The Committee of Safety chaired by Weare administered the oath of allegiance to all white males over twenty-one trying to identify those Loyalists who would spy, discourage enlistments, counterfeit money, circulate propaganda, and in any other way hinder the cause of the Revolution. Private citizens and groups of citizens took steps, legal and extralegal, to control the Loyalists. Mob violence, boycotts, and destruction of property were not uncommon, while confiscation of property and jailing were adopted as standard legal punishments. Some were tried before the Committee of Safety and convicted of Loyalism on the flimsiest of evidence—hearsay and gossip being admitted as evidence, there being no bill of rights to assure fair treatment of dissenters.

But acts committed against the Loyalists did not meet with unanimous approval. Portsmouth, always sympathetic to men of property, held a town meeting in 1779 that expressed disapproval of the confiscation of property owned by Loyalists. Later State President John Sullivan, perhaps because he was an attorney for a wealthy Loyalist family, refused to confiscate property of the hundred or so Loyalists who fled the state. He claimed that the impoverished state government profited little from the property which it confiscated, much of which was lost through mismanagement or corruption. After the war New Hampshire hastened to comply with the terms of the peace treaty which repealed the confiscation laws. Loyalists were allowed one year to return to settle their affairs, though the reason was not necessarily humanitarian since Loyalists owed the merchants of New Hampshire more than the merchants owed them.

The threat from the Loyalists inside the state was less alarming, however, than the military threat from the British outside the state. Though New Hampshire was the only state not invaded by the British army during the Revolutionary War, the people lived at the mercy of rumors of invasions and battles, and they were always prepared for a possible offensive by the British. The local militia continued to drill, and each man between sixteen and sixty was required to provide himself with a musket, bayonet, knapsack, cartridge box, one pound of powder, twenty bullets, and twelve flints. Each town was required to keep one barrel of powder, two hundred pounds of lead, and three hundred flints for every sixty men and provide equipment for any man unable to provide it for himself. Besides these local precautions, the state supplied three regiments to the Continental Army, though how well the state equipped these regiments is questionable.

The two most vulnerable areas for British invasion were Portsmouth harbor and the Connecticut River Valley. John Sullivan supervised the construction of defenses of the harbor which in the end escaped attack. Though the British chose to invade via Lake Champlain rather than the Connecticut River, it was New Hampshire that provided the troops and the leader to stop that invasion in one of the crucial battles of the war. In July 1777, Vermont sent an appeal to the New Hampshire Assembly for assistance in defeating General Burgoyne's march down the Champlain Valley. John Langdon, the Speaker of the House urged them to comply. In a speech attributed to him by Isaac Hill, Langdon reputedly said, "I have a thousand dollars in hard money; I will pledge my plate for three thousand more. I have seventy hogshead of Tobago rum which will be sold for the most it will bring. They are at the service of the state. If we succeed in defending our firesides and our homes, I may be remunerated. If we do not then the property will be of no value to me."[4]

To lead these troops the Assembly persuaded John Stark, who had served in the French and Indian War with Rogers Rangers, to come out of retirement. Stark, miffed that he had been passed over for promotion three months before, had resigned from the army. Fortunately, a belated promotion to general lured him back to arms; Stark not only had experience, he was a wily tactician and a charismatic leader who kept his troops together when most commanders suffered wholesale desertions during the grim days of the war.

The colorful Stark, who had once fought his way through an Indian gauntlet yelling, "I'll kiss all your women!,"[5] according to one Colonel Potter had attracted fourteen companies to his standard in as many days after the first battle at Lexington. Now he had no trouble finding volunteers to follow him to Bennington. Perhaps they were attracted by his bravado. At Lake George during the French and Indian War when his wounded commander, Robert Rogers, urged retreat, he declared he held a good position and would "fight on until dark."[6]

At the Battle of Bennington Stark lived up to his reputation for leadership and quick wits. Burgoyne, the leader of the British troops, planned to march down Lake Champlain and the Hudson River cutting off New England from the rest of the colonies. Stark fought the British and the Hessians from the woods as he had the French and Indians rallying his men with the cry, "There, my boys, are your enemies, the red-coats and tories; you must beat them or my wife sleeps a widow to-night."[7] The victory at the Battle of Bennington foiled the strategy of the British who aimed to cut New England off from the rest of the states. It also raised the morale of all the colonies in a dark period of the war because it demonstrated that by fighting in the woods the ill-equipped Americans could offset the advantage British soldiers had in training and cannons.

In general, however, privateering turned out to be a more popular enterprise in New Hampshire than serving in the army since it offered the possibility of rewards for the hazards of war while the army offered only discomforts and danger. The privateer served his country and himself at the same time, a familiar role for the Piscataqua shipowners and shipbuilders who raised the private navy which would plague the British cause. After all, in a "state of nature" almost any useful and profitable venture was fair game.

A New Economy: Piscataqua Shipbuilding Prospers

The Piscataqua's maritime economy adjusted to war just as it had adjusted to earlier obstacles and opportunities. As emphasis shifted from international timber trade to internal transportation and shipbuilding, the region's carpenters, known since the 1650s for their skill at building fishing vessels and larger cargo ships, claimed just recognition as superior shipwrights working in a major shipbuilding region. Soon these artisans would be a major force in the Revolutionary War, producing vessels for the Continental Navy as well as for a regional navy of privateers.

The shipbuilding industry had expanded along with the overseas lumbering trade in the eighteenth century. During this period, New Hampshire-built vessels increased in size and quantity. Between 1687-1695, thirty-four vessels of an average tonnage of 28.9 tons were built; in 1727, forty vessels of an average tonnage of 72.5 tons were built, and in 1742, eighty-two vessels of an average tonnage of 83.2 tons were built. The Piscataqua area, therefore, approached the Revolution ranking second or third in ship production in the New England region, or producing 17 percent of the ships' tonnage in the thirteen colonies. Risking capital to encourage shipbuilding, the clever merchants of Portsmouth had found yet another way to achieve prosperity and prepare the colony for economic as well as political independence.

At first glance, the American Revolution dealt a sharp econom-ic blow to the prosperous Portsmouth oligarchy and its Piscataqua constituents. While most of the young province's citizens continued their accustomed agricultural, trading, and pioneering enterprises, the Piscataqua region's life was unalterably affected by the gathering war clouds. England, major partner in the growth of the region's maritime economy, was now the enemy and trade on the seas was severely limited. Certainly the Piscataqua trade shrank drastically during the war years, but it quickly regained the vigorous health of the prewar years principally through privateering. The rationale for privateering was clear: using privately owned, armed vessels, the colonies would attack Britain's most vulnerable point — the commer-cial vessels the Navy used to resupply its warships — thereby gaining an otherwise extremely limited naval advantage. Quick to see the advantage of this "marine militia" or "volunteer navy," the Continen-tal Congress authorized ship's captains to seize all British ships car-rying cargo to their naval vessels, designating the captured ships legal prizes to be awarded to the privateers by regional admiralty courts. The proceeds from the sale of the ship's cargo would then be distributed proportionally among the ship's captain and crew.

Between 1775 and 1783, Portsmouth contributed at least a hun-dred ships and three thousand men to the total Revolutionary "guer-rilla" force of two thousand ships and thirty thousand men. Owned by men in all parts of the district, the ships ranged in size from small sloops to ships of several tons, sailing with crews of from 10 to 160 men. The roster of the owner's names included most prominent Portsmouth merchants, notably John Langdon, and even a judge of the local admiralty court. Choosing life on a privateering vessel over starving in George Washington's army or being flogged in the navy seemed easy for crewmen, who also received a percentage of the cap-tured ship's worth.

Nonetheless, privateering was a risky business. Thousands of colonial seaman were captured; many were impressed into the Brit-ish Navy or imprisoned in most unpleasant conditions. Others faced death and disfigurement. Young Andrew Sherburne's story reveals the dangers many sailors faced. Sailing from Portsmouth at fourteen on a Continental Navy vessel, which was later captured at Charles-ton, Sherburne returned to his home port to sign on as a crew-member on several successful missions by newly commissioned Pis-cataqua privateers. But his luck soon ran out. Captured first in

Newfoundland, he narrowly escaped death at the hands of an angry mob of British sympathizers through the good offices of a woman Sherburne's memoirs describe as "an old English lady of distinction who appeared to have an excellent education."[8] Imprisonment in England followed nevertheless, until he was freed in an exchange of prisoners, only to return home, join another privateer crew and face capture and brutal treatment once again. Such were the risks many investors and sailors were willing to take—perhaps for profit or perhaps for patriotism.

Lest we impute uncomfortably mixed motives to the Piscataqua merchants and shipowners, it should be noted that this same group's skill produced three warships for the Continental Congress—the 32-gun *Raleigh*, the 18-gun *Ranger*, and the 74-gun *America*. All three ships saw considerable and successful naval action and greatly impressed their rivals. The legendary Captain John Paul Jones supervised the construction of the *Ranger* and the *America*, the latter of which he turned over reluctantly but obediently to the French as a gesture of thanks from the Continental Congress. Captured later by the British in the Anglo-French war, the *America* so impressed her captors that she remained a Royal Navy ship of the line until as late as 1846 and became a model for several British ships.

If the Piscataqua's shipwrights could boast of their dramatic effect on the war effort by building and refitting ships for both a private and the Continental ocean-going navy, the region's farmers and jacks-of-all-trades could boast of developing and perfecting yet another essential but unassuming, non-seagoing craft, the gundalow. In fact for more than two hundred years, this nautical workhorse, quickly and easily built and highly practical, moved through the Piscataqua waterways, unacclaimed and dependable. The gundalow illustrates as eloquently as any feature or character of the region the degree to which successful adaptation to circumstance has been a crucial element in the state's economic history. While very few of the seagoing vessels built in the region's "inland" ports such as Exeter, Newmarket, Durham and Dover ever returned to their home ports once launched from shallow waters and headed downstream, the gundalow was built to stay and work.

Crudely designed and quickly built in the seventeenth century to bear heavy loads in shallow waters along narrow river banks yet nimble enough to negotiate fast-moving, open-water currents, these

Gundalow working on the Squamscot River. Peabody Museum of Salem, Massachusetts.

bulky, broad-beamed craft were also capable of surprising speed as they took advantage of wind and tidal currents. The earliest design was later modified to become more and more efficient and sophisticated until the regional prototype, unique to the Piscataqua, the lateen-sail version of the nineteenth century, evolved. Like the early fishermen of this region, the reckless, hard-drinking, profane gundalow captains and crews were regarded with scorn by other seamen, so much so that even the Revolutionary privateer captains avoided hiring gundalow men if possible. With the hyperbole these lusty crews inspired, a resident who remembers the earlier gundalow days has said: "An old sea captain made the statement that a man who would sail a gundalow would rob a churchyard."[9]

Beneath whatever legends their crews may have inspired lies the demonstrable reality that the gundalows provided a crucial regional transportation system for years. They hauled cargos of local bricks and granite; cord wood (up to sixteen cords at once) and coal for fuel; cotton and other raw materials to mills; marsh hay and grass cleared from the bay's fields. And they ferried civilian and military cargoes between Piscataqua towns.

During the Revolution the native craft proved indispensable in defense of the Portsmouth harbor, working as both military landing craft and cargo vessels. Never as glamorous as the region's schooners, or warships, or nineteenth-century clippers, this maritime delivery truck was a hearty survivor. Well-adapted to the Piscataqua's geography and economy, it alone among the region's vessels continued to ply her twentieth-century waters.

REGIONAL CONFLICTS CHALLENGE THE NEW STATE

As the state grappled with the economic and political problems created by the war, regional differences among its citizens threatened to unglue the territorial unity of the state, and neither the threat of war nor the rudimentary constitution the state adopted welded the regions into a comfortable political unit. So violent was the dispute, that at times the government in Exeter seemed almost isolated within the sixty-mile arc of land originally granted to Mason, the western towns claiming that they owed no allegiance to the central state government. That radical opinion now challenged the territorial integrity of New Hampshire.

From the days of the earliest settlements, the regions of the state developed differently and separately. The first settlements in the state — the four first towns, Dover, Portsmouth, Exeter and Hampton, all located near the Piscataqua, the tidewater, and the coastal plain — had dominated the political and economic life of the state until the Revolutionary War. By 1776 there were more towns in the region, and political, social, and religious attitudes had not changed a great deal. Portsmouth, the center of trade, still enjoyed the pleasant style of life established by the Wentworths. The fine houses, carriages, parties, and servants did not vanish with the royal governor but remained part of the life of Portsmouth well into the nineteenth century when journalist Isaac Hill complained of the influence the style of life in Portsmouth had on politics of the state. It was more conservative in its politics and less zealous in the Revolutionary cause being, perhaps, still a little enchanted with the glamor of the royal governor. Besides, the port city still focused its attention on overseas trade much disrupted by the war.

Exeter, the town of land-owning Puritans, had traditionally grabbed political power from the royal governors whenever the opportunity arose. And the Revolution presented just such an opportunity. With the exit of John Wentworth, the Gilmans, Weares, Bartletts, and others moved the capital to Exeter. It seemed another turn of the wheel of fortune in the old game that the two political and religious antagonists had been playing out in the Piscataqua since Mason received his grants.

But times had changed. There were new players, new regions of the state that could not be ignored. Only a few miles west of Exeter lay the Merrimack Valley and the southern towns extending as far west as Charlestown that had been granted during the quarrel between New Hampshire and Massachusetts over the southern boundary. Except for properous Londonderry, which was settled by Irish immigrants, these towns, whether granted by Massachusetts or New Hampshire, had been settled by people from Massachusetts. In the rich valley of the river lay twenty flourishing farming towns. And within the old Mason grant lay thirty-five more town corporations. Most of these people scorned the political and social institutions of England as did their Massachusetts neighbors with whom they had strong religious, social, and economic ties.

During the 1740s and 1750s, when Benning Wentworth assumed that his grant extended as far west as Lake Champlain, he had granted a spate of over a hundred new towns on both sides of the Connecticut River which became the fourth contrasting region of the state. Over the protests of some of the citizens of New Hampshire, these towns were settled in large part by pioneers pushing up the Connecticut seeking the rich valley farmland. Neither shipbuilders nor merchants nor Puritans, these settlers lacked bonds not only with England or Massachusetts, but also with the rest of New

Hampshire. Lack of roads running east and west and forbidding winter weather inhibited communication between the Connecticut Valley and the eastern coast. Furthermore their trade flowed down the river to Connecticut, not east to Portsmouth or south to Boston. Settlers on both sides of the river shared common interests and identified with each other rather than with faraway Exeter or Bennington, Vermont.

The White Mountains and northern part of the state which formed a fifth region geographically were so sparsely settled at the time of the Revolution that they were politically insignificant (except for the episode of the Indian Stream Republic) until later in the nineteenth century.

Small though the territory of New Hampshire was, the disparity in the people of the various regions made it difficult to mold them into a cohesive political unit. Certainly the lawmakers in Exeter working under the first constitution which many regions found unsatisfactory watched the state nearly break apart.

It was at the signing of that first state constitution in 1775 that the western towns first protested that the system of representation was unfair. After being outvoted at the constitutional convention, the towns that lay east of the Connecticut began to question the authority of the government in Exeter and began to withdraw from participation in the state government.

The landowners on the western bank of the river (in what is now Vermont) felt particularly uneasy because they had been granted their land by the authority of the royal governor of New Hampshire, and now their land fell under the authority of New York which might or might not recognize their legal claim to it. Furthermore, the towns on the western bank of the Connecticut felt as remote from towns west of the Green Mountains as the towns on the east bank from the eastern part of New Hampshire. Thus the "New Hampshire Grants," as these towns were called, shared common discontents, a common history, and now they wanted to share a common political future.

Unlike most frontier regions, the Connecticut Valley had a spokesman for its discontents, or rather an institution that made a case for its claims. Pamphlets from Dartmouth College expressed the argument that sovereignty rested with the towns and not the state, that the independence of the United States reduced them to "a state of nature" which allowed them to form any political bonds they liked. These towns boycotted the Constitutional Convention of 1778 and refused to send representatives to the General Court. Two delegations from Exeter, one led by the indomitable Weare, himself, made the arduous journey to the Connecticut Valley to try to persuade the people that Exeter had their best interests at heart. Both missions failed.

If Dartmouth College claimed the towns were in "a state of nature," Ethan and Ira Allen, landowners from Bennington and leaders of the Green Mountain Boys, threatened to throw them into a state of anarchy. Not only did they fear New York might declare their land grants invalid, they also recognized that since they lived outside the Connecticut Valley they could not count on sharing the collective fate of the New Hampshire Grants. They took matters into their own hands and revolted against New York, established the state of Vermont, and threatened violence to anyone who defied their decrees. The conflict became so acute that it endangered the very existence of New Hampshire.

Finally New Hampshire and New York appealed to George Washington to review the matter. In a masterful letter to the governor of Vermont, he laid out the case and suggested that Vermont relinquish claims to land east of the Connecticut ending, "There is no calamity within my foresight, which is more to be dreaded than a necessity of coercion . . . and consequently every endeavor should be used to prevent the execution of so disagreeable a measure."[10] Even the Allen brothers heard the warning and acknowledged the boundary at the river. Rancor lingered, but the state of New Hampshire was preserved whole and honored Washington for his perspicacity by naming a town after him — the first Washington in the country.

The state government resented the whole secessionist movement, particularly the college's role in it. The towns were not happy and retaliated with an obstructionist policy in the courts. The state responded by adopting an amendment to the state constitution prohibiting college professors from serving in the legislature. Only gradually did animosity fade, flaring up in the nineteenth century in the famous Dartmouth College Case. State President John Sullivan adopted a lenient policy toward rebellious individuals of the western counties. More citizens from the west were appointed to state offices.

Furthermore the new Constitution of 1784 provided for more liberal representation from western towns in the Assembly and Council, all of which soothed their ruffled feathers.

A NEW CONSTITUTION SOLIDIFIES THE NEW GOVERNMENT

As if the problems with the war and internal revolts were not enough, the government in Exeter suffered from its own inefficient organization. Though the Constitution of 1775 had been unsatisfactory from the beginning, the people were as divided over revising it as they were divided over so many things. But reformers were hard at work by 1776 campaigning for a new state constitution. In 1777 when John Langdon became Speaker of the House, he led the Assembly into another historic first. As New Hampshire in January of 1775 became the first state to establish its own constitution, so in June of 1778 it became the first to call a constitutional convention in which "a common people [were] allowed to elect themselves into convention for creation of their own government, with a key proviso that it had to be returned to them for final ratification or rejection."[11]

Several issues worried those who agitated for a new state constitution. Most people saw the need for a chief executive of the state. John Langdon, who mistrusted the royal governors, now saw that a legislature alone could not run the affairs of the state effectively. Many people were also disturbed by the fact that a few men were being appointed to so many offices. According to Daniell, one contemporary writer observed: "I know of an Assembly who have given amongst themselves almost every place of honor or profit in the colony, civil, military, executive, judicial and legislative."[12] On the other hand, Weare, Bartlett, Thornton and many others not only saw nothing wrong in holding more than one post, they contended that it was the only way the government could operate efficiently. The western towns were unhappy with the system of representation outlined in the first Constitution. And finally, of course, many people questioned the legality of the first Constitution since it had been drawn up by the same men who served in the legislature outlined in the document they had written.

In 1779, the convention produced a document which curtailed plural office holding but neither provided for an executive branch of government nor improved representation by the western towns. Jeremy Belknap, who did not limit his writing to impartial histories, referred to the proposed government as "a lousy chick of the degenerate British breed, vulgarly styled omnipotent" and led Portsmouth to vote against it 87 to 2.[13] The western towns refused even to vote on the new proposals. In short, the electorate took the opportunity offered by the revolution to reject the government proposed by their representatives and sent them back to design another that met with their approval.

In the absence of both Weare and Bartlett, George Atkinson of Portsmouth, heir of an old Royalist, Theodore Atkinson, chaired the next convention. It was enough to make any Revolutionary nervous. Nevertheless, it was under the intelligent leadership of Atkinson that the convention produced three more proposed constitutions until finally, overcoming voter apathy by sheer persistence, in 1784 the convention found a combination that suited the mood and ideas of the voters well enough so that they were unwilling to reject it totally. The war had ended and the old constitution was outmoded. The new constitution kept a tight rein on the executive, it forbade plural office holding, it separated the branches of government and provided a system of checks and balances of power between the branches. It would be impossible for a small clique to appoint one another to overlapping jobs in the new government, and more difficult for the government to be dominated by a few men.

At the insistence of the western towns, the incorporated town was "fixed so firmly in the fundamental law as the basis of representation that no subsequent effort could remove it. It is there today, making the New Hampshire lower house almost as large as the national House of Representatives"[14] which is, perhaps, a dubious distinction, but one that reflects not only the long struggle to unify the eastern and western regions of the state, but also the attachment that the citizens of New Hampshire feel for their towns and their belief in a grass roots democracy.

In 1784 the new constitution went into effect — the constitution which remains through many revisions the basis of the government of the state to this day.

Seventeen eighty-four proved to be a banner year for New Hampshire. The state constitution was put into effect, the Revolutionary War ended, and the boundaries of the state were nearly complete. The state had become a stable and complete physical and political body. By replacing the picture of a fish and a pine tree on the state seal with a picture of a ship being built and the rising sun, New Hampshire commemorated a year in which the state had found a fresh direction after struggling through the uncertainties of the revolution. That same year when the Piscataqua Bridge was built from Newington to Durham, a half-mile span that was an engineering wonder at the time, the political and economic focus of the state turned away from the eighteen miles of coastline facing international waters and focused inland. Since its inception New Hampshire had been obsessed with that port. No longer. Though Portsmouth remained important in shipbuilding, the port never again dominated the state as it had before and during the Revolutionary War. Instead, the people turned to the land and expected their new government to promote the welfare of a rural society based on agriculture. Politically, as a member of the new republic, the state would turn its attention to cementing relations with the other states of that republic.

4

The Farm

IF IN THE AGE of the exploration and settlement of New Hampshire, exploitation of her resources — fur, fish, and timber — had been the chief source of economic and social well-being, cultivation of the land's resources consumed her citizen's energies for much of the period which immediately followed. By Jeremy Belknap's reckoning, and he spoke for his contemporaries, the pursuit of husbandry promoted a partnership with the natural environment and provided the basis for development of country towns, where by diligence and industry one might achieve as much "social happiness" as this world could afford. Ordinary folk, politicians, and philosophers promoted the virtues of a rural yeoman's republic, fostering the assumption that such a society was possible in New Hampshire. By the mid-1800s the effects of geographic isolation and market realities, however, challenged these assumptions, shaking the faith of politicians and citizens alike and setting the state's economy and politics on yet another course.

In the first two centuries of settlement, New Hampshire became a landscape of fields and fences. Until the mid-nineteenth century in fact, most citizens whether artisans, ministers, merchants, storekeepers, or lumbermen were also involved in farming. Nevertheless, the degree to which New Hampshire's farms ever constituted the source of its economic prosperity is arguable; the balance between expectation and reality constantly shifted. In the seventeenth century the men who traded in fur, fish, and lumber also for the most part provided their own food. Later at the time of the Revolution farming was the state's largest single industry. But the fact that the fishing, lumber, and shipbuilding industries formed the backbone of a highly profitable overseas trade in the eighteenth century at the same time suggests that the region had already learned a good deal about the value of what the land would yield. In 1784, the same year the state adopted its constitution, the half-mile Piscataqua Bridge built between Newington and Durham began to shift the state's economy to interior resources. Later the census of 1820, which for the first time classified Americans by occupation, listed 52,384 people in New Hampshire who gained their livings by agriculture, 1,068 by commerce, and 8,699 by manufacturing. By the twentieth century a manufacturing economy replaced the agrarian economy almost completely as it drew the work force away from the farm to a source of steady wages, and as the age of the railroad shifted sources of supply and demand. Yet the state's farms were never largely "abandoned" and changed to the refuge of the summer visitor; the success of the region's dairy industry belies that assumption. And so the balance between fact and fiction shifts.

To understand the relationship between the myth and the reality of farmers' place in New Hampshire's history and economy, it is necessary to consider the same determinants which affected the state's maritime economy — geographic and market realities. Like the experience of the latter-day backyard gardener struggling with crops of rocks, poor, thin soil, and fickle weather, a key element in the story is the interaction between the settler and the land. The farmer's economic and ecological assumptions about the land — its uses, its possibilities, its limitations — largely determined the direction of nearly three centuries of farming in the state. In each century the decisions the farmer made and the risks he took permanently changed the land he settled.

Farming in provincial New Hampshire was never easy. The English settlers who came directly to New Hampshire's Piscataqua Basin in the 1600s, and particularly those who emigrated a little later from the Massachusetts Bay Colony, brought with them certain strict assumptions about settlement and land use. As Roderick Nash has argued in *Wilderness and the American Mind*, the wilderness which the settlers confronted posed both physical and symbolic dangers. On the physical level, the wilderness offered a direct challenge to survival. Taking the abundant resources required difficult labor;

cultivation of the wooded wilderness required a formidable battle for conquest. And the settlers hadn't come for trouble. On a symbolic level, as Nathaniel Hawthorne later dramatized so convincingly, the wilderness acquired significance as a dark and sinister symbol. The settlers shared a long Western tradition of considering the wilderness empty of morality — a wasteland. Subduing and battling the wasteland, therefore, became a call to personal survival and a call to enlighten the darkness, bring order to chaos, in short, change evil into good. As late as 1769 Eleazar Wheelock characterized his mission to found Dartmouth College in this same mold when he chose for the college's motto, "Vox Clamantis in Deserto," "A voice crying in the wilderness."

The Settlers Meet the Natives

New England's native inhabitants posed an early external threat to the farmer. Information about New Hampshire's native population is scarce and often based as much on conjecture as fact because European settlers were more concerned with survival than historical record and the largely nonliterate Indian populations left virtually no records. In the 1600s when the English arrived, about three thousand Algonkian Indians lived in the region settled in well-established villages. This population included Sokokis (probably Abenakis) in the White Mountains; Pigwackets near Conway; Pocumtucks and Ashuelots near the Connecticut River; and the population's most numerous and powerful group, the Pennacooks, which loosely included other southern groups, the Pemigawassets, the Souhegans and Nashuas, the Piscataquas and Squamscotts.

The pattern of the native Americans' life is familiar: they engaged in hunting, fishing, and agriculture, using tools of their own making and moving from hunting and fishing grounds to food-producing areas according to seasonal cycles. In the first decades of the 1600s the native population was strongly attracted to the guns, metal fishing hooks, cutting tools, and domestic commodities like kettles which fur-trading with the settlers provided. Even at the time of European settlement the Indians probably considered that Mohawk tribes from the west posed a more distinct threat to their existence than did the newcomers. Coexistence worked and was in fact promoted by tribal leaders until the English population overtook the native population in numbers in the mid-1600s; English settlements directly affected the Indian's access to hunting and fishing grounds, and English livestock wreaked havoc with accustomed growing fields. Indian leader Passaconaway and his son Wonalancet constantly warned their tribes against open warfare, urging either survival by accommodation or migration, and limiting their aggressiveness to incantations and spells. But peace did not last indefinitely.

One clue to a major source of tension between the natives and the European settlers lies with several New Hampshire town names of Indian origin. The town of Sunapee, near one of the state's largest lakes, derives its name from Algonkian usage in which "suna" means goose and "apee" means lake; the name Ossipee is derived from two tribal names Cossuck, or Cowass, later Coos, which means pine tree, and "sippee" meaning river; Pennacook, near Concord, takes its name from the local tribe, whose name bears the meaning "crooked place" or bend in the river; Nashua, also near the home of the Nashaway Indians, means "beautiful river with a pebbly bottom"; and finally Amoskeag is a Pennacook word meaning "abundance of fish." For the native Indians, place names reflected their discovery and use of places where they could gather necessities. In this way the landscape became a map which inhabitants could study, and find sources of food and shelter. Thus land, agricultural and nonagricultural was not so much "owned" as "used"; or put another way, the Indians considered that they "owned" the bounty which they moved from place to place to gather, not the gathering-place itself.

For the English settler, on the other hand, land granted individually or communally by proprietary agreement deriving from the Crown brought with it the exclusive right of permanent ownership, a condition regarded as the basic requirement for settlement. Displacement of the Indian was then most certainly inevitable as the settlers acted on their Divine imperative to "improve" the land, which from their point of view had been so cavalierly treated by the Indian. As early as 1675 settlers were faced with increasing opposition from the Indian population, whom they generally displaced and whose seeming lack of industry they criticized. As a result, for nearly forty years around the turn of the eighteenth century and later from 1744 to 1760, northern New England was a battleground between settlers and Indians in conflicts often arising out of conditions beyond both parties' control—the European struggle for North America. These wars were the most devastating New Hampshire ever experienced, and they affected life at every level. Population grew very slowly as did inland or frontier settlement. Scarcely any family escaped the effects of sudden houseburning, scalping, slaughter, captivity, and looting, activities frequently undertaken in the season New England now ironically regards as a dispensation, "Indian summer."

Constant threats of violence during these years altered a farm family's sense of freedom and well-being and the garrison life which such conditions imposed in many ways resembles the enclosed life of some modern city-dwellers. Many berries went unpicked in the woods and many mothers admonished children to stay within sight of the house in those years. And with the men and boys so often off the farm fighting the Indians, numerous responsibilities for planting, cultivating, harvesting, and managing fell to the women.

Certainly the most animated accounts of frontier farming in this period are reserved for the so-called captivity narratives, and New Hampshire lays claim to Hannah Duston's tale of terror, remembering her with native pride. Between the late 1600s and early decades of the seventeenth century close to three hundred women, men, and children were taken captive in northern New England, many from the towns surrounding Hannah Duston's home in Haverhill, Massachusetts, many others from the vulnerable settlements on the Oyster, Cocheco, and Piscataqua rivers. Unlike many of her sister captives, Hannah returned home safely, continued to bear children, and even became a public convert, so that her tale, exalted and elevated by Cotton Mather, the famous Bay Colony Puritan minister, survives where many others have slipped into obscurity.

On March 15, 1697, at about seven in the morning, Hannah Duston's house along with several others was attacked by Indians, resulting in the death or capture of about forty persons. Hannah, who had given birth less than a week before and was still attended by a nurse, Mary Neff, first endured an attack on her house and then the murder of her newborn child. Then with her nurse and a boy who was visiting the house, she was marched over a hundred miles into the wilderness, to rest finally near Pennacook in New Hampshire. By stealth and cunning Duston directed and participated in the killing of her sleeping captors, and after second thought returned to remove and reclaim ten scalps to present proof positive of the deed. For the scalps she received a bounty from the General Court of twenty-five pounds. For her bravery she received near canonization from the New England pulpit and inclusion in Cotton Mather's 1702 *Magnalia Christi Americana*, where she became an archtypal heroine of the New World frontier. For Nathaniel Hawthorne, who later described her with undisguised disdain, she was a "bloody old hag" who he wished "had sunk over head and ears in a swamp, and been there buried, until summoned forth to comfort her victims at the Day of Judgement."[1] As a woman accustomed to heavy farm labor, animal slaughter, and identification of the Indian with evil, however, her revenge for her child's death gains credibility.

THE GOAL WAS SELF-SUFFICIENCY

In the first two centuries of settlement self-sufficiency was the farmer's goal, not mere subsistence. To achieve self-sufficiency, the farmer would become a year-around small production and manufacturing unit, evaluating his resources and his needs. He would become an extensive farmer, producing a variety of crops for food, raising and pasturing livestock for food, hides, and wool and in some instances producing a marketable surplus, which would allow him to barter for goods he could not produce. Each year the cycle of producing, storing, saving, and exchanging would be repeated.

New Hampshire poet, Donald Hall, writes of the "Ox Cart Man," who walks one hundred miles to the Portsmouth market and repeats this cycle:

> When the cart is empty he sells the cart.
> When the cart is sold he ⌐lls the ox,
> harness and yoke, and walks
> home his pockets heavy
> with the year's coin for salt and taxes,
>
> and at home by fire's light in November cold
> stitches new harness
> for next year's ox in the barn,
> and carves the yoke, and saws planks
> building the cart again.[2]

Farm Scene in Warner. Painted by Harry E. Greaves. New Hampshire Historical Society.

Clearly, unlike the rowdy coastal fishermen and lumbermen, the farmer's life was one marked by diligent, sober work, close family interdependence, and communal responsibility.

The pattern of settling-in was both typical of New England and peculiar to New Hampshire. The provincial government gave grants of land for townships to groups of proprietors, who then agreed to certain conditions governing the development of the settlement. These conditions often included a specific time period (usually three to seven years) for settlement, specifications about house and houselot sizes, standards for divisions of common meadow and grazing lands, provision for the establishment of a meetinghouse and school, and later for the building of roads and bridges. Houselots were then divided among the settlers according to the degree of their investment in the settlement.

With land in hand, the farmer began the slow and difficult process of clearing the land for planting a suitable succession of crops and providing fields for grazing animals. Sometimes the pioneer farmer was lucky enough to find that some of his land had already been cleared by Indians. More often, however, he was faced with either girdling the trees and allowing them to die standing or practicing the more time-consuming method of cutting and burning. Each method had its trade-offs. Cutting an incision in the bark and leaving the tree to die was quicker and provided nearly immediate open ground for tillage, but once dead the trees became dangerous obstructions. Burning and cutting, on the other hand, took longer, but provided building and fencing material, fuel, and the important early cash crops, pot and pearlash. Removing stones and making walls would come later. After sowing a crop of winter rye the first year, the principal crop was usually the New World's sustaining grain, Indian corn or maize. Following the Indian habit of planting corn as soon as the leaves on white oaks were the size of a mouse's ear, the farmer quickly learned the advantages of growing this crop which ripened easily during the short and fickle growing season inland and required little cultivation. Even though Mason's plantation on the Piscataqua received seven hundred bushels of Virginia corn in 1631, the provincial farmer, according to Belknap, could hope to produce thirty to forty bushels of corn per acre on his own. Cultivation of accustomed European grains such as wheat, barley, oats, rye, and hay followed later, particularly as the need for forage crops for livestock became clear. Other early crops included squash, beans, pumpkins, again food crops whose worthiness the Indians had tested and passed along to the settlers.

As the colonial farm approached the eighteenth century and came of age, it was the agricultural "immigrants," however, not the native crops, which like their yeoman counterparts, began to take center stage. And taking center stage meant making indelible changes in the landscape. The relationship between the "newcomer" and the native is a very old story in New Hampshire.

The Indians had kept no domestic animals other than dogs, but European agricultural practices included domestic animals, and these were introduced. Grazing animals, used both as draft animals in tillage and for transportation, greatly increased the quantity of land the farmer could plant, and laid the foundation for commercial agriculture. Cattle, of course, were the stars, presenting as they did several benefits: they could be used as draft animals; slaughtered for meat; or kept as milk, butter, and cheese producers. Their value was local and international, for salted and preserved surplus beef found an eager market in the West Indies. Cowhides were also invaluable once tanned. From sheep, the domestic spinner clothed the family.

Swine, mercifully easy to take care of, were hearty survivors in the region. Horses appear to have been used principally for transportation and by the military.

But the economic value of domestic livestock also had interesting ecological side effects. While the pressing need for more land for grazing had the obvious effect of heightening interest in new land and dispersing farms within settlements, it also produced the immediate visual effect of creating a world of fields and fences. Good fences made for civil tranquillity and were sure evidence that the wilderness was under cultivation. Of more far-reaching significance was the shortage of native forage crops for the animals and the subsequent need for a new wave of "green immigrants," the bluegrasses, timothys, and clovers of western Europe. Initially introduced accidentally in the dung of the imported animals, the clovers quickly took over the fields of New England, adapted as they were to the demands of pastoralism at home. Later, apples from the continent and potatoes, native to the Andes but introduced into New Hampshire by Irish immigrants in Londonderry, became successfully assimilated plant immigrants crucial to the region's agricultural prosperity. Several other less desirable species also found their way to New England's fields on shipboard; amongst these were the ever-present "weeds," dandelions, chickweeds, mulleins, and nettles, and, as Belknap reported, the ubiquitous and irritating black fly. Each sturdy survivor followed the settlers eagerly and, as we know today, with enduring genetic success.

Despite the physical and symbolic obstacles which the wilderness presented to New Hampshire's early settler-farmers, despite the challenges presented by isolation, recalcitrant and easily exhausted soil, fickle weather and a short growing season, earthquakes, diphtheria, wolves and bears, by the time of the Revolution, New Hampshire's principal economic unit was the family farm. The peace following the French and Indian War largely put an end to the Indian threat and in turn initiated considerable expansion of settlements. For most of the seventeenth century, as we have seen, population had been concentrated along the narrow coastal strip, but by the late eighteenth century population and farm settlements were fairly dense in an area comprising a one hundred mile arc from Portsmouth.

Whereas in 1690, four thousand persons had populated the four coastal towns, by 1790 about fifty thousand persons populated fifty towns. Or put another way, of the 240 townships in New Hampshire today, 60 percent were settled between 1715 and 1765. Between 1761 and 1775, the province of New Hampshire grew faster than any of the other twelve colonies that took part in the American Revolution. The New Hampshire farmer took advantage of whatever opportunities he could to advance his well-being. While the merchants of Portsmouth suffered during the Revolutionary War, for instance, the farmer prospered in face of a heavy demand for grain and livestock for the army. Wars, internal and external, provided good growing weather for farm products. By the late 1700s surplus crops and livestock reached markets in increasing quantities. Nevertheless, New Hampshire was not the only region which was growing and establishing an internally successful economy, and the fruits of her summer of agricultural self-sufficiency would soon be affected by the chill of an autumnal decline in agricultural fortunes.

SIGNS OF CHANGE

While population trends continued to support a picture of healthy rural expansion well into the nineteeenth century, by even the first decade it was clear that changes were underway — dramatic changes, which would drastically affect the farmer's life for the rest of the century. The agents of this change are well-known: the coming of the railroad, the lure of new land in the West, and salaried jobs in the new urban manufacturing centers. Each contributed in some way to a significant decline in the rural population and to readjustments undertaken to promote the survival of the much-exalted farming life. Between 1820, when the census showed the majority of New Hampshire residents were farmers, and 1830, sixty-one of the state's 228 towns declined in population.

As early as 1812, practically all farming land available in the southern two-thirds of the state was already under cultivation. And because of inadequate transportation large portions of northern New Hampshire would remain sparsely populated until the rise of the tourism and wood-processing industries later in the century. It has been estimated that at the turn of the eighteenth century the population density near Portsmouth and along the Merrimack and the

Connecticut rivers reached about fifteen persons per square mile, about half again as much as that of Massachusetts, and almost twice that of New Hampshire's western neighbor, Vermont. Nonetheless politicians and legislators and commentators continued for most of the nineteenth century ardently to believe that the state's economy could rest on a backbone of diligent yeoman labor. And the traditionally conservative farmer was probably too busy promoting and guaranteeing his self-sufficiency to offer public contradiction. Despite legislative action to "help" scientifically by promoting the formation of some of the earliest agricultural societies in America, in 1836 Governor Isaac Hill noted officially to the General Court what was already apparent elsewhere: sections of New Hampshire, particularly the Merrimack River Valley, no longer produced enough food for themselves, and had begun to rely on exchange of manufactured goods with other areas for food supplies.

The testimony of farmer, Thomas Coffin of Boscawen, whose matter-of-fact record of farm life from March 27, 1825 to March 28, 1835, is notable as much for what it leaves out as for what it includes, suggests the outlines of the farmer's situation at this time. Daily entries always began with references to weather, the daily determinant of activity. References to crops show a farmer and his family and several hired hands living fairly independently producing flax, wool, barley, wheat, beans, peas, potatoes, corn, cider, milk, veal, beef, pork, lamb, and mutton. Coffin's main cash crops appear to have been cider, cheese, and timber. Buried in details of weather, mowing, raking, and timber-cutting are one-line comments on his first wife's death, his remarriage, a neighbor's suicide attempt, service on a bank board and in the legislature, as well as an account of President Andrew Jackson's visit to Concord on horseback. Coffin's diaries are summarized by one of his readers in this way:

> From year to year, as from day to day, he was busy performing varied but repetitious, incessant, demanding and arduous tasks. The man himself is only dimly seen behind the homely details, but the glimpses we get show a farmer so solid and substantial as the granite of the New Hampshire hills. [3]

Self-sufficiency was a demanding goal and one, which having for all practical purposes the weight of an article of faith, would die hard.

Effects of New Transportation

Each of the external agents of change affecting New Hampshire's farmer—the coming of the railroad, the lure of the West, and the promise of the cities—was similarly related to the more deeply rooted change in the farmer's life, his relationship to the market.

Portsmouth's colonial dependence on timber markets overseas and along the Atlantic coast and the colonial and postcolonial farmer's favored practice of self-sufficiency both arose as realistic responses to the state's location. Early attempts at circumventing the effects of an isolated port(Portsmouth) and two rivers(the Connecticut and the Merrimack) flowing away from regional markets laid the groundwork for the changes the coming of the railroad would have on the rural economy in New Hampshire.

The Middlesex Canal, begun in 1794 and completed in 1803, established a twenty-six mile link between Boston and Lowell in Massachusetts. By 1814 a connection to the hinterland of Concord, New Hampshire, opened new routes to and from developing industrial cities such as Manchester. Similar attempts to make the upper reaches of the Connecticut River accessible by erecting locks and canals to by-pass natural obstacles proved more difficult. At the same time there was a great deal of road and turnpike building. Locally and privately financed, this spurt in transportation resulted in 460 miles of roadways by 1819. Most new roads lay on northwest and southeast axes, linking the Connecticut River valley with the Merrimack River valley and Boston. Exceptions were the Tenth New Hampshire Turnpike through Crawford's Notch to Portland and the New Hampshire Turnpike from Portsmouth to Concord; these provided other crucial market links.

It was the advent of the railroads, however, that accelerated the movement of products to market and changed the future of New Hampshire farming and the state's economy in general. Beginning in the 1830s, the railroad tied New England to the nation and facilitated regional trade. The pace of railroad building between 1840 and 1870 was impressive. From 35 miles of track in 1840, figures escalated dramatically: 92 miles in 1845; 467 in 1850; 657 in 1855; 661 in 1860; and 900 in 1870. By 1870 the state's previously separated regions were largely united by railways.

Twin Bridges, Hooksett. J. B. Bachiolder. New Hampshire Historical Society.

The first spur, following the Merrimack Valley, radiated from Boston to Lowell, pushing six miles into New Hampshire at Nashua and connecting Manchester with Concord by 1842. At about the same point in the 1840s the Boston & Maine reached Exeter, pushing by mid-decade to Portsmouth. (Much later, in 1867, this spur completed its eastern linkage by reaching North Conway.) With a brief respite imposed by legislative constraints, expansion continued full tilt in the 1840s with the next significant extension being north and west from Concord through Franklin to White River Junction and access to northern and southern routes along the Connecticut River. Another route beginning in the central part of the state eventually connected Concord, Tilton, Plymouth, and Wells River, Vermont, a route which affected the development of east-west spurs north of the White Mountains. Numerous short spurs followed in the wake of these major intrastate routes bringing transportation to many towns previously almost totally isolated. By the 1870s most sections of the state boasted of rail service and entered either reluctantly or willingly into a new age.

When the Northern Railroad reached Lebanon in 1847, there was a large public celebration attended by stockholders, officers, and guests from the Boston office and several thousand local residents. With Daniel Webster on hand, few could have been disappointed with the occasion. He spoke, he declared, as "one who had been the steadfast friend of internal improvements, thro' whose farm this railroad went, connecting the home of his adoption [Boston] with the home of his nativity [Boscawen] and his Alma Mater (Dartmouth College in Hanover)."[4] Few observors suspected that this progress in transportation was a double-edged sword.

Certainly the formerly isolated rural communities now had access to cheap transportation for their bulky livestock and fresh dairy products. And as manufacturing communities developed in the southern part of the state, the farmer gained natural markets for his products. Despite the apparent advantages in both access to, and demand from, city markets, however, the rural population of New Hampshire had passed its maximum point by 1840. In bringing regional cities within the farmer's reach, the railroad also brought to the region an influx of cheaper western farm products and manufactured goods and made attractive, abundant, and cheaper farmland equally accessible. And of course it was New Hampshire-born

Horace Greeley who popularized the practical advice, "Go West young man."

Consider the facts: in the West in the 1850s land went for about a dollar and a quarter an acre; in New England it went for about thirty dollars an acre (if available); and by the 1850s it cost a New England farmer forty to fifty cents to produce a bushel of corn, while in Illinois it cost twelve to fifteen cents. If the boys left New Hampshire farms for the promise of Western success, the girls responded to the glittering attraction of salaried jobs as mill girls in the fast-growing mill towns in the southern part of the state. The market for both farm products and manpower, which the railroads, the western land boom, and mill towns promoted was by the last several decades of the nineteenth century acting as a selective force in the state's rural economy.

THE WINTER OF HILL COUNTRY FARMING

Under the accumulated weight of developments in transportation, shifting trade routes, western competition, and the growth of manufacturing, New Hampshire farmers in the closing decades of the nineteenth century entered what hill country historian, Harold Wilson, calls the chilly "winter" of farming. Faced with the question of whether much of the land under cultivation was really suitable for farming at all, old arguments over upland versus lowland advantages yielded to the need to abandon both submarginal lands and submarginal crops. Intensive farming—cultivation and production of single crops or products—replaced extensive or multicrop farming. By 1910 the farmer, for instance, was tilling only one quarter of the land he owned, allowing unused land to revert to forest cover. A brief mania for sheep, thought jokingly to be perfect for New Hampshire since their long noses would allow them to reach down between the rocks for blades of grass, was followed by intensive emphasis on the advantages of dairy production.

At the same time many farmers realized that if the West was to become Boston's granary, New Hampshire had good shot at becoming its dairy. With advances in cooperative processing, marketing, and winter silage, the hill country could adapt its farming to the urban population's demand for fluid milk, butter, and cheese. By the beginning of the twentieth century circumstances were slowly changing northern New England from a meat-wool-and-grain region to a dairy-fruit-potato-poultry and truck-crop territory as well as other innovative forms of agriculture to be discussed later. At the same time advances in postal delivery, electrification, telephone service, and radio communication helped staunch the effects of the isolation which the farmer might otherwise have felt acutely in the winter of his endeavors.

If few actual historical characters emerge from the record of farming in New Hampshire, there is little doubt that a vivid general type exists in most people's minds. Locked in a fierce battle with stubborn soil and fickle weather, the diligent, patient, resourceful, adaptable, versatile yeoman emerges as a universal favorite. No wonder Jeremy Belknap places the farmer and his family at the center of his picture of a happy society; the farmer's life in his heyday of self-sufficiency and even in its eventual decline was one characterized by virtues most admire, if not envy. Fostering close family life, development of various crafts and skills, and even hints of egalitarian relationships between the sexes, the rural life served as a natural nursery for sturdy character-building.

In a day when the new "first, second, and third persons rural" of regional author Noel Perrin's world are exurbanites emigrating to simpler surroundings and learning to adapt to new challenges, Ralph Waldo Emerson's "sturdy lad from New Hampshire or Vermont" comes to mind. Emerson wrote:

> A sturdy lad from New Hampshire or Vermont, who in turn tries all the professions, who *teams it*, *farms it*, *peddles*, keeps a school, preaches, edits a newspaper, goes to Congress, buys a township, and so forth, in successive years, and always like a cat, falls on his feet, is worth a hundred of these city dolls.[5]

The type endures in the minds of intellectuals and politicians and casual observers even in the face of all the obstacles which New Hampshire's fields and hills and mountains have always posed to the farmer.

5

Organizing the Government

IRONICALLY, AT THE END of the Revolutionary War when farming had emerged as the chief occupation of the state and the mainstay of its economy, the farmers were hit hardest by the economic crisis that followed. Now instead of the rampant inflation of the war years, the economy settled into a chilling depression which provoked a great many questions about the nature of the new government and its relationship to the people. The small farmers who comprised the majority of the electorate saw their representatives ignoring their wishes while Langdon, Sullivan, Belknap, Plumer, and other political leaders believed that the people were unwilling to sacrifice personal interest for the public good, choose wise leaders, and accept the decision of elected officials, duties, as they saw it, of a responsible electorate.

The crisis in the economy was emblematic of the split between the people and their leaders. The depression following the war, the economic counterpart of the inflation of the war years, drove desperate farmers to clamor for paper money to spark an economic recovery. Towns began to send their delegates to the legislature with non binding instructions to support paper money. When the representatives ignored the nonbinding instructions, the voters resorted to binding instructions. When the Assembly still did nothing, the western towns held county conventions to plan ways to control their representatives.

The first such convention was turned to ridicule by eleven lawyers led by a twenty-seven-year-old lawyer named William Plumer,

William Plumer.
New Hampshire Historical Society.

soon to be a powerful figure in the state government. Plumer and the eleven other lawyers posed as delegates favoring paper money. The eleven false delegates planned to urge the real ones to demand that the government print more and more paper money but found that they could hardly keep pace with the extravagant demands of the convention. As one delegate, Dr. Jonathan Gove from New Boston, suggested, "While we are money-making, tis best to emit as much as will discharge all our debts, public and private, and leave enough to buy a glass of grog and a quid of tobacco, without being dunned for them twenty times a day."[1]

John Langdon, the Speaker of the House, who was in on the joke, received the delegation from the convention with mock solemnity, but the hoax was soon uncovered, and Gove left without presenting the petition. Though for the moment the joke rebuffed the paper-money faction, the currency problem was not solved.

So serious did the situation become and so disillusioned were the citizens with their government, that the next protest turned into near rebellion of the sort Massachusetts had experienced only a short time before.

In September of 1786, an armed mob of some two hundred men presented the General Court with demands for paper money, equal distribution of property, and abolition of debts. When the legislators refused to consider the petition, the men surrounded the First Church of Exeter in which the Court was meeting and held the members captive until nightfall when the townspeople led by Colonel Nathaniel Gilman frightened them away. The next day the militia led by the former general, President Sullivan, dispersed the mob and imprisoned the leaders.

There followed great rejoicing that order had been restored and government by force had been resisted. The citizens of Exeter and the militia were lauded for their zeal and public virtue in supporting the constitutional authority of the state, and the offenders were lightly punished or magnanimously allowed to go free. Thereafter President Sullivan discouraged conventions, observing "they have a tendency to overturn and destroy all constitutional authority and government,"[2] an interesting observation by a veteran of the Revolution which drew its power from unauthorized conventions of disgruntled colonists.

Just as Plumer's hoax had foiled one conventional protest, so quick action had foiled the insurrection; however, the small farmer's feelings of disillusion and discontent with the government were not banished, and the economic depression did not go away. The spring elections revealed how alienated these voters were when almost 25 percent of the towns decided not to send representatives to the General Court, and another 15 percent did not elect anyone. Travelers reported that inhabitants in the interior were indifferent to both Sullivan and Langdon and did not care who became president. Nineteen residents of Wolfeboro actually voted for former governor John Wentworth.

CONSTITUTION MAKING: FEDERAL AND STATE

New Hampshire was not alone, of course. All the states struggled with financial problems after the Revolution; no one was sure how the new representative governments would succeed in solving these or any other problems facing the states. Certainly under the Articles of Confederation the states were not helping each other.

From the beginning New Hampshire had demonstrated its belief that the central government should organize the relations of the individual states. It had sought instruction from the Continental Congress before writing its first state constitution, and after the war it appealed to the central government to regulate trade and ratified a 5 percent tariff proposed by the national Congress. In 1784 Jeremy Belknap wrote a letter ridiculing the idea of the national confederation as "combined sovereignty, subject to be checked, controuled, and negatived by thirteen individual sovereignties . . . our present form of federal government appears to be inadequate to the purpose for which it was instituted."[3] In 1786 Belknap's letter was published and became a powerful piece of propaganda for a new federal constitution establishing a stronger central government.

More immediately and practically the prospect of a strong federal government aroused high hopes among the leaders of New Hampshire that many of the state's more pressing financial problems might be solved. Just before the passage of ratification of the proposed federal Constitution, John Langdon said, "The deranged State of our finances, the almost annihilation of our commerce are objects truly important, but I look forward with pleasure to the time which I trust is not far distant when by the blessing of divine providence we shall be relieved in a great measure from those and many other embarrassments by the adoption of the proposed federal constitution."[4] Such had been the sentiments of the Langdons, Bartletts, Plumer, and other leaders of the state.

Despite the enthusiasm of its leaders for the Federal constitution, in 1787 the legislature could not afford to send the four delegates they had elected to the Constitutional Convention in Philadelphia. Two of the delegates never made it to the convention, but John Langdon finally paid his own and young Nicholas Gilman's expenses so that New Hampshire was among the twelve states to sponsor the federal Constitution in September of 1787. While young Gilman's chief distinction in Philadelphia lay in being one of the youngest and handsomest men at the Convention, Langdon expressed his views on several issues. He advocated power for the federal government to call out the militia, regulate slave trade, veto state laws incompatible with those of the union, admit new states to the union, and regulate international trade. He opposed taxes on trade between states such as the ones Massachusetts had imposed on New Hampshire's goods. While he advocated allowing the federal government to assume a debt, he wanted to outlaw paper currency. With the exception of his stand on paper currency, Langdon's opinions generally reflected the situation in his home state which, being small and relatively poor, saw great advantages in subscribing to a strong central government.

The voters in New Hampshire were more wary than their leaders. They feared, said William Plumer "that the liberties of the people were in danger, and the great men, as they call them, were forming a plan for themselves" as well they might considering how the "great men" had ignored their wishes in the past.[5] Those federalists favoring the Constitution campaigned for it from the pulpit, through newspapers, and in private conversations. Still there are times when the people refuse to be led. In February when the state's specially elected convention met to consider the federal Constitution, State President John Sullivan realized that he did not have the votes to ratify and hastily moved for adjournment.

But by June when the convention met again to consider the matter, the "great men" had campaigned and explained so vigorously that, totally persuaded, the delegates were eager to vote quickly for ratification to beat Virginia for the honor of becoming the ninth state to pass the Constitution of the United States, thus putting it into effect. This honor they captured on June 21, 1788.

It is revealing to note that Strafford and Rockingham counties on the seacoast and the Piscataqua, particularly, where merchants and traders could see the advantage of a central authority to establish uniform trade policies solidly favored the new Constitution. So did the towns in the Connecticut Valley where trade flowed down the river to Connecticut and which, perhaps, still smarted from the failed secessionist movement and so did not identify with the government in Exeter. Opposition was concentrated in the center of the state where isolated and debt-ridden farmers who had little to trade with other states or abroad had judged from the paper money fiasco that the government promised them little help out of their problems.

In general, however, the new federal Constitution produced a surge of confidence in New Hampshire. Even those who opposed it recognized the serious problems facing the state, and after the Constitution was ratified, they only hoped the new federal government would work out. And, indeed, times improved dramatically whether through the new federal government or through the new optimism, or through the outbreak of war in Europe that increased the market for fish, lumber, and agricultural products is hard to say. In any event, by 1791 there was plenty of money for trade and by the next year farm produce brought the highest prices ever. For these improvements in economic conditions the new federal government got much credit.

A visit to the state by George Washington and the selection of John Langdon as the new United States Senate's temporary presiding officer further raised the morale of the state. The passage of the Bill of Rights helped alleviate fears of the power of the federal government, and reappointment of customs and post office officials reassured many.

Revisions to State Constitution

No sooner had the state coped with the problem of the federal Constitution than its own hard-fought Constitution of 1784 came up for the revision that that document stipulated. Experience had showed men in public office that the constitution had serious flaws, besides which certain things needed to be changed simply because New Hampshire was now part of the federal union, not a loose federation.

It was easy enough to change the name of the chief executive from president to governor to distinguish him from the President of the United States. And it was not hard to change the way representatives to the national Congress were chosen from appointed by the legislature to elected by the people. Other aspects of the constitution presented more complicated problems. All three branches of the government needed changes. The authority of the judiciary and the legislature overlapped. As a result of the concessions made to the western towns in 1781, the legislature had grown to unwieldy proportions as each new town sent another representative. Complaints about the administration of justice were widespread, and the weak president (soon governor) like the judiciary needed to be further distinguished from the legislature and given more authority.

William Plumer, the lawyer who had made a joke of the paper money convention, was the most enthusiastic member of the constitutional convention. Plumer headed a Committee of Ten to produce a thoroughly revised constitution dealing with all these problems. Though the convention as a whole vetoed much of the reform of the legislature and gave the legislature authority to reform the judiciary proposed by Plumer's committee, it still generally agreed with the committee's recommendations concerning the strengthening of the executive and other provisions which eliminated abuses of power and overlapping appointments. Among other reforms, Plumer favored the abolition of the religious establishment in the state including the articles in the constitution which obliged residents to support the town's Congregational church and which made Protestantism a qualification for officeholding. The convention moderated these proposals, but still supported some loosening of the religious restrictions. The electorate, however, rejected any idea of change in those articles.

But it was not just religious toleration that the electorate rejected. The whole idea of considering another constitution left the electorate cold. Under the responsive and judicious presidency of Josiah Bartlett following the contentious incumbencies of John Sullivan and John Langdon, the political scene was peaceful and the economy was thriving. In fact, when the constitution was submitted for approval amendment by amendment, fewer than half the number of votes were cast for or against any single amendment than had been cast in the nearly uncontested election of Bartlett for governor two months before.

In hopes of salvaging some of their work, the convention met again, clearing up minor problems; then they presented the document to the electorate once more to be voted on as a whole. The revised constitution was passed with even fewer voters considering this version than had considered the first. Though all steps toward religious toleration were eliminated, "Plumer's Constitution" as the revision is sometimes known, made some major reforms in the Constitution of 1784. This revised constitution strengthened the governor's authority, forced legislators to be more responsive to voters, and held all public officials to stricter accountability than the original one had done.

THE INDIAN STREAM REPUBLIC

From the days of the first Masonian grants, settling the boundaries of New Hampshire was a rocky process. The eastern boundary with Maine had been amicably established by the Masonian grants, but the southern border was established later by the Crown under the influence of Thomlinson and the Wentworths only after a long battle with Massachusetts. The western boundary had been settled at the Connecticut River by George Washington during the Revolutionary War after the western towns had threatened to secede from the state. Just where in the river the boundary ran remained a sore point between New Hampshire and Vermont until 1934 when the Supreme Court of the United States declared that the river belonged to New Hampshire to the low-water mark on the western bank. The short northern boundary between Canada and New Hampshire remained in dispute until 1842 and promised to be just as stubborn and colorful as the other boundary disputes in the state had been.

Article II of the treaty which ended the Revolutionary War states "the boundary was to follow certain highlands until it reached the northwesternmost head of the Connecticut River and was to proceed thence down the middle of the said river to the forty-fifth parallel where began the northern boundary of Vermont." But, of course, the treaty was drawn up in Paris, a long way from the wilds of northern New Hampshire where it was not at all clear which exactly of the three principal branches of the river constituted the "northwesternmost head" of the Connecticut. The province of Lower Canada maintained that the main head of the river, or at least the Indian Stream, was the northwesternmost head while New Hampshire maintained that Hall Stream was the northwesternmost branch. Between thirty thousand and eighty thousand acres were disputed (what is now the town of Pittsburg) and became known as the Indian Stream Territory.

Border disputes are seldom easily settled, and this one, small though it was, soon became encumbered with nothing less than the making of a tiny and thinly populated nation. In 1832 the fifty-nine inhabitants of the territory, weary of their uncertain status, drew up a constitution and founded the Indian Stream Republic, declaring themselves to be an independent country. Once they established their independence, they clung to it for eight years, resisting the political authority of both Lower Canada and New Hampshire. In 1840, New Hampshire finally sent the militia to seize the territory which subsequently was incorporated as the town of Pittsburg. In 1842 yet another treaty upheld New Hampshire's claim to the territory, and thus ended the last secessionist movement in the state.

BEGINNING OF PARTY POLITICS

During the colonial period in New Hampshire, long before there were political parties identified with names like Whig or Federalist or Republican, there were political alliances among groups of men who shared economic ambitions, social visions, and most of all religious affiliations. The conflicts between the Anglicans (early Warnerton, later Wentworth) with their vision of an agreeable life and the Puritans (the Waldrons and the Vaughans) and their sober view of the good life underlie much of colonial history in the state. After the Revolution, when many of the Loyalist Anglicans had left the state, those who had gained power, mostly Puritan Congregationalists, supported the Federalists during the debate over the federal Constitution. While the early town charters required the towns to set aside ground for the building of a church, the state Constitution of 1784 also required that the towns support a settled minister (who was almost always Congregationalist) and restricted public officeholding to Protestants. Thus, despite the first amendment to the federal Constitution, in New Hampshire politics and religion were almost inextricably bound together. An attack on the Federalist power structure was also an attack on Congregationalism and ministers who addressed their flocks weekly from pulpits in every town in the state. It is not surprising, then, that the Jeffersonian Republicans, who swiftly rose to challenge the Federalists in much of the country, found a cooler reception in New Hampshire—particularly since religious liberty was one of the Jeffersonians' most cherished tenets.

Aside from the stumbling block of religious liberty, however, many of the principles of Jeffersonian Republicanism dovetailed remarkably with the kind of government that New Hampshire had inscribed in its constitution—small government with checks against executive power, wide representation by the people, and rotation in office, all of which were designed to guard against the usurpation of power by one or a few leaders and insure that the electorate had as much control of their leaders as possible. Coincidentally, both the puritanical Congregationalists and the religiously tolerant Jeffersonian Republicans agreed that the self-sufficient farmer was the cornerstone of society. Thus when Jeffersonian Republicans (and later the Jacksonian Democrats, who espoused similiar principles) finally gained a foothold in the state, New Hampshire turned out to be among their more fervent supporters.

These ideals sparkled on the surface of the rhetoric of politics which was, like most human enterprises, more often controlled by private ambitions and expediency than by philosophical visions. Certainly before the end of the eighteenth century, the voters in New Hampshire viewed political parties and even political campaigning not as means by which they could influence the government but as unattractive displays of personal ambition. Both Sullivan and Langdon campaigned vigorously for the governorship during those years, but they did it through their friends and supporters, both outwardly behaving like reluctant debutantes. Even so, the voters found their rivalry disruptive and favored Josiah Bartlett who so eschewed the spirit of competition that he appointed his rival for the governorship and a man he had helped send to prison as a Loyalist to important political positions.

However, during his term in the United States Senate, John Langdon, who had been an ardent supporter of the federal constitution, learned to admire the Jeffersonian Republican's position on many other issues and established himself head of the Jeffersonian Republicans in New Hampshire. Particularly in 1794 did he break with the Federalists over their sympathy for England which was disrupting New England's shipping in the course of prosecuting its war with France. The issue struck close home in Portsmouth, for the French had opened their ports, including those lucrative ones in the West Indies, to neutral American ships while the English seized any American ship engaged in trade in those ports.

During the 1790s in New Hampshire the Federalists included all of the state's leaders like John Taylor Gilman, who succeeded Bartlett as governor, William Plumer, and Jeremiah Smith and most of the state's voters as well. The Exeter Junto, as these Federalists were called, were alarmed at the results of the French Revolution which popularized among other things deism and government by the people, both of which were antithetical to the Federalist's reverence for property and the established Congregational church. They called the southerners who admired the French "Jacobins" after the French revolutionary party which had organized the reign of terror. The eminent scholar of jurisprudence, Jeremiah Smith, spoke for many when he explained to William Plumer why he voted to leave as many southerners as possible unrepresented in the national government: "I am clearly of the Opinion that the people Southward of Pennsylvania are in a state of barbarity when compared with the New England States."[6] These "barbaric" southerners threatened to dominate the national government, and so, as one New England writer observed, "The federalists must make State justice and State power a shelter of the wise, and good, and rich, from the wild destroying rage of the Southern Jacobins."[7]

Many of the small landowners, the natural constituency of the Jeffersonian Republicans, who had sacked Castle William and Mary and fought with Stark at Bennington, now viewed with horror the disintegration of order in France after the French Revolution and the unsettling extremes to which revolution can go. The Congregational minister, who viewed with equal distaste the deism of Thomas Jefferson and French Catholicism, did not hesitate to ask these farmers from the pulpit, if not face to face, "Would it afford you pleasure to see the guillotine erected on your land?"[8]

It was not as though the Federalists' policies were universally approved. The Jay Treaty which favored the British enraged some in Portsmouth where a mob burned effigies of John Jay and Senator Samuel Livermore who had supported the treaty. When rioters were brought to court, the crowd expressed such ardent support for the defendants that the judge postponed the trial until the following term.

Even so, the Federalists with John Taylor Gilman as governor were too firmly entrenched for the fledgling Jeffersonian Republicans to make much impression. Besides, the Jeffersonian Republicans concentrated so hard on being a national party rather than a state or regional one that they often failed to take advantage of local issues which could have boosted their influence in the state. On one occasion the Federalists supported Boston shipowners in a court battle against New Hampshire shipowners. On another occasion the Federalists petitioned the United States government to appoint to the federal bench Judge Pickering who was on the point of going insane and whom they wished removed from the state bench.

Nor did the Federalists handle state funds with the utmost prudence and honesty. Through some suspect borrowing and lending of state funds that may or may not have been an outright swindle by the Gilman family and others who held key positions in the government, the state was left so short of funds that the legislature was forced to levy a tax of eight thousand pounds to pay off the debt. The Republicans complained about this bit of dirty business but did not capitalize on it. To cap it all off, Governor Gilman vetoed a bill taxing unimproved land, further provoking beleaguered farmers.

The Republicans, however, failed to organize all the factions that these decisions by the Federalists might have alienated: the Portsmouth merchants, the western towns, the aggrieved taxpayer, the outraged citizen. They fielded an uninspired leadership which failed to expand the influence of the party from Portsmouth to the inland towns. John Langdon, their most astute politician, spent most of his time in Washington serving in the Senate.

Monarchies and aristocracies can go on almost forever exploiting their power and making mistakes, but the Federalists in New Hampshire in 1800 finally abused their authority so recklessly that the Jeffersonian Republicans only had to publicize their actions to establish a viable two-party system in the state. When John Langdon and other wealthy Republicans organized the Union Bank, issued notes, and applied to the legislature for incorporation, there was only one other bank in the state, the New Hampshire Bank of Portsmouth organized in 1792 and owned largely by the Exeter Junto and particularly by Governor John Taylor Gilman. Oliver Peabody, treasurer of the state and president of the New Hampshire Bank, was alarmed. He proposed that the legislature not only refuse to incorporate the new bank, but that it restrain the Union Bank from issuing notes.

The new bank made loans on easy terms, had twice the amount of stock of the New Hampshire Bank, and sold shares in small denominations throughout the state in a direct appeal to the middle-sized farmer who was always a little short of cash. Even some of the Federalists hesitated to disallow such an obviously appealing enterprise and wanted to let the bank continue to issue notes, but Gilman insisted that the Union Bank was an intolerable "POLITICAL MACHINE . . . that would ruin the Politics of the state."[9] With carrot and stick he whipped the Federalists into line so that the legislature refused to incorporate the bank and restrained it from issuing notes. The Federalists were so delighted with their victory that in a fit of politically suicidal arrogance, the state senate sent down a petition authorizing the treasurer to buy twenty-four more shares of the New Hampshire Bank of Portsmouth for the state.

The Republicans had a field day. One Republican editor pointed out that the "junto of individuals, at one stroke, benefited both their Politics and their Purse"[10] and that the government was so heavily invested in the old bank that it would never charter a new one. The incorporation of the Union Bank would surely not have hurt Exeter as much as the bad press it received for these political and financial shenanigans.

In 1800 Governor Gilman, who had not faced a serious rival in the six elections since 1794, faced serious opposition. The Republicans supported Judge Timothy Walker of Concord who was billed as a moderate Federalist (those Jacobins from Portsmouth still couldn't have counted on a vote outside of their hometown) and they ran a real, two-party campaign sending "runners" to the interior to campaign for Walker, telling the story of the "scandalous conduct of the legislature in regard to the Union Bank."[11]

In August of 1800, the *New Hampshire Gazette* quoted from an article in the *Massachusetts Mercury*, "'Naturally there can be but two parties in a Country; the friends of order and its foes. Under the banner of the first are ranged all men of property, all quiet, honest, peaceable, orderly, unambitious citizens. In the ranks of the last are enlisted all desperate, embarrassed, unprincipled, disorderly, ambitious, disaffected, morose men.'"[12] But the campaign and the bank scandal were influencing public sentiment. The possibility of changing the political party in power no longer frightened the electorate — even change in the direction of Republicanism — as the state's electorate learned the value of having two political parties to choose between.

Not that the Republicans really won. Gilman did with 61 percent of the vote, but that was against 86 percent of the vote in the previous election. And Walker won almost all the remaining 39 percent of the votes instead of having them spread around among many candidates as they usually were. Clearly, the two party system was working in the state.

Furthermore, the Republicans had found their constituency and the platform. They appealed to the interior by choosing a candidate from Concord. They appealed to the farm vote with a policy of easy money. And they painted the Federalists as the party of the privileged few — aristocratic, monopolistic, and Congregationalist — while they championed the cause of small farmers and workers.

In 1801 the Federalists made a serious strategic mistake. John

Langdon's term in the United States Senate expired, and they pulled out all stops to have James Sheafe elected in his place. The New Hampshire delegation in Washington was now triumphantly Federalist; on the other hand, John Langdon was free to harry the Exeter Junto from his home base. In 1802, Langdon ran for governor against Gilman and cut the incumbent's majority to two thousand votes. In 1804 the Republicans gained control of the legislature and in the presidential election in the fall they carried the state for Thomas Jefferson. After 1804 it was a rout. In 1805 Langdon defeated Gilman with a majority of 3,800, and perhaps equally important, 65 percent of the eligible voters cast their ballots. The new party spirit had also inspired the electorate to use the franchise which they had fought for and lately neglected.

Almost at once the new majority party was faced with unpopular decisions made not by the state party leaders, but by the national leaders. Jefferson's Embargo Act of 1807 against the English hurt New England shipping, displeased many New Englanders, and caused some Federalists to turn against the president and do their best to thwart the policies of the federal government actions. Seldom and reluctantly did nationalistic New Hampshire fail to cooperate with the federal government's actions even when its shipping industry suffered from those policies. Nationalistic Federalists, among them New Hampshire's William Plumer, left the party to join the Jeffersonian Republicans. Even so, in the federal elections of 1807 the Jeffersonian Republicans could not withstand the backlash against the Embargo. Ex-Federalist Plumer wrote, "at no election since the establishment of our government, has there been so much time & money spent in New Hampshire as at this."[13] (What would he think of New Hampshire's recent presidential primaries?) In this fray appeared a young newspaper publisher, Isaac Hill, fated to be one of New Hampshire's greatest rabble-rousers and a leading force in New Hampshire politics for forty years, who delivered slashing attacks on the Federalists. Even so, Madison, who had vowed to continue Jefferson's Embargo, won the presidency without the help of a single electoral vote from New England.

The new Jeffersonian Republican party under able leadership of Langdon, Plumer, Isaac Hill, and a young lawyer named Levi Woodbury held its own against the Federalists led by Jeremiah Smith, John Taylor Gilman, and the formidable young Daniel

Webster. The regions of the state remained fairly consistent in their political views. Exeter and the rich Connecticut and Merrimack valleys voted mostly Federalist, Portsmouth and the hill towns voted Jeffersonian Republican, and the frontier split.

That the city of Portsmouth, whose economy was based on trade and shipbuilding, voted to support the party which enacted the embargo can partly be explained by the fact that it could turn its ships and its shipbuilding to wartime uses. Piscataqua commerce and shipbuilding had thrived for thirty years immediately following the War for Independence. In the absence of British restraints, old overseas trade patterns had revived and expanded; 1783 to 1812 were good years. More lumber and fish were exported, more ships were launched, and more fortunes were made in this period than ever before in the Piscataqua region's history. With local costs for shipbuilding about one half of those in English, French, and Dutch shipyards, the area's shipbuilders found eager clients. In the accompanying boom in overseas trade, the Piscataqua's docks were jammed with schooners and other ships loading and unloading pine boards and planks, barrel staves, dried fish, cattle, sheep, horses, bricks, cider, flaxseed, molasses, rum, sugar, cocoa, coffee, cheese, and salt.

This resurgence of prosperity had not escaped the attention of the young country's first president, who visited the Piscataqua ports in October of 1789. After a barge trip in the harbor, a trip which included a break for cod fishing, Washington recorded in his diary that he was impressed with the good anchorage, the many docks, and the amount of shipbuilding.

The Embargo Act of 1807 and the War of 1812 disrupted the port's properity; however, the port also cushioned its trade losses by engaging in privateering once again, though on a smaller scale than during the Revolution. In the peacetime period which followed, overseas trade declined significantly. Ironically, during the 1830s and 1840s most of the foreign goods brought into the port at Portsmouth supplied the growing railroad industry, as a new era dawned. In the meantime the region tried with varied success to encourage local production of such imported manufactured items as iron fittings, rope, and sailcloth. Historically successful enterprises such as fishing and shipbuilding continued as the region returned to local and coastal markets to compensate for the loss of foreign markets.

The last stars of the shipyards, the sleek Piscataqua clippers built in the decade before the Civil War, certainly gave credit to the region, though the purchasers in Boston and New York ports were the very agents of the decline in Portsmouth's role in the overseas market.

At the beginning of the War of 1812, hearing, sight, and memory all weak, one of Portsmouth's most famous merchants, John Langdon, tried to retire from politics, but the Jeffersonian Republican Party prevailed on him to run for governor once more. The next year Langdon, who had sacked Castle William and Mary, attended the Constitutional Convention in Philadelphia, served as the first Chairman Pro Tem of the United States Senate and governor of the state many times, retired from politics. He had joined the revolutionary party early and supported it to the end; he had seen the advantages of a strong union and favored the federal Constitution. He had expressed his support for both individual freedom and national cohesion in founding New Hampshire's Jeffersonian Republican party. He left the Jeffersonian Republicans so solidly entrenched in the state that on the eve of the War of 1812 which drove much of New England into noncooperation and near-rebellion against the federal government, New Hampshire elected a Jeffersonian Republican government, choosing once again to cast its lot with national rather than regional interests.

6

Testing State and Federal Governments

WITH LANGDON'S DEATH died the last of the revolutionary leaders in the state; the problems of the revolution ended as well, for the state had devised a stable government and stable boundaries. The new challenge was to use that stable government for the benefit of the people of the state and to reaffirm a satisfactory relationship between the state and the Union of which it was a part.

Langdon named William Plumer, the former Federalist, to succeed him. Plumer, whose service to the state already included lending his leadership and careful intelligence to the revision of the state constitution, was more interested in political theory than many of his colleagues, reading Jeremy Bentham with admiration. When the ailing John Langdon asked him to run for governor, Plumer confided to his diary without undue modesty, "If a Langdon & a Gilman had sufficient abilities to perform the duties of governor, I may perform the task, in case I am elected."[1]

In 1812 Governor Plumer, like Governor Langdon before him, cooperated with orders from the President of the United States to prepare the state militia to serve under the command of the War Department. As always the state was vulnerable to attack by the British navy at Portsmouth and by the British army from Canada. The residents of Coos County were particularly alarmed and sent Plumer a letter declaring they "were in great terror" over possible attack from their neighbors whom they described as "Counterfeiters of bank notes, thieves, swindlers, violators of all laws, prison breakers, and other escapes from Justice."[2] However, the company of militia de-

tached to the county quickly became unpopular when the Coos inhabitants realized that their lawless neighbors would rather buy
goods from them than invade their territory, and the militia hampered what could have been a bit of lucrative smuggling.

Plumer managed to extort from the legislature barely enough
money to equip the army, but he believed the war would silence its
critics. However, in November after Plumer's election, critics of the
war were more vocal than ever, and New Hampshire sent an entirely Federalist delegation to Washington headed by antiwar activist
Daniel Webster.

As the combination of the war and the embargo began to hurt
not only the shipping industry (which rallied via privateering), but
also the farmers, antiwar sentiment caught on. In 1813 the Federalists, protesting the government's authority to call out the state militia
and to impose taxes to support the war, campaigned against the general bungling of the war effort and returned Gilman to the governorship and kept him in office for four years thereafter. By the end of
the war John Taylor Gilman had been elected governor of New
Hampshire fifteen times. Despite the state's determination to have
the governor elected every year, a man who represented the will of
the people as Gilman did by opposing the war but not becoming an
extremist could still make a career of the governorship. Ironically,
Daniel Webster of Portsmouth opposed the war in the name of commercial interests while his home town, the most commercial of New
Hampshire cities, consistently voted Republican and supported the
war. Webster would not have been elected if New Hampshire had
been divided into congressional districts at the time.

Gilman had his own troubles resisting prosecution of the war
when the people of Portsmouth became nervous about the possibility
of attack from the British. He opposed calling out troops in response
to orders from the president as his Republican predecessors had
done; if he called out troops on his own responsibility, the state of
New Hampshire would be responsible for financing the defenses of
the harbor at Portsmouth. In a dramatic gesture, Daniel Webster
took shovel in hand, led the people of his town to begin building
their own defenses, and pressed the governor to follow the lead of
Plumer and call out the militia in response to federal requisition.

But antiwar sentiment in Massachusetts far outstripped such
feelings in New Hampshire, and the Bay State pressed its northern

neighbor to join in some antiwar conventions and schemes that began with noncooperation and nullification and finally verged on rebellion. At one of the antiwar conventions at Rockingham, the young orator, Daniel Webster, later the staunchest defender of the Union, declared the government hostile to commerce and protested that the states had no grievance against England for impressment. Finally he warned of possible separation of the states or even civil war if the federal government made an alliance with France, sentiments that caused him some embarrassment in his later defense of the Union against southern restiveness.

As the war dragged on, resistance stiffened until in 1814 the governor of Massachusetts officially called on Governor Gilman and invited the state to send representatives to a secret convention in Hartford which, presumably, would consider stronger measures of resistance than noncooperation with the federal government's war efforts. Since the legislature was not in session, the governor turned to the Council and his personal advisors for guidance. The slender thread of the Republican majority of one in the Council prevented the governor from embroiling New Hampshire in the seditious conventions of its neighbors. Fortunately, before the resolutions from the Hartford Convention could foment any more unrest, the War of 1812 ended.

THE DARTMOUTH COLLEGE CASE

With the war over several more local issues claimed the attention of the state: the issue of religious freedom, the responsibility of the state for the education of the people, the relationship between the state and federal government, and finally on a federal level the power of the state to nullify private contracts. All these primary social and political issues were tangled together in the famous Dartmouth College Case which reflected fundamental differences of opinion between the Federalists and the Republicans.

The case did not begin as a test of philosophical or political positions, however, but as a power struggle between Presbyterian John Wheelock, who had succeeded his father, Eleazar, as president of the college, and the board of trustees of the college who were largely Congregationalists. It is astonishing that Federalist, Calvinist-Pres-

Eleazar Wheelock. Painting by Joseph Steward (1794-96). Hood Museum of Art, Dartmouth College.

byterian John Wheelock and the Federalist, Calvinist-Congregationalist trustees could find enough religious differences to cause any real hostility between them, but they did. John, who was president for thirty-six years, and the trustees clashed again and again. When in 1809 Governor Jeremiah Smith, ex officio trustee of the college, cast the deciding vote for a majority faction against Wheelock in a crucial vote by the trustees, Wheelock lost his undisputed dominion over the college.

To regain his hold on the school, Wheelock flung the battle into the public and political arena by publishing anonymously an attack on the college trustees accusing them among other things of using the college to establish "a politico-religious hierarchy in New England based upon the close alliance of Federalism and Congregationalism"[3] and then openly appealing to the legislature to rectify the situation. Ever since the days when the college supported the attempted secession by the western towns, the state government and the college had rubbed along together uneasily. Though the legislature had appropriated funds from time to time to help the struggling institution, the legal status of the relationship between the two had never been defined and the extralegal one was not always cordial. The college (which Eleazar Wheelock had established to produce ministers rather than to educate the Indians as had been rumored at the time) was religiously as well as politically conservative and supported the Federalists. Since many Republicans saw it as a bastion of conservative elitism and religious bigotry, the legislature might very well have agreed with Wheelock's accusations.

But before the legislature could consider the case, the trustees fired Wheelock and hired a recent graduate, Congregational minister Francis Brown, to replace him. The move galvanized public opinion against the trustees. Isaac Hill leapt to Wheelock's defense with editorials warning darkly of schemes which merged law and religion and put political power in the hands of the "rigidly righteous."[4] He pointed to the founding of Andover Academy by fundamentalist dissidents from Harvard and the flowering of rigid orthodoxy at Williams and Yale where the scheme to catapult religious establishment into theocracy was already underway. He cited laws forbidding Sunday travel and a decision by Judge Jeremiah Smith exempting clergymen from direct taxation as steps toward creating a privileged class which controlled people's lives. All these freedom-threatening schemes could be nipped in the bud by the Republican party, according to Hill, overlooking the fact that John Wheelock, the beleaguered president he was defending, was a Federalist and an ardent Presbyterian.

Meantime Republican Governor William Plumer, at the prompting of Thomas Jefferson, the advocate of public education, pressed the attack on Dartmouth College aiming to remove the college from private control and make it a state university. But before he could reorganize the college into a state university, he had to face litigation and for that he had to "reorganize" the state superior court with enough sympathetic judges to support his case against Dartmouth. To this end he appointed twenty-six-year-old Levi Woodbury to the bench. The appointment caused cries of outrage, but Plumer now had enough of his men on the bench to be sure of a favorable attitude, and Levi Woodbury was launched on his career as a political power in the state.

Thus armed, Plumer drew up the Dartmouth College Act in 1815 changing the name of the school to Dartmouth University and appointing enough new trustees to raise the number to twenty one, giving him a substantial majority over the eight anti-Wheelock trustees dubbed "the Octagon" by Isaac Hill. Plumer chose the most prestigous men he could find to fill the new positions on the board. However, Plumer failed to ensure that he commanded a quorum as well as a majority of the trustees.

And what he also failed to take into account was the intense loyalty commanded by the tiny college with a total teaching staff consisting of the president, three professors, and two tutors. The Octagon was willing to go to the wire for the school, raising money and travelling up and down the east coast drumming up support. They persuaded the three most eminent lawyers in the state, Jeremiah Smith, Jeremiah Mason, and Daniel Webster, to take the case.

The situation which produced a precedent-setting case in the Supreme Court of the United States produced some ridiculous spectacles on the college campus as the newly minted university operated side by side with the old college. The university took over the buildings and the account books, but the students mostly continued to meet the old faculty in their homes, paying them directly. In 1817 there were two graduations; the university graduated eight students while the college graduated thirty-nine. At one point the college students took all the books from the library and, armed with clubs, barricaded themselves in the building. The university students, encouraged by their professors, broke down the door but retreated after a short fracas.

When Plumer tried to convene his new board of trustees, none of the Octagon would attend. The governor huffed around the campus for three days with his prestigious trustees in tow but could not get together a quorum for a meeting. During the same visit to the

Daniel Webster. Painted by Francis Alexander. 1835. Hood Museum of Art, Dartmouth College.

campus the governor admitted in an unguarded moment that the new state university could expect little financial support from the legislature but would have to rely on private donations to keep itself afloat.

But if the battle being fought at the college looked like a circus, the legal battle was being fought like a chess match. Smith and Mason drew up a finely reasoned case which orator Daniel Webster, alumni of the college, argued before the Superior Court stating in essence that Dartmouth College was a private, charitable institution not subject to state regulation. Webster ended with a rehearsal of the oration that he would perfect before the Supreme Court of the United States. The three Republican justices, Richardson, Bell, and Woodbury ruled against the court in an equally carefully reasoned decision. Richardson observed that "It is a matter of too great moment, too intimately connected with the publick welfare and prosperity to be thus entrusted in the hands of a few."[5] Despite political biases of the participants, the arguments were formidable on both sides of the question.

Plumer, Hill, Woodbury, and company thought that the Superior Court's decision finished the case, and they were unprepared for the trustees' appeal. The trustees and their attorneys, who had known all along that they would have to take the case to the United

States Supreme Court, sent Webster to argue the case in Washington based on the same brief prepared by Smith and Mason for the state court. Unable quite to believe the case would have to be argued again, Plumer settled for a second-rate attorney then belatedly buttressed him with U. S. Attorney General William Wirt who got sick and appeared to plead the case ill-prepared.

In 1818 in the Supreme Court of Chief Justice John Marshall, Daniel Webster presented the college's case. He claimed the college was a charitable institution, and that though it benefited the public, the trustees had rights to it through the founder. He also asserted that they could be deprived of those rights only through court action and not through the decision of the legislature. Most pertinent to the court's final decision was Webster's last argument that under the Constitution of the United States the government could not violate a legal contract such as the grant Eleazar Wheelock received to establish Dartmouth College under a board of trustees. Webster finished with a shattering oration, long famous because an influential teacher of oratory heard it and described it to his students, in which he maintained that destroying Dartmouth College would lead to the destruction of all private institutions and ended, "It is a small college sir, as I have said yet there are those who love it." Observers claimed that Chief Justice John Marshall was moved to tears by Webster's speech.

The judges took a year to give an opinion on the case. Realizing how dismally the state's attorneys had performed, Plumer mustered a team of legal brains hoping the justices might call for new arguments, but they did not. When the court reconvened, the judges issued an opinion that under the federal Constitution Dartmouth College was a private institution under the authority of the trustees and that the state of New Hampshire had no power to take the college from them.

In the long run this decision, cited daily in courts of law in the United States as crucial to the protection of private enterprises against interference from the government, struck a blow for liberty. In the short run, however, the Republicans saw it as a setback for public education in the state and as a blow to religious freedom. It was not until 1896 that the state started its own university in Durham, and not until 1923 that it became known as the University of New Hampshire. Meanwhile the struggle for religious liberty shifted to other fronts.

SOCIAL IMPROVEMENTS

The question of religious freedom which Hill had raised with respect to Dartmouth College proved to be irrelevant in the outcome of the case, but the struggle emerged in other arenas during the same period. The turning point in the battle for religious liberty came when the legislature passed the Toleration Act of 1819.

Before that law was passed, under a 1791 statute the voters in each town were required to designate a church (almost always Congregational) which the town would support through taxes. Only people who proved they contributed to another officially recognized sect were exempt, and towns were slow to grant exemptions, especially to sects of which they disapproved such as the Roman Catholics or the Universalists. Since the Federalists established tax support for the Congregational Church, Congregational clergy emerged as a leading Federalist influence as early as 1795. Furthermore, the clergy abhorred the French, finding little to choose between their traditional Roman Catholicism and the deism which many of the revolutionaries espoused; by extension they distrusted that francophile, deist, and proponent of religious freedom, Thomas Jefferson, who founded the Republican Party. It is understandable, then, that the Republicans would lead the fight against the established clergy in the state.

Among those who struggled for religious toleration were the new frontier churches, the Baptists and the Methodists, who had no settled ministeries but were served by circuit riders travelling from town to town preaching in thinly settled areas. These ministers were not well educated, nor were their congregations, nor did they approve of education, sneering at the dull sermons of the settled preachers, their own making up in fire what they lacked in learning. The Congregational ministers in return generally showed little Christian charity toward their brother ministers who not only lacked education but threatened their livelihood and the cohesiveness of their flock. The *New Hampshire Gazette* in August of 1804 cautioned its dissenting readers, "Remember, my Brethren, that the truth you [Baptists] believe, is not supported by the friends of State Religion."[6] These religious dissenters naturally gravitated toward the Republican Party and as these denominations grew they affected political events.

From this group a young Methodist minister named Daniel

Young joined Isaac Hill, Episcopalian, and William Plumer, deist, to lead the legislature to pass the Toleration Act of 1819. Young was not a professional politician, as were the other two men; he ran for the state senate with the sole intention of ending the religious establishment in New Hampshire.

Though in 1818 New Hampshire, Connecticut, and Massachusetts were the only remaining states with religious establishments, the proposed Toleration Act brought a storm of hysterical protest based on the fear that, like the decrees of the French National Assembly in 1793, it would abolish religion. In fact the Toleration Bill was not nearly as dramatic as these extreme reactions implied. Far from separating church and state, it simply allowed towns to incorporate more than one religious sect and gave each sect the right to tax the polls and property of its members. Though the bill protected the privileges of existing ministers, it was obvious that the Toleration Act would water down the system of tax-supported religious institutions and undermine the powerful political influence of the Congregational Church in New Hampshire.

Meantime in the twelve-man senate in 1816, Daniel Young mustered three votes for toleration, the following year, six, and in 1818 a majority. The mood of the state clearly favored liberalism and toleration even against opposition of the established church, and finally the next year while the Supreme Court mulled over the Dartmouth Case, the Toleration Act became law.

To the surprise of many the meeting houses were neither deserted nor forsaken. The next year after the passage of the Toleration Act, there was a revival of religious fervor in the state that vitalized the Congregational Church as well as other Christian sects, and soon the churches themselves found it not in their best interests to enforce the powers of assessment that the Toleration Act gave them. Though religious bias did not fade at once from the public mind, the Toleration Act was the beginning of its decline from the legal code and the death knell of its political influence.

The impulse toward social improvements which had emerged during the years following the War of 1812 spread to other areas of the public domain and continued until the eve of the Civil War. For almost thirty years the state tried to improve both the social and physical conditions under which its citizens lived, including such liberal social programs as penal reform, public education, religious toleration, better treatment for the insane, better working conditions, and major public construction of canals, roads, bridges, and public buildings. By the 1840s New Hampshire had become a leader among the states in social programs.

The programs began under Governor William Plumer whose most liberal ideas might surprise a moderate liberal today. In 1818 Plumer proposed to abolish imprisonment for debt, an idea the legislature rejected though it did pass a law prohibiting imprisonment for debt less than $13.34 which just happened to be the sum owed by a seventy-year-old Revolutionary War veteran, Captain Moses Brewer. When Brewer was returned to jail because he could not pay the three thousand dollars in court costs for pleading his case, Benjamin Pierce, himself a Revolutionary War veteran and the father of Franklin Pierce, paid Brewer's debts out of his own pocket. Imprisonment for debt was clearly on its way out. By 1827 debtors were no longer jailed, though they were confined to their towns. By 1840 under Governor Dinsmoor and Governor John Page, debtors were no longer confined at all.

Capital punishment, which no longer exists in the state, was losing favor. Governor Page would have disallowed capital punishment altogether, but the legislature managed to reduce the number of capital crimes from nine to two.

Schemes improving buildings and social institutions burgeoned. Under the auspices of Governor Plumer a new penitentiary was built with an administration modeled on the most progressive theories of the day. Plumer also almost singlehandedly saw to the construction of the capitol building in Concord, an assumption of authority that irked the legislature. Their protests, however, came after the building was well underway. The senate approved appropriating one thousand dollars to send deaf and dumb children to an asylum in Hartford, Connecticut. In 1838 the legislature established a "charitable home" for the insane.

During the early years of these reforms there was great enthusiasm for improving public transportation. The state built a new toll bridge across the Connecticut at Claremont, continued a road from Boston to Quebec, and finished a canal that linked Boston and the Merrimack in 1815. Some wildly ambitious projects were ditched: a canal from Lake Winnipesaukee to Portsmouth and another from the Merrimack to the Connecticut never materialized.

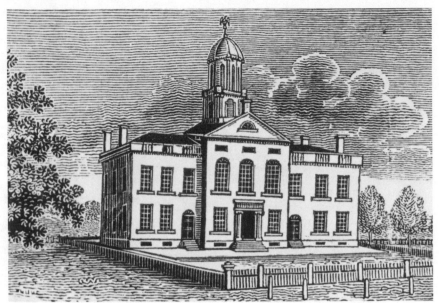

Southeast view of the State House in Concord. c. 1830. New Hampshire Historical Society.

Not until the 1840s, however, did the state begin to pass laws protecting workers. Then a child labor law was passed that prevented children under fifteen from working in factories if they did not attend school and that required parental permission for them to work longer than a ten-hour day. The legislature also pegged the normal working day at ten hours, and all workers had to sign a special contract to work longer than that.

In a quixotic gesture that exposed a paradox that has existed in the state government ever since this time of reform, Governor William Plumer demanded that his own salary be reduced as well as that of the state's judges and the treasurer, a gesture which won him praise from Thomas Jefferson. Thus though the drive to improve the state continued through the 1830s and 1840s, there was also a strong desire for a frugal state government and on the national level a resistance to federal spending for improvements. It was a paradox that existed in the political thinking of both Jefferson and later Andrew Jackson, both of whom were enormously influential in the state during their tenures. And those same conflicting impulses continue to plague the state government today as it strives to provide services for a burgeoning population at the same time it keeps a lid on the size of the government by keeping taxes low.

Even so, these years before the Civil War were a time when, as Levi Woodbury observed, most politicians were espousing the cause of "the plain people of the North," farmers, small businessmen, artisans, and mechanics. As Woodbury observed, "The great mass of society" was "very sagacious about its interests and rights and, though liable to be misled for a time" soon used their judgment to ensure "the greatest good for the greatest number."[7] Thus in their own interests the people balanced the value of reform and the cost of reform as well as they could.

THE NEW JACKSONIANS

That the popular Governor Plumer and often the legislature, too, as well as one of the most powerful papers in the state supported this social legislation reflects just how broad was the consensus on social issues in New Hampshire after the War of 1812. But by 1822, there was a new breed of Jeffersonian Republicans. Langdon, the founder of the party in the state was gone, and William Plumer, Langdon's successor, who had begun his career as a Federalist, found the young blood in the party disturbing.

Isaac Hill, the combative journalist from Concord, and Levi Woodbury, the lawyer who had been appointed Superior Court judge by William Plumer, now commanded positions of leadership in the state. Hill, who had become socially prominent through his marriage and rich through his various enterprises — his newspaper, a printing shop, a bookstore, and investments in real estate, banks, factories, and the Concord and Union Boating Company — nevertheless spoke for the interests of the common man. Hill never lost a passion for the spirit of revolution and a suspicion of the conservative seacoast towns, the Connecticut Valley communities and Washington, D.C.

Though he served as U. S. Senator and governor of the state and became a powerful advisor to two presidents, Hill continued to wear the black coat of a printer to remind himself and others of his humble beginnings and his sympathy for the common people; this attire may have inspired the voters with confidence, but it failed to endow Hill with any noticable personal humility. Hill lashed out in his editorials, mocked his opponents, sneered at his rivals, and never doubted his position as defender of the poor and weak.

Isaac Hill. New Hampshire
Historical Society.

The other new power in the state, Levi Woodbury from Portsmouth, was of quite a different stamp. Woodbury claimed a distinguished ancestry and a fine education. Though he was related to John Langdon and espoused the same republican causes, Woodbury would never be labelled a firebrand. He was circumspect and sometimes noncommittal, characteristics that caused Hill to distrust him and sometimes caused him to waffle. Even so, Woodbury, like Hill, espoused the Jeffersonian causes such as frugal government and rotation in office and associated them with the Puritan tradition. In the sixteen years between 1816 and 1832 he served as justice of the state Superior Court, governor, representative to the state legislature, United States senator, and secretary of the navy. Meantime he and Hill formed an uneasy alliance that dominated state politics from the War of 1812 until the 1840s.

The alliance travelled a rocky road. Hill was outspoken and aggressive, a real political infighter. Woodbury was tactful and sometimes evasive. The very fact that Woodbury was from a wealthy family made Hill wary. And Woodbury, patient man that he was, must have suffered from Hill's relentless vulgarity. When they worked together, they created an enormously effective political machine, but they did not always cooperate.

To begin with, in the election of 1822, Hill refused to support Woodbury who was running for governor, observing tartly that, "To run for governor a man must remove either to Portsmouth or Exeter, erect or purchase a large, three-story house, keep his coach, four horses, and servants,"[8] and worrying that Concord would be neglected by the state government in favor of Portsmouth. When the Federalists swung their support to Woodbury, Hill's suspicions deepened and his opposition created a split within the Jeffersonian Republicans between Portsmouth and the interior, an alliance the party depended on.

While the amiable Woodbury continued to seek common ground with Hill, William Plumer, Samuel Bell, and others in the party inched away. On national issues the split was particularly sharp since Hill refused to support John Quincy Adams whom he suspected of federal principles while, for some mysterious reason of his own, Plumer cast his lone ballot for Adams in the electoral college of 1820 — the only vote Adams received. The differences between the older Republican leaders and the younger ones was driving a wedge in the party as ties of state leaders to the national parties affected the state political structure.

Meanwhile on the state level, Woodbury and Hill were patching up an alliance. A canal proposed between Portsmouth and Lake Winnipesaukee proved impracticable, and the new turnpike between Concord and Portsmouth not only carried goods but also goodwill between the two towns, which helped revive the political alliance of the towns and the two men who led them. Furthermore, in the race for governor in 1825 they had found in Revolutionary War veteran Benjamin Pierce a candidate they could agree on.

In 1825 Hill had marched firmly into the camp of Andrew Jackson. When Senator Samuel Bell tried once more to conciliate the wayward Jacksonians, defending the Adams administration by calling it "strictly democratic,"[9] he succeeded in alienating both the Jacksonians who hated Adams and the Federalists who hated democracy. By 1826 Woodbury, too, was sidling away from the Adams administration because the president was "aloof more than was expected from the antient and firm democracy of the country."[10] By 1827 Woodbury had certainly moved into the Jackson camp, and once committed Woodbury became an important force in the emerging party in Washington and in New Hampshire.

In the 1827 gubernatorial election in New Hampshire Bell ran against Benjamin Pierce in a fiercely contested battle pitching Jacksonians for Pierce against National Republicans for Bell. Though they lost the election, it established the new Jacksonian Democrats as the beginning of our modern Democratic Party.

The contest between Jackson and Adams for the United States presidency was as dirty as the one for governor of New Hampshire. Hill may have peaked in his career as a yellow journalist with a story that asserted that while the Puritanical Adams was minister to Russia, he had tried to procure a servant girl to assuage the sexual appetites of the lecherous Tsar Alexander. In turn the Adams campaign charged that Jackson had murdered seven militiamen, two British agents, two Indian chiefs, and one American — the latter in a duel. To which Hill responded, "Pshaw! Why don't you tell the whole truth? On the 8th of January, 1815, he murdered in the coldest blood 1,500 British soldiers for merely trying to get into New Orleans for Booty and Beauty."[11]

The response delighted Jacksonians all over the country, but Hill and Woodbury still could not muster enough strength to deliver New Hampshire's electoral votes to Jackson. Even so, the Democratic party burned with enthusiasm. They held rallies and dinners and meetings. In the spring elections their energetic campaigning paid off when Pierce won the governorship. Furthermore the Democrats dominated the Council and the Senate in Concord, and six Jacksonians were sent to represent the state in Washington. By 1828 the Democrats were firmly in control in New Hampshire.

The new Democrats revived the rhetoric of class warfare with which the Jeffersonian Republicans had attacked the Federalists at the turn of the century, stressing democracy, opposing privilege, appealing to the common man. As many had foreseen, the Democrats sided with the South and the West. Hill and Woodbury, both now in the Senate, opposed tariffs, the Bank of the United States, and most internal improvements at federal expense, all issues that the state would face in the next few years. They supported the right of the South to have slavery. On the other hand they disagreed with the other Democrats on the issue of states' rights. New Hampshire, like the Jacksonians, disapproved of the idea of nullification now just as it had during the War of 1812.

THE BANK WAR

A national bank war erupted in 1833 when President Jackson removed federal funds from the Bank of the United States; it began with a crisis in the Second Bank of the United States in Portsmouth. Since 1799, when John Langdon had started the Union Bank that offered small loans at low rates to compete with the New Hampshire Bank, banking had been a political as well as a social and financial issue in the state. As the economy and particularly manufacturing expanded in the early years of the nineteenth century, so did the need for banks. After the founding of the Union Bank, the number of commercial banks increased to twenty-one in 1831, and the state chartered six savings banks. However, the new banks were mostly located in the southeast—around Portsmouth, Exeter, and Dover. Only three of the new commercial banks were in the hill country in the middle of the state. Furthermore, the powerful Bank of the United States opened a branch in Portsmouth in 1817, thus complicating the regional issues by involving the federal government. The concentration of such power and wealth on the seacoast aroused all the old regional hostilities, but it was the involvement of the federal government that precipitated the crisis which followed.

In 1828, though Biddle, the head of the Bank of the United States, later denied it, he followed the recommendation of Daniel Webster, one of the bank's directors, and appointed Jeremiah Mason president of the Second Bank of the United States in Portsmouth. The appointment of such a staunch Federalist in the middle of a presidential election infuriated the Democrats. Not only was Mason a Federalist, he favored manufacturers over merchants and farmers, ruthlessly cutting back on what he referred to as "country loans" in order to get the affairs of the bank in better order but leaving merchants and the poor hill farmers in financial straits. The angry citizens of Portsmouth hanged Mason in effigy.

Woodbury and Hill circulated two petitions which they sent to the directors of the Bank of the United States with a covering letter declaring "Mason's conduct partial and oppressive." Hill further persuaded the legislature to sign a petition to the secretary of the treasury urging him to transfer United States pension agency funds to the Merrimack County Bank, which happened to be Hill's own bank but also had the advantage of being located in Concord. Secretary of the

Treasury Samuel Ingham sent a letter obliquely warning Biddle not to play politics. Biddle responded that there were not "in the whole country, any five hundred persons of equal intelligence so abstracted from public affairs," as were the legal administrators. After spending a week in Portsmouth where he heard conflicting reports of the bank's affairs, Biddle endorsed Mason and went home. From his olympian heights Biddle observed that it "was a paltry intrigue got up by a combination of small bankrupts and Demagogues."[12]

He soon, however, received a reply to his letter to Ingham in which the secretary of treasury declared he was surprised at the "confident . . . assertion of the universal purity of the bank," observing drily that no "body of five hundred men, not selected by an Omniscient eye" can "be fairly entitled" to such "unqualified testimony."[13] Biddle bridled. He reminded the secretary of the treasury that the Bank had helped pay an installment of the public debt, but he didn't stop at that. He said he was responsible to the Congress alone and not to the secretary of the treasury or even to President Jackson. The haughty response proved to be a bad idea. Ingham reminded Biddle that the administration had the power to remove federal deposits from the bank. Biddle decided to sue for peace.

But the Jacksonians in New Hampshire continued to harass the bank. Woodbury tried to get the bank moved to Concord, though he waffled when the opportunity finally presented itself. Meantime, Hill, unlike the hesitant Woodbury, printed anti-bank speeches from the U. S. Senate on the front page of the *Patriot*, and claimed that the bank would be "a more powerful enemy to the people than an invading army of half a million men."[14]

In 1833 when President Jackson made the final decision to remove federal funds from the Bank of the United States, he justified the decision on grounds that spoke to New Hampshire Democrats. The bank would make "the rich richer and the potent more powerful" giving "the humble member of society, the farmers, mechanics, and laborers . . . a right to complain of the injustice of their government."[15] It was Woodbury and Hill who selected the pet banks to which federal funds would be transferred, and to no one's great surprise by 1836 the pensions were distributed from the Merrimack County Bank of which Hill was a director. Whether in the long run the attack on the bank helped the farmers, mechanics, and laborers, or not, it had increased the number of people who shared in the money and power that banks have, and to that extent it accomplished some of the democratic aims that its instigators professed.

THE LOCOFOCOS

In 1836, when Hill left the United States Senate to become governor of New Hampshire, he had led the state in its efforts to achieve a grassroots democracy, sympathetic to the farmer striving for self-sufficiency. However, when he became governor, Hill discovered in the state ambitious and vocal young agrarian Democrats, eager to curb business, who were far more radical than he. A new wing of the Democratic party called the Radical Democrats (no relation to modern radicalism), sometimes called "locofocos" (because at an early meeting in New York where the party originated they had used locofoco matches for light), led by Thomas Treadwell of Portsmouth and Edmund Burke of Newport opposed business expansion in general and railroads and banks in particular.

Isaac Hill had opposed banks and railroads and business and supported agrarian interests against the Federalists for years, but times and Isaac Hill had changed. Treadwell and Burke represented the Connecticut Valley and the coast, two regions of the state that Hill never trusted; this time, though, Hill represented the middle of the state against both east and west, but this time he was on the opposite side of the issues. While Hill had always courted the vote of the "yeoman farmer," the new Radical Democrats, these new agrarians, far outdid Hill in their antagonism to industry, particularly the railroads. Instead of seeing the farmer as a moral example, the locofocos tried to reduce the whole industrial segment of New Hampshire until the state's economy rested entirely on farming — this in a state that in 1840 ranked ninth out of thirty in the percent of capital invested in manufacturing.

In 1835-36 the Radicals lacked the votes to stop the legislature from chartering six railroads. However, in 1837 the Radicals managed to limit railroads to six rods of land along the tracks, but in fact they disapproved of allowing the railroads to take land by eminent domain at all.

Ignoring the displeasure of his fellow Democrats, Hill pushed ahead with attempts to raise money from both state and national governments for the Concord Railroad of which he was a director. Insisting that all of Concord would benefit from the railroad, he persuaded a special town meeting to invest seventy thousand dollars in eight hundred shares of the railroad—forty thousand dollars of school and parsonage funds and thirty thousand dollars borrowed. When the state received nine-hundred thousand dollars of surplus federal funds, he proposed that the money be lent at low interest to four railroads, "most important" to the one to Concord. This last proposal the Radicals succeeded in blocking. Thus ended the first skirmish in the Railroad War which lasted until 1844.

In 1838 Hill fought a hard race against the Whigs (whom the *Patriot* claimed were Federalists) and barely retained his office—the first time the Democrats had been challenged seriously since the War of 1812. Convinced that Hill's unpopularity was hurting the party, the next year the Democrats nominated Senator John Page, and at fifty-two Hill was sick and out of a job.

Radical Democrats moved rapidly to stop the railroads from expanding further. By 1840 they had passed a law granting chartered railroads the right of eminent domain only if every claim for damages had been paid and repealing the right of eminent domain for future railroads. Another law permitted farmers who felt they had not been paid fairly to remove tracks from their land. Such stern measures effectively delayed railroad construction in New Hampshire, and in the next five years only fifty-seven miles of track were laid in the state. The Concord Railroad alone continued to build—to Manchester to accommodate the Amoskeag mills and the Boston & Maine continued on down to Boston by 1842.

Beginning in 1840 the Radicals were equally effective in blocking industrial growth. For the next two years the legislature chartered not a single mill or manufacturing corporation. By 1842 the Radicals were so powerful that they not only postponed four bills to extend bank charters, they managed to pass the Unlimited Liability Act which made stockholders of corporations responsible for the debts of the corporations in which they held stock. Since most states had established a principle of limited liability, New Hampshire for a time became a very unattractive location for new businesses.

In 1842 Hill gained the patronage of President Tyler to fight a rearguard action for the railroads against the Radicals by backing

John H. White for governor against Radical Henry Hubbard. However, not only did the engimatic Levi Woodbury choose this moment to come out in support of the Radicals, but Franklin Pierce returned to the state to join the political fight against Hill and the railroads, banks, and manufacturing.

When in 1843 Hill once again challenged the Radicals, the Radicals appealed to Woodbury to clarify his position on the railroad's right of eminent domain. Woodbury hedged by explaining that if a corporation is public, then lands could be taken, but if railroads were private, then they could not take land under the law of public domain. Since railroads only ran their own cars on their own tracks, they were private, and thus could not buy land under eminent domain. With that careful statement of support by the most eminent man in the New Hampshire Democratic Party and with the diligence of Franklin Pierce, the Radicals won control of the state party as well as the governorship.

Then, as quickly as it had begun, the trend reversed itself. Men such as philosophy Professor Charles Haddock of Dartmouth seeing the economic threat of "the youthful giant States of the West" and thinking the railroads would help New Hampshire compete, urged that the state "stimulate the enterprize and reward the industry of our own commonwealth."[16] The democratic, rural bias against corporations was assuaged with reminders of the Puritan morality of social improvement and progress. Even fears that corporations would be controlled in Boston rather than New Hampshire were allayed with the promise that stockholders from the state could vote by absentee ballot.

By June 1844, petitions favoring the railroads poured into the capital. Woodbury's wary opinion on the subject of eminent domain had given the state a way out of the dilemma. The railroads declared themselves public, and the Radicals believed them. The law of eminent domain was restored, and the railroads began expanding again, though since they were declared public, the state could and did regulate many of the railroads' affairs besides stipulating that after twenty years the state could buy the railroad, a law that, in the long run, would fail to prevent another crisis between the state and the railroads. There ensued a truce between New Hampshire and the railroads, though the conflict resumed again a few years later.

Gradually the Radical Democrats made peace with the Conservative Democrats, leaving some of the locofocos quietly grumbling but regaining party harmony and encouraging economic development in the state. By 1846 the law on unlimited liability was repealed, and other laws encouraging industry were passed. The Radicals did not lose their control of the state, they compromised. They changed their policies towards industry; however, in their efforts to circumscribe business they delayed New Hampshire's recovery from the depression of 1837 and helped slow economic growth of the state.

Even so, the Radical Democrats fulfilled some of the promise of social progress favored by the Jacksonians. They foresaw some of the problems arriving with the industrial revolution, and they set an example for legislation protecting workers and children and regulating industries which might threaten the economic well-being of the people of the state.

Franklin Pierce, John Parker Hale, and the Slavery Question

Quite overshadowing these local questions loomed the slavery debate. Though New Hampshire had almost no first-hand contact with slavery, during the 1840s the issue reverberated through the state. Most notably two former slaves who lived in the state wrote famous narratives about their experiences. In Weare, Fredrick Douglas worked on his autobiography *Narrative of the Life of Fredrick Douglas, An American Slave,* published in 1845, and in Milford, Harriet Wilson wrote *Our Nig,* published in 1859.

Meanwhile the issue of slavery changed the course of New Hampshire politics forever. Two men from the state, very nearly the same age, graduates of the same college, friends, and colleagues took different positions on the issue of slavery which would divide the nation for the next twenty-five years. Each of the men took his stand on the national political stage. For two years John Parker Hale alone in the Senate of the United States fought slavery against such giants as John C. Calhoun, Daniel Webster, and Stephen Douglas. He was nominated for the presidency by the abolitionist Liberty Party in 1848, though he later lost out to men more radical than himself. Franklin Pierce, on the other hand, stood firmly by his commitment to keep peace by allowing states and territories to decide the issue for themselves. The stand brought him to the presidency in 1852.

As a young senator in Washington, Franklin Pierce, an ardent

Franklin Pierce. Painted by Francis M. Potter. 1892. Hood Museum of Art, Dartmouth College.

anti-abolitionist, had voted more than once for the gag rule by which the Senate accepted petitions from the abolitionists and failed to debate them. But the abolitionists, whose antislavery stand caused them to be labelled fanatics, were beginning to protest that the rule denied the people their right to petition, and Pierce was beginning to doubt its further usefulness. Nevertheless, he certainly was not wavering in his commitment to the Democratic Party's alliance with the South which was both anti-tariff and anti-abolitionist.

The Democratic Party's stance did not reflect the opinions of the whole state. Congressman John Parker Hale, once a rabid anti-abolitionist, had changed his mind about the issue. Like Pierce, he had attended Bowdoin College, but unlike Pierce who had chosen Bowdoin over Dartmouth because his family found Dartmouth too Federalist and too Congregational, the Hale family was Federalist. Only gradually did Hale's views become Democratic. (Perhaps Hill's particularly vitriolic attacks on Hale when Hale joined the Radical Democrats stemmed partly from his late arrival in the party.) In any event, for his first few years as a Radical Democrat he certainly showed every sign of being a loyal member of the Democratic party and anti-abolitionist. In 1835 he made a heated response to an abolitionist speaker in which he declared slaves were "BEASTS IN HUMAN SHAPE AND NOT FIT TO LIVE FREE."[17]

But through unrevealed stages and for unrevealed reasons, the sociable and easy going Hale abandoned his violently anti-abolitionist position, though he did not quickly abandon the Democratic Party. In 1845, the question before the Congress that was most crucial to the issue of slavery was the annexation of Texas to the Union. Projecting that Texas was likely to be slaveholding, the abolitionists opposed its annexation. The legislature of New Hampshire sent instructions to the state's representatives in Congress to support annexation, but after Hale made a proposal testing the assurances that Texas would be more free than slave and discovered that there was not much support for Texas as a free soil, he determined to vote against annexation.

In January Hale sent a letter to his constituents explaining his determination in the matter. When Party Leader Franklin Pierce got word of Hale's letter, he flew into action to prevent the party from renominating Hale. With the support of Levi Woodbury and most of the party leaders, Pierce organized the state against Hale. From one end of the state to the other through the snowstorms of the New Hampshire winter he denounced Hale for his insubordination, accusing him of betraying "the party that had so long supported him"[18] and using the issue for "schismatic purposes." Nothing was such an anathema to Pierce as disloyalty to the party, and he determined to chuck Hale out. He prophetically accused Hale of "planning a bargain with the Whigs and Abolitionists which should make him senator and the leader of a great new party."[19] Whether or not Hale had any such ambitions at the time is debatable, but that is what eventually happened.

For the moment, however, Pierce called a special convention to nominate someone to replace Hale on the March ballot and found most party leaders, including the Conservatives, willing to jettison the renegade Hale. The issue of Texas annexation was immaterial. The point was party discipline, and on that point there was agreement. The convention was sparsely attended because of a snowstorm, but Pierce was taking no chances. He hastily called for a vote and got Hale expelled before any latecomers could object.

Though Hale refused to return to New Hampshire to defend himself or campaign for the nomination, others, most notably Amos Tuck and John Hayes, carried on his fight against the party powers under the banner of Independent Democrats. The new Independent

Democrats could not elect Hale, but they mustered enough votes to prevent either the Whig or the Democratic candidate from gaining a majority, leaving the seat vacant until another election could be held in September. As one witty stage driver observed to Amos Tuck the day after the election, "there had been a terrible Hale storm" in the state.[20]

In the summer of 1845 Hale broke his silence and stumped the state campaigning for reelection. In a historic debate Pierce denounced Hale as an abolitionist and a Whig. Hale countered with an emotional speech ending with a wish that his tombstone would read "He who lies beneath surrendered office, place, and power, rather than bow down and worship slavery."[21] As Pierce had predicted, the Independent Democrats forged an alliance with the Abolitionists and the Whigs and some disenchanted locofocos. In 1846 this new alliance sent John Parker Hale to the Senate and Whig Anthony Colby to the governor's office as the voters of New Hampshire responded to a national issue in their own local elections.

The next year Pierce went off to fight in the Mexican War — the same war that John Parker Hale denounced to the state legislature. Before he left, Pierce helped compose what became the model of Democrats' position on the issue of slavery:

> That we affirm the sentiments and opinions of the democratic party and democratic statesmen of the north entertained from 1776 to the present day, in relation to slavery — that we deplore its existence, and regard it as a great moral and social evil, but with this conviction, we do not deem ourselves more wise than Washington, Franklin, and their associates, and that patriotism, common honesty and religious principle alike bind us to a sacred observance of the compact made by those wise men.[22]

Before Levi Woodbury died in 1851, chances looked good that he would be the moderate Jacksonian candidate the Democrats needed to run for president. After his death, the party scrambled to find another suitable candidate. The candidate needed to fill a complicated list of requirements, but ultimately he would have to be agreeable to both the North and South. The burning issues were the fugitive slave law, the admission of new territories to the Union, slavery in the District of Columbia, and, above all, the preservation of the Union in the face of increasing antagonism between the North and South. Such giants as Webster, Calhoun, Douglas, and Clay had been wrestling with these and related issues for some time and found compromises that put patches on the wounds but did not heal the cankers that infected the nation. The latest such patchwork was the Compromise of 1850, and Franklin Pierce from New Hampshire agreed to run on that platform. So it was Pierce who provided the party with a compromise candidate in 1852.

Pierce was an amiable man who, as his nickname suggested, wanted nothing so much as to follow in the footsteps of Old Hickory, Andrew Jackson. He clung to the ideal of the Union, and he strove to protect it by erecting a shaky structure of advisors and supporters from both sides of every question. But though Pierce had served as a brigadier general in Mexico, he was no Jackson, and even Jackson would have been hard pressed to heal the nation in the 1850s. As one of Pierce's best friends, Nathaniel Hawthorne observed, " . . . it would ruin a noble character (though one of limited scope) for him to admit any ideas that were not entertained by the fathers of the Constitution and the Republic."[23]

To make matters worse, during a family trip following the election there was a train wreck in which Pierce's only child, Bennie, was killed. Neither of the child's parents could cope with his death. Inconsolable, Pierce's wife, who hated politics anyway, remained behind with relatives, and Pierce took office already a demoralized man.

He returned to New Hampshire after his undistinguished term in the White House and sacrificed his popularity in Concord by maintaining his opposition to Lincoln and the Civil War, believing to the end that the war could have been prevented. So unacceptable was his position that when Nathaniel Hawthorne died while the two friends were on a trip together in 1864, Pierce was not asked to be a pall bearer at his funeral. Perhaps that he held his convictions so tenaciously in face of such disapproval casts doubt on the general assessment that Pierce was simply an amiable nonentity.

THE NEW PARTY

In the period between the War of 1812 and the Civil War, New Hampshire produced several political figures who molded the state into a strong political unit. So strong was their leadership that the Democratic party dominated New Hampshire from 1828 until 1852. Even in the election of 1840 when the Democrats won only two seats in the national elections, New Hampshire was one of them. But this solidarity was shaken by the expulsion of John Parker Hale which not only laid the groundwork for a party split but provided the foundation for a new political party, a party that had its conception in New Hampshire and became one of the two major political parties in the nation.

Allied as they were to the South, the Democrats clung to the anti-abolitionist position, and so long as the abolitionists clung to their antipolitical policy, there was no trouble for either of the political parties. However, Hale's expulsion from the Democratic Party over an antislavery issue coincided with the movement among the abolitionists to press their case through political channels, and Hale emerged as a ready made rallying point.

When in 1853 Amos Tuck returned to Exeter from Washington where he served in Congress for six years, a jumble of political parties were contending with the Goliath, the Democratic party. Tuck conceived the idea of uniting all the factions in New Hampshire that opposed the Democrats--the Whigs, the Free Soil, the Liberty, the Know-Nothing or American party, and the new Independent Democrats; many of them opposed slavery and favored protective tariffs on imports. To this end he called a secret meeting of the leaders of these various groups—George Fogg, Asa McFarland, William Plumer, Jr., D. H. Batchelder, Ichabod Bartlett, and, of course, John Parker Hale. The meeting did not remain secret long, for Horace Greeley published an account of it in his paper before the end of the year. This meeting formed the alliance that became the Republican party, the party which has more or less dominated the state every since.

As antislavery, protariff sentiment grew in the state, and as the Democrats persisted in their loyalty to the positions favored by the South, the Democratic party lost its long-held supremacy in the state, and the influence of the Republican party flourished. At the end of the Civil War the Republicans were almost as unassailable as the Democrats had been in the first half of the century. The new party would face massive economic and social changes as the industrial revolution swept through the state, and it would have to organize the government of the state to handle the problems these changes created.

7

The Mill

By the 1830s as New Hampshire's politicians continued to struggle to put the state's house in order, its economy like its politics came more and more under the influence of forces outside both its expectations and its borders. It became increasingly clear that economic well-being rested in the developments and cultivation not of its farmlands but of its manpower and the waterpower which could turn the wheels of mills and factories.

For New Hampshire the journey from the mercantile trading society of the colonial port, to the self-sufficient farm, to the commercial manufacturing economy of the mill was natural enough. After all, following temporary log home shelters, the sawmill and the gristmill emerged as the first buildings in a new settled town, long before the meetinghouse or the school was raised. Early in a town's development the air was filled with the sound of waterpowered saws slicing timber for buildings and waterpowered millstones grinding Indian corn for bread. And of course farm children had long learned and practiced a variety of home manufacturing skills from whittling to weaving. Nonetheless the changes — social, economic, ecological, and political — initiated by the shift toward large-scale manufacturing created a whole new world of opportunities, challenges and problems for the state.

In 1774 Abel Twitchell left his home in Sherborn, Massachusetts, to settle on a heavily forested, hilly, rough and rock-strewn lot near a steep gorge and turbulent brook in the southern part of New Hampshire near a town now called Harrisville. The area's first settler, Twitchell learned of the land through his father who had been an agent for the proprietors, who traced their holding to an old Masonian grant. Settling on land unattractive to farmers, Abel, and later four of his brothers and two of his sisters, recognized the value of the waterpower at hand. Brother Samuel, the third settler, built a sawmill before acquiring complete control of the area's water power. Abel Twitchell also built a square, two-and-a-half story frame house which still stands. The story of the development of the three closely related towns of Dublin, Nelson, and Harrisville follows both well-known and unpredictable patterns. Following the surveying for houselots, clearing boulder-filled land, planting, building rude log houses, putting in roads, and erecting mills, agrarian communities emerged. According to contemporary accounts, the principal hardships which the early settlers faced were the relentless winters, meager arable lands, devastating fires, and natural enemies to livestock, bears and wolves.

By the nineteenth century the framework of settled community life was in place, and the community was poised for its golden years — but not as a rural agricultural community. Abel Twitchell's mills set a standard for the development of the waterpower which by 1860 enabled the growth of two competing woolen mills. During Harrisville's most vigorous period of economic growth, 1850 to 1870, and in fact until the present, this town's life has been dominated by its woolen mills. Though they may never have attained the star quality of their giant sisters in Manchester, Nashua, Dover, and Somersworth, their history and the town's adaptation to modern industrial times is illustrative of the state's experience in a number of ways. John Borden Armstrong, the town's chronicler, has observed that Harrisville's history includes on a small scale many developments important in the history of the nation: a frontier community of self-sufficient farmers, the utilization of waterpower to run small mills, the building of a factory village, the conflicts brought by mass immigration, the growth of the railroads, clashes between farmers and mill population, and the effect of economic booms and busts.

For Harrisville and for many other towns in the state, the seeds of the industrial revolution were planted early in the community's history as natural responses to the settler's domestic needs, the geography of the land they settled, and later their grasp of the opportunities for economic growth.

In the years before the Revolution, manufacturing in New Hampshire was a small and principally home industry whose production costs were so high that products, even if marketed, could rarely bring a profit. And of course, at the same time the English carefully protected their own commercial interests by promoting colonial consumption of English manufactured goods. The flax and linen production of Scotch-Irish settlers of the Merrimack valley, whom Belknap praises lavishly for their industry, frugality, and hospitality, was a notable exception.

Early in the 1700s they spun and wove linen thread and cloth of a very high quality in Londonderry. Turning a home industry into a professional and commerical venture, using skills brought from their homeland, the "sanguine and robust" men and women of "lively dispositions" saw quickly the advantages at hand.[1] Soon they were growing their own flax, carding, spinning, and weaving cloth, which commanded such profit and respect that by 1748 Londonderry's citizens voted to preserve 'the credit of our manufactory's' by appointing inspectors of local linens and hollands to stamp each piece of approved cloth with the town's seal.[2] In 1768 Governor Wentworth noted that at least twenty-five thousand yards of linen were manufactured each year for regional markets. Aside from the masting trade and its allied trade in wood products, Londonderry's unusual flax production, and grist and cider mills, most other manufacturing in New Hampshire before the Revolution was either an outgrowth of farming or a related extractive enterprise like bog-iron, tar, pitch, pot, or pearlash production. Finally, while the Revolution reduced dependence on English manufactured goods and encouraged home production, at the end of the war infant industries once again suffered the press of foreign competition.

Yet in the early nineteenth century, in southern New Hampshire, on a typical small town's streams and millponds one might find tanneries, cabinetmakers' shops, blacksmitheries, starch factories, hat works, and other small industries. Managed and financed locally, small industries like these gradually began to supplant many towns' agricultural economy.

THE MILL IN THE CITY

If the local sawmill and gristmill were natural enough features of the state's emerging towns, soon so too were the textile giants in Manchester, Nashua, Dover, Somersworth, and Exeter which offered stable wages and social independence to the new generation of workers. Though most of these sites were established after 1820, the 1810 census had shown twelve cotton mills operating in the state. By 1812 the Cocheco Mill had opened in Dover; by 1821 the Great Falls Manufacturing Company created a factory town on the Salmon Falls River; by 1822 two factories were active in Somersworth; and in 1823 the Nashua Manufacturing Company was underway. Building upon small cotton-spinning works operating as early as 1809, by 1831 the soon to be world-famous Amoskeag Company began operations in Manchester. In 1832 the state had forty cotton mills operating.

At the same time, somewhat less dependent on massive water-power resources, the woolen industry developed. James Sanderson, a Scotsman, is credited with founding in 1801 the state's first sizeable woolen mill in New Ipswich, where he became well-known for his indigo dyeing. In Keene in 1815, the Faulkner and Colony Company began a successful operation weaving flannel cloth, which ultimately achieved fame among the California forty-niners for red shirts and the New Orleans stevedores for blue shirts. By 1823, the state is reported to have had fifty-six woolen carding mills.

Just as textile and woolen production developed naturally from home industries to large-scale manufacture, industrial mechanization contributed to the founding of the state's other major industry, the shoe industry. The first shoe factory was opened in Weare in 1823 by Allen Sawyer, whose factory soon produced over twenty thousand pairs of shoes each year. Other factories followed in Farmington, Rochester, and Dover beginning an industry which at one point in the 1920s outflanked even cotton production in value. Responding to the demand for cheap shoes in the South and work shoes in the West, the shoe industry differed somewhat from the textile and woolen industries in its method of production. Until the Civil War, instead of centralized production units, the shoe industry distributed components to small shops and households for finishing, the last hold-out perhaps of home manufacturing.

Whatever far-flung fame and fortune the New Hampshire textiles and woolens and shoes created for their native factory owners,
whatever profits their sale produced, the social changes their production caused should not be underestimated. To understand the magnitude of the changes afoot requires a look at the new work force
which the manufacturing economy created.

In the years before the Civil War, the larger mills in southeastern New Hampshire and Lowell, Massachusetts, depended on a
new class of workers, young farm women who were prepared to respond to opportunities for economic independence and social well-
being. Schooled in the rigid seasonal patterns and deprivations of
farm life and accustomed to shouldering "male duties," these young
women adjusted to mill life more easily than might be imagined.
(And it was not unusual either for farm wives to take their sons and
daughters to the mills, leaving husbands and grandparents behind to
manage the farm.)

Typically the young women who went to the factories came
from established hill farms, were about eighteen when they started
at the factories, and about twenty-two when they left to be married.
Significantly, their principal motivation was a desire for economic
and social independence; letters collected from the spinners and
weavers of this period are filled with references to urban amenities
such as cultural events, recreation, and clothes stores.

While the new mill jobs produced steady wages and hence some
economic independence, on the face of it the country girls' living
conditions were as safe and strict as those at home. In fact by providing strictly run boarding houses for young workers, the textile companies reassured their operative's nervous fathers. Substituting orderly schedules of work, meals, bedtime, and church attendance for
accustomed family schedules of cooperative effort on the farm, the
companies exercised benevolent paternalistic control and created
stable if not rigid environments. Few workers actually complained of
the lifestyle other than to fill their letters with references to the long
hours, their exhaustion, and homesickness.

If their environment was tightly controlled, it was also support-
ive; workers cared for each other and often took the intial step into
the mill with a sister or cousin or close family friend. Such was true
with Sarah Hodgdon of Rochester, who was shepherded at her
Lowell factory and boarding house by an older cousin, Wealthy

Page, whose offices included helping Sarah over the difficult matter of deciding which church to attend in her new home. From both the farm and the mill flowed strong kinship ties, which mill life failed to erode, indeed may have reinforced. In letters to his foster daughter, Delia Page, Luther Trussell of New London writes to "My Dear Factory Girl" with details of the family's life, neighbor's illnesses and deaths, and constant mention of the weather. With unfailing concern, letters from this period express fear for the girl's safety and well-being.

The early textile industries of New Hampshire created a whole new world of opportunity and change, and neither the family nor the economy would ever be quite the same again. Women were on the payrolls as wage earners and were moving into new circles of influence. Though most young women in the antebellum years of industry left the labor force after several years to marry, few married farmers, a number went West, and an occasional free spirit like Mary Paul tried out a utopian agricultural community in New Jersey. The wheels of industry had replaced the hearthside spinning wheel for women, and economic and social life began to be organized differently.

PORTRAIT OF A QUEEN: THE AMOSKEAG

While the wheels of industry spread throughout the state and the mill on Main Street became a prominent force in the life of many New Hampshire towns, the queen of them all for nearly one hundred years was the Amoskeag Manufacturing Company of Manchester. From the company's founding in the 1830s until its death by southern competition, antiquated machinery, changing fashions, labor relations, and natural causes (flood) in 1936, thousands and thousands of workers were induced to leave European and French Canadian homes as well as New Hampshire farms for the millyard on the Merrimack. The principal elements in the story of the Amoskeag Manufacturing Company — its physical development, its management policies, its workforce, its products, and its demise — come together to create a history as uniquely textured as its world famous A.C.A. cotton ticking and ginghams.

Even today as one passes the elegant, now silent, brick factories which stretch along the Merrimack River for a mile and a half on one side and a half of a mile on the other, it is easy to imagine smoke rising from its smoke stacks, the hour tolling from its commanding clock tower, and the whistle blowing to announce the end of another twelve-hour work day. As the whirring of thousands of looms is stilled, the gigantic millyard suddenly fills with thousands of men, women, and children — seventeen thousand in its heyday — pouring out of the gates of the world's largest textile factory. Carefully, extensively planned by a close knit group of Boston entrepreneurs known as the Boston Associates, the Amoskeag and the town of Manchester emerged in the 1830s to become a major force in cotton manufacturing in the nineteenth and early twentieth century.

Placed strategically at the falls of the state's second largest river, the development of the factories and the city which grew around them was carefully controlled by the Boston developers, who wished to avoid the environmental problems of the town's English namesake. To this end the company erected and maintained an elaborate physical, social, and political design for its workers. Manchester was the Amoskeag; the Amoskeag was Manchester. Not only was the millyard with its thirty major mills covering a total of eight million square feet of floor space (about equal to that of the present World Trade Center) a carefully designed architectural unity, but also the development of adjacent tenement housing for the workers, with town lots for management, followed a master plan. Using its own engineers and craftsmen, the company constructed most of the mills, twenty-four mechanical and electrical departments, three steam power plants, and hydroelectric power station, exercising an aesthetic control which extended to matching the color of bricks in successive buildings. Furthermore, the company manufactured much of its own machinery in foundries used later to manufacture locomotives and rifles for the Civil War.

In its early years the company recruited young farm girls, providing safe housing, and carefully controlled social and religious opportunities. In the mid-nineteenth century it began employing more and more cheap immigrant labor. Employing first a wave of Irish immigrants, the company labor force by the turn of the century was distinctly French Canadian. Other ethnic groups followed: Germans, Swedes, Scots, Greeks, and Poles. To all its employees, native and immigrant, the corporation intentionally and deliberately became the responsible but strict parent, who expected in return diligence and obedience from its children. With profitable production as its goal, the corporation sought to maintain this careful equilibrium with its workers — whose loyalty was after all crucial.

Although the company's overall operations were controlled by the Boston-based directors, most of whom were completely unfamiliar with the Manchester mills, the local operations were supervised by a treasurer, also Boston-based. He, too, had only limited contact with the Manchester workers and managers. In fact, until the 1922 strike, most of the workers barely knew of his existence. At the Amoskeag mills, the agent, a local, salaried official, who answered to the Boston office, directly supervised production and personnel relations. Much of the corporation's management success derived from the unusual continuity in its employment of agents — only six in its history and three from three generations of the same family, the Straws. And in the worker's mind, the hierarchy was an acceptable equivalent to accustomed family and religious patriarchal authority.

The Amoskeag's paternalism reached beyond the comfortable hierarchical management of production to what the company later called its welfare and efficiency programs. Designed to improve employer-employee relations, socialize immigrants, and create an Amoskeag consciousness, these included provision and maintenance of corporation housing; centralized employment records and procedures; social clubs combining comradery and lessons in cooking, gardening, sewing, and English; playgrounds, parks, and recreation opportunities; health services; and provisions for house mortgages. Since the company employed over two-thirds of Manchester's residents, it is not surprising that the town's politics were under its thumb as well. About the only service that the company did not provide was a company store for foodstuffs.

Amoskeag's Children

In several important ways Amoskeag's workers were as distinctive as the company product in which they took such pride. No matter where they came from or what reservations Amoskeag's workers developed about their work life in Manchester, they agreed upon and ardently believed one thing: everything about life and work for the corporation was an improvement over either the deprivations, isolation, and tedium of farm life in New England or Quebec or cramped living and limited economic opportunities in Great Britain or western Europe. Manchester was the "new world" and became a whole world.

Whereas earlier and competing corporations had relied heavily on native employees and especially native girls, the labor force at Amoskeag by the mid-1880s underwent a transformation which affected its situation in a number of ways. The transformation involved the shift toward cheaper immigrant labor, a change so encompassing that by 1890 the foreign-born constituted 45.5 percent of Manchester's population; of these French-Canadians constituted the largest single group, 28 percent. Major train service linking Manchester and Montreal encouraged the steady influx of families attracted to the giant mills. The immediate effect was positive: French-Canadians came to Manchester as families, often with as many as sixteen children, and as working families moved easily in the Amoskeag world. In fact rather than disrupting the family unit, as was supposed by sociologists for some time, Amoskeag's world of work actually reinforced family unity. Factory time was flexible enough to allow mothers in and out of the system as the demands of child-bearing allowed; children began working in summers; family members not only smoothed the way into the system for younger members or relatives, but they also frequently worked side by side. In a sense kinship ties within mill workrooms acted as surrogate labor unions and operated successfully so long as the company kept its part of the family bargain as responsible parent.

Strong ethnic and kinship ties in the mills presented some problems for workers as well, especially as ethnic groups clustered in certain workrooms and created in effect "closed" shops. Many factory overseers had to learn French, for instance, in order to manage certain areas of the mill. While the family became the principal working unit at Amoskeag, it is important to note that of its members women constituted more than half of the work force, in part because a number of the jobs within the mill could be performed by either men or women. By affording women wages which in some jobs were equal to men's, many women of Amoskeag gained a sense of pride and accomplishment unknown to them before. While domestic obligations remained, women nonetheless could become breadwinners and in many instances became the principal breadwinners at their husband's death. Children also had many opportunities for employment at the Amoskeag, though New Hampshire child labor laws in 1905 prevented full-time employment until the age of fourteen. So compelling was the factory life, however, that many sons and daughters of mill workers falsified their age in order to join the ranks earlier.

While an unusual workroom atmosphere of interdependence, sociability, and even jollity evolved from the close family and kinship ties at the Amoskeag, ultimately discontent common to the industrial worker of this period expressed itself in Manchester too. Despite steady wages, most working families were very poor and worked very long hours — twelve hours, six days a week was not unusual. Work schedules were rigid; the very scale of production was sometimes intimidating. Workrooms were vast in size — noisy, hot, fiber-filled, often roach-infested, and always regimented. And since the mill paid the highest wages in town, workers often sensed that they were trapped.

UNTIL THE WALLS CAME TUMBLING DOWN

The early successful equilibrium between management's production goals and the worker's sense of well-being rested in good part on each constituent's relationship to the company's world-famous product. Management spared no opportunity to remind workers that Amoskeag textiles by 1851 were winning prizes at the Crystal Palace in London and later was the textile of choice at the new Ford automobile plant. Later after record wartime profits in the second decade of the twentieth century, when southern competition forced both bosses and workers to increase output, and when the quality of the raw materials and environment declined, the earlier equilibrium between labor and management was threatened. Management first responded by speeding-up production and increasing laborer's workloads, with the result that worker's sense of competence and identification with the product was challenged — and the worker was exhausted.

In February of 1922, the peace in the formerly strikeless city

Amoskeag mill yard in Manchester. Photograph by Ann Page Stecker.

collapsed under the weight of management's sudden announcement of a 20 percent reduction in all hour and piece rates and an increase in the work week from forty-eight to fifty-four hours. The queen of the textile mills essentially never recovered from the nine-month strike which began eleven days later. The United Textile Workers never gained the control and credibility they sought; management never regained its worker's absolute loyalty; the town of Manchester's civil and religious authorities failed as intermediaries. Though the strike was fought, and in part won, over wages and hours, the real issue was the loss of mutual codes of behavior between corporate parent and corporate children. Some mills reopened; some workers were rehired; but the Amoskeag like all New England textile companies eventually lost its markets as its machinery aged and its labor and materials costs soared.

The Boston management protected its investment in a 1925 reorganization which put its $18 million cash reserve in a holding company called the Amoskeag Company, while continuing production under the name of the Amoskeag Manufacturing Company, an entity now virtually lacking liquid capital. Violent strikes in 1933 and

1934 and a devastating flood in 1936 from the falls which had been the mills' original power source, followed by bankruptcy ended a hundred year corporate history unique in New Hampshire if not in New England. In its wake the Amoskeag's workers and managers, and indeed the whole city of Manchester, experienced a local depression of devastating proportions.

The queen was dead. About ten years later, the state's other textile giant, the Nashua Manufacturing Company, was forced to end its textile production under the famous Indianhead label. Like Amoskeag, its buildings eventually became a home for the state's newer industries. The old mill buildings of the Nashua company became the first home of the electronics giant, the Sanders Corporation, an immigrant from Massachusetts; in the 1970s it became the state's largest employer.

Most New Hampshire communities were irrevocably changed from their bucolic beginnings after their entrance into the industrial age. Whether they produced linen or woolen goods, gingham or denim or mattress ticking, hosiery or shoes, cordwood or flooring or clothespins, coaches or newsprint, the community's life was never quite the same after the mill came to Main Street. Whether the adjustments involved recognition of the role of women and immigrants in the work force, or the effects of regimented work schedules or the hazards of the workplace, or absentee management practices, new economic opportunities brought new social and political challenges. Whatever the case, as the twentieth century arrived, New Hampshire was on the move; her sons and daughters were on the road looking for new opportunities, and her mills and factories, released first by steam power and later by electricity, were no longer bound to the millstream.

8

The Power of the Iron Horse

AT THE TIME THE FIRST railroads were built in New Hampshire, the state had been wary of their influence. As new railroads acquired land on which to build, some people doubted that the benefits of the railroad would be worth the land they occupied while the government suspected the power that the new transportation system might wield in the state. So the General Court took steps to control the railroads. As early as 1836 when the first line ran from Lowell, Massachusetts to Nashua, New Hampshire, the legislature began supervising the railroads, and four years later the state established the State Railroad Commission to carry on the process. As we have seen, the Locofocos curtailed the expansion of the railroads for several years; even when they loosened the reins of control, they did not abandon them altogether.

During the first stage of development, a multitude of short lines crisscrossed the state, sometimes competing with each other and undercutting each others fares. Through the 1870s and 80s there was a rush to consolidate these lines and make them more profitable and efficient, a process that concluded in the 1890s when the Boston & Maine Railroad with its headquarters in Boston took over the Concord Railroad, the last of the state's locally controlled lines.

When the Democrats loosened restrictions on the railroads in 1844, railroad charters multiplied, and every new charter needed legislative approval. Groundbreaking for each new line, driving the first spike, operation of the first train, commencement of regular service all called for public display and political hoopla. The Republicans, who followed the Democrats into power just before the Civil War, did not mistrust the power of the railroad companies as had the Democrats. The farmers' initial mistrust dissipated as railroads proved their usefulness in delivering farm produce as well as manufactured goods to market. In the midst of all this optimism, the legislature loosened its regulation of the railroads just as the railroad corporations were establishing a powerful political base in the state. In fact, in 1862 Joseph A. Gilmore, a Concord Railroad superintendent, was elected governor having distributed an untold number of free railroad passes in the process. (The railroad pass, as valuable as an airline pass might be today, was a powerful tool that the railroads used lavishly to create good will and cooperation in the hearts of useful citizens.)

No longer did the legislature restrict the corporations; rather it refereed the battles among them as they struggled with every device their uninhibited wits could conceive to destroy their competitors. The legislature was deluged with generous lobbyists each time the corporations fought for control of feeder lines or sought permission for mergers as larger, more aggressive, or better-placed railroads swallowed up the smaller and more vulnerable ones. Ultimately, the legislature became a pawn among the contending railroads rather than a regulator as regulations that had been imposed forty years before were ignored or repealed. The state assessed railroad property at a very low rate and regulated fares only tokenly.

While the government in Concord mostly acquiesced to the will of the railroads, occasionally the legislature made some efforts at reform. In 1878 the legislature created a Board of Equalization to increase railroad taxes, but so pervasive was the influence of the railroad corporations that the courts nullified its influence. When the General Court tried to curb excess profits, the railroads plowed the profits back into building fancy railroad stations, some of which are still standing and admired today. In 1883 the legislature passed the Colby Act which removed the legislature from contests for leases of feeder lines, but the Supreme Court of the state declared the leases invalid except by unanimous consent of the stockholders or by action of the General Court. These reforms were, perhaps, designed to be just as ineffectual as they turned out to be. Certainly they lacked the clout needed to curb the powerful railroad corporations.

However, in 1881, the son-in-law of John Parker Hale, William

E. Chandler, a lawyer and master politician who filled many governmental positions during his life, but was then a member of the General Court, took up arms against the railroad. He introduced three bills that would curb the power of the railroads. He proposed that the state impose regulations on rates the railroads charged, that railroad property be assessed and taxed more fairly, and that free passes be abolished. Only the proposal to abolish free passes ever reached the floor for a vote, and that was soundly defeated, one member complaining that without his pass he would never reach home.

With the opening volley Chandler had begun a thirty-six-year crusade to curb the growing power of the railroad. To this end he enlisted his newspaper, the *Independent Statesman*, based in Concord, which was sometimes the only voice in the state raised against the railroad, using it much as Isaac Hill had used the *Patriot* (perhaps with more wit and scruples).

The effect was not noticable or immediate. Henry M. Putney, editor of the *Manchester Mirror*, was appointed to the post of chairman of the Railroad Commission, a job he held for twenty years, defending the interests of the railroad to the best of his considerable ability at a salary two and a half times that of the governor of the state. In 1885 banker Moody Currier of Manchester observed that "So far as I can judge, the new policy [of consolidations of railroads] is generally approved by the people."[1] And, indeed, the larger lines ran more smoothly and provided more efficient service. In the 1850s passengers had to change trains six times between Boston and Montreal, an inconvenience which buying, leasing, and merging of lines would alleviate.

Of course, the policy of consolidation was self-limiting, and the fewer the number of lines became, the more desperately the corporations battled for power. In 1887 there was a five-month struggle in the legislature (which regulated the railroads and had to give permission for mergers and leases of lines) between the Concord Railroad and the Boston & Maine, the two remaining contenders for control of the railroad systems in New Hampshire. Even the Railroad Commission decried the five-month legislative battle as "more expensive, more demoralizing and more unsatisfactory . . . than any other that ever destroyed the substance and sacrificed the dignity of the State." The Boston & Maine won; but the governor vetoed the bill because of the corrupt contest.

By 1889 when the competitors had arrived at their own compromise which left the Boston & Maine dominant in the state, it became clear that, bad as had been the influence on the state government by the many small railroads, the control of all the railroads by one corporation based outside the state was more alarming. A vestige of the old Radical Democrats' wariness of the railroads existed in the charter of 1844 for the Concord Railroad which gave the state the right to purchase the Concord Railroad Corporation for cost plus a 10 percent return on its investment. Having enlisted the aid of wealthy businessman, Austin Corbin, Chandler invoked this law in attempting to stop the final merger of the Concord and the B & M. Corbin, a native of Newport, who had lived in New York for some years, controlled the Long Island Railroad. He had moved back to the state and had invested in a large game park, which still exists, near Newport. Now Chandler induced him to offer to buy the state's interest in the Concord Railroad if the state would purchase the railroad under the clause in the railroad's charter that gave it that right. Of course, the purchase price would be bargain basement for the Prince of Wales state. Corbin found the opportunity amusing and potentially profitable.

The offer threw the General Court into a funk. Not the tamest of railroad supporters relished returning to his constituents with the news that he had voted to reject this offer of hard cash. The legislature turned to the Supreme Court of New Hampshire for help.

Chief Justice Charles Doe of Rollinsford, who ran the court, was a brilliant and eccentric jurist who wore a horseblanket in his courtroom which he insisted on keeping well ventilated even in the dead of winter. To Doe the law was both vocation and avocation, and he amused himself by mulling over legal points unrelated to cases he was hearing. Jeremiah Smith described him to President Arthur as "a great constitutional lawyer,"[2] and whether political intrigue or his own idiosyncrasies prevented him from being appointed to the U. S. Supreme Court is not clear. This original jurist, who must have pondered the points of law involved well before the case ever came before him, issued the court's decision the day following the closing arguments: the state might buy the company under the general laws of eminent domain at fair market value, but it could not take the Concord Railroad under the provision made in the company's charter.

Having issued this decision, Doe did not elaborate for two years while Chandler hurled such accusations of incompetence and even dishonesty at the court that he was in danger of being cited for contempt. After two years Doe explained that when the legislature passed a law governing all railroads in 1844, that law superseded the charter of the Concord Railroad. The eminent jurist had based the opinion on a view that had not occurred to lawyers of the railroad or the state, but the railroad was happy. Doe's decision ended the hopes of those opposing the monopoly of the Boston & Maine in New Hampshire. Not only did the B & M control the railroads, it also dominated the government of the state. A naive newspaper editor once wrote that "the Boston and Maine has always given the State a good government, and has always been regardful of the interests of the Republican Party."

The man at the top, the president of the corporation, Lucius Tuttle, ran the line from corporate headquarters in Boston's North Station. However, the operation of the railroad machine in New Hampshire was in the hands of three New Hampshire natives: Benjamin Kimball, a railroad mechanic who had risen to be the president of the Concord & Montreal line which the B & M leased; Frank Streeter, the aggressive counsel for the corporation; and John Sanborn, who handled public relations and vetted candidates for political office. There was also staff of agents, political managers, and lobbyists who implemented the policies of these three men. A number of somewhat unsavory political bosses delivered votes for the corporation, but more numerous were many honest, successful, and respected men like the able Henry M. Putney, who regarded the railroad as generally right and so supported the railroad's policies when he served on the Railroad Commission.

For services actual or potential the railroad also awarded a small retainer or a free pass to almost every newspaper editor and lawyer in the state silencing most vocal opposition to railroad policies and making it difficult to find a lawyer to represent a case against the corporation.

On the political side John Sanborn handed out railroad endorsements to candidates whose views were sympathetic to the railroad, being especially mindful of the governor, the five Council members (whom the electorate often ignored but who had the power to negate the governor's appointees), the Speaker of the House, and

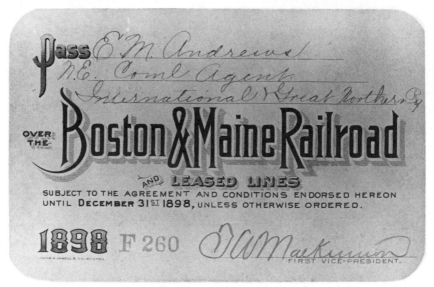

Boston & Maine railroad pass. In the Chase-Streeter collection of Baker Library, Dartmouth College.

the leaders of the General Court. Most important he saw to it that the Railroad Commission was packed with appointees congenial with Chairman Henry Putney.

It is a mistake, however, to imagine that the men who ran the affairs of the corporation thought of themselves or were thought of as unscrupulous, opportunistic, or malevolent. They were public-spirited, useful citizens. They served on boards of charitable institutions, including Dartmouth College, and performed other good works in the state. And there was little ill-feeling toward them or the corporation among the rank and file of the voters. True, as businessmen they had little respect for politicians (ignoring the fact that the ethics of business were hardly superior to that of politics), but the railroad ran efficiently. It brought the citizens of the state closer together by making travel between towns possible during most of the year—a boon to isolated, rural areas. It carried goods into and out of the state, and it opened the remote regions of the state, particularly the North Country, to economic development.

THE NORTH COUNTRY OPENS

While towns and cities in southern interior and coastal New Hampshire negotiated an entrance into the industrial age in the 1830s and 1840s, the resources of the upper half of the state remained virtually untouched until after the Civil War. Here, with the exception of farms close to the Connecticut River, lay one third of the state's land mass under a cover of virgin forest of spruce, balsam fir, hemlock, and mixed hardwoods.

The opening of the north woods awaited the action of Governor Harriman under whose administration in 1867 the state's extensive land holdings in the White Mountains (172,000 acres) were sold to local landowners and speculators for about twenty-five thousand dollars. The sale, ironically, benefited a "literary fund" for school financing and maintenance. Of this questionable political decision (reminiscent of similar arguments in the 1980s over development of resources on public lands), William Robinson Brown has written: "Suffice it to say that by 1867 the state parted with all its timberlands at a small percentage of their subsequent worth."[3] By 1904, when it has been estimated that several large companies owned the state's timberland, there was little idle woodland.

In a state and region undergoing rapid expansion after the Civil War in domestic and industrial construction, the woods offered riches — if they could be reached. The railroad was poised to become, with the land owners and speculators, the cooperative agent in opening hitherto inaccessible timber stands. Before long the region had the beginnings of a lumber and paper industry whose growth between 1890 and 1900 eclipsed that of any state in the Union. The story of the opening of the north country is one of excesses as extreme as the region's towering mountains, deep gorges, and swiftly running rivers — none perhaps as striking as the stories of the human agents. Take J.E. Henry, whom newspapers dubbed "King Contractor of the Mountains," "Heartless Lumber King," "Mutilator of Nature," and "Grand Duke of Lincoln." Henry is reported to have said of his lumbering activities: "I never see the tree yit that didn't mean a damned sight more to me goin' under the saw than it did standin' on a mountain."[4]

Paradoxically, by the fateful turn of the economic wheel of fortune, as farming became a marginal occupation the hill country farm contributed part of the raw material for the state's modern timber industry: the once-cleared, now increasingly abandoned fields, returned to forest cover.

Before being swept away by the torrents of exaggerated language inspired by the logging industry, it would be helpful to look at the map and see where the forests, men, and railroads met in the White Mountains. Intensive logging activities were centered in the area surrounding and bounded by the Androscoggin, Saco, and Swift rivers to the east; the Mad and Pemigewasset rivers to the south; and the Ammonoosuc and Connecticut rivers to the west. While some white pine remained untouched by colonial cutting and was harvested in the eastern region as late as the twentieth century, the principal cover was the valuable, high-altitude, cold-loving spruce. On the heels of the land speculators and their complicated maneuverings to secure land or cutting rights, came the woods surveyors, who like their royally-appointed colonial counterparts, cruised and marked virgin forest stands for potential investors.

Cutting, transporting, and milling the region's riches finally depended on the competition which developed among railroad giants like the Boston & Maine, Maine Central, and Grand Trunk to establish major rail lines through the area by the 1880s. Such companies, quick to see the advantage of leasing their equipment, promoted the growth of seventeen smaller railroads built by the individual lumbering operations to carry the timber from cutting sites to mills and markets. The entrepreneurs became immensely rich, the "robber barons" of the woods: J.E. Henry, nearly penniless at birth, is said to have been worth $10 million when he died in 1912. Furthermore, although lumber and later pulp mills were the principal producers and money-makers, the vast timber operations spawned the local manufacture of everything — bobbins, veneer, ladder rounds, crutches, clothespins, boxes, ice-cream freezers, and excelsior.

On the other hand, three decades of intensive lumbering nearly destroyed a natural source of wealth, creating "death valleys" out of primeval forests. By 1900 lumber production had escalated dramatically, culminating in 1907 with the record production of 650 million board feet. Characteristically, hasty forest clearing frequently caused devastating forest fires, finishing off the axe-handler's work, leaving a lifeless natural environment, and retarding growth for up to thirty years. Usually ignited by lightning, a locomotive spark, or a carelessly tossed cigarette, the highly combustible "slash"—branches discarded after a wooded area had been virtually leveled—was the villain. In the region's worst fire in 1903, over twelve thousand acres of timber were lost, and ashes from the inferno reached Nashua. By September of that same year, there were over 554 separate reports of fires. Public outrage at the often reckless, usually shortsighted harvesting of north country timber, soon created another industry by-product—improved methods of forest management and state and national legislation to protect wilderness area from any future exploitation.

A Few Who Succeeded and How They Did

Though the forest cover now has returned to the White Mountains, the present-day hiker will find many evidences of the nineteenth-century logging operations. In fact many of the area's marked trails follow the abandoned railroad beds of the seventeen small railroads, which inched and poked their way into the mountains and valleys of the north country. Using rails, ties, locomotives, trailers, and switching equipment leased from the larger railroad companies, the logging companies built these small spurs, usually only five to ten miles long and short-lived, to gain access to the edge of the campsites where interior logging operations were conducted. At these sites, loggers generally practiced "clear-cutting," that is, all growth—healthy, sick, young, old—was harvested off a lot at the same time. Marketable timber was graded and sorted; the leftover "slash" was abandoned and left behind to become natural kindling for fire. Logs were then rolled or hauled by horse teams along tote roads, which girdled the mountains, to landings alongside the railroad tracks. Here the logs were moved onto waiting flat cars. Once loaded, the trains headed to the company-owned mills over remarkably steep and twisted routes, protected from disaster by only air brakes on the locomotives and hand brakes on the flat cars. Once an area was successfully stripped of its timber, the temporary, portable camps and sawmills would be moved to other locations.

While the region's place names still recall the friends, family, and patrons of the eighteenth-century Wentworth governors who granted and chartered most of the north country towns, tales of the "newcomers" like the Saunders family of Livermore, J.E. Henry of Zealand and Lincoln, Oakleigh Thorne of Conway, or George Van-Dyke of the upper reaches of the Connecticut abound.

In its heyday, the Saunders' Sawyer River Railroad (1877-1937) created a highly profitable logging operation, more or less founded and abandoned the town of Livermore, and left a permanent mark by enabling one of the few early logging operations to practice selective tree cutting. Operating in an area of about thirty thousand acres at the southern end of Crawford Notch, "the biggest little logging railroad of its day,"[5] created employment for over two hundred loggers as well as fifty or more employees in Livermore's steam-powered sawmill. Despite three carefully spaced cuttings over its forty-year history, the company-created town of Livermore, whose population reached one hundred and sixty in 1890, was disincorporated in 1951 when its population dropped to zero. Even selective tree cutting, it would seem, had built-in problems.

If Saunders' family operations inspired praise, the massive logging operations begun several years later by J. E. Henry near Carroll inspired nearly universal distrust and criticism — from beginning to end. Henry's logging operations took place on probably the largest privately owned tracts of north country land; it employed the efficiency of two logging railroads, involved the destinies of two towns, and created both lumber and pulp mills, all with what logging historian, C. Francis Belcher calls a "devastating efficiency never again equalled in the White Mountains."[6]

The Zealand Valley Railroad (1884-1897) opened up the riches of the virtually untouched virgin forest growth of the Pemigewasset River valley, and conveyed timber to company-owned mills in Zealand and Fabyan. Having finished with both the area's timber and the village of Zealand, Henry moved his operations to Lincoln in 1892, where he brought new life to the town he finally dominated. From here he expanded his logging and railroad operations and built the East Branch and Lincoln Railroad (1893-1948). In both the town of Lincoln and his twenty-four or so nearby lumber camps, Henry exerted the sort of paternal control earlier evident in the state's textile mills. Lincoln's original twenty-eight taxpayers suddenly found themselves in a thriving company town, with company-built saw and paper mills, houses, a coal steam plant, stores, a hotel, and even a hospital. In the surrounding forest tracts, the Henry operations' famous portable red frame camp buildings were often filled with as many as 250 or more loggers (many French-Canadian and Irish). Henry's was an embracing presence, right down to forty or so rules and regulations posted in each camp. While most of the rules related to a Henry commitment to careful care of the firm's horses, others reflected J. E. Henry and Son's attempt to impose social order in the rowdy camps. One rule read: "Any person found throwing food or making unnecessary and loud talk at the tables will be fined."[7] Few argued with J. E. Henry's authority, and few dispute the magnitude of the alterations his logging operations made in the north country's forests.

Wall Street banker Oakleigh Thorne, who at the turn of the century established the Conway Company operations and three logging railroads on the yet undeveloped eastern slopes of the White Mountains, was as refined a gentleman and sophisticated a businessman as the north country's logging industry would see. He attracted attention by his new management practices (including subcontracting of both logging and railroad building operations), his complex corporate structure, and bringing his New York-trained supervisory staff to manage his three-story Conway Lumber Company (1906-1922).

No consideration of north country logging would be complete without a glimpse at the activities of the industry's brawny, unsophisticated, premier riverman, George Van Dyke. There is disagreement about whether J. E. Henry or George Van Dyke owned and exploited the most north country timberland, but there is no dispute over the fact that both men were very successful in their efforts. Born in Canada in 1846 and reputed to have had only four years of schooling and to have gone shoeless until the age of eleven, life-long bachelor George Van Dyke was a woodsman through and through — including his powerful nineteen and one-half inch neck. His canny sense of opportunity opened venture after venture to him to the point that this riverman, who is said to have known everything about logging and river-driving first hand, owned most of the northern tip of the state and considerable adjacent land in Canada.

It was his legendary river drives along the tricky Connecticut River, from his mills in Pittsburg as far south as Holyoke, Massachusetts, which inspired the most hyperbole. In an average spring river drive, fifty million feet of logs would either inch down the easily jammed river or be flung like firecrackers into farmer's fields and meadows. Either situation required the agile acrobatics and nimble footwork of accomplished rivermen. Van Dyke, who had cajoled and maneuvered his way to success and fame, died as he had lived — working. Barely recovered from a serious three-month illness, he followed the largest log drive of his career — fifty three million feet of timber — as it inched and lurched southward along the Connecticut. One morning in 1909, while watching his rivermen easing logs through a dam just below the Massachusetts border, Van Dyke and his chauffeur died tragically as their car jerked over the seventy-five foot embankment, which had been their vantage point.

The Legacy

Two major industries emerged from the tangled history of land-grabbing, railroad building, extensive clear-cutting of timberland, mill construction, and lumber and pulp marketing in the north country. The first, of course, is the papermaking industry, which began to replace the lumber industry in production as early as 1900. With advances in pulp processing and in the machinery needed for full-scale production, northern New Hampshire became an important papermaking region, with one company, the Berlin Mill Company (later the Brown Company, now the James River Corporation), dominating the market. Founded in the late 1800s, the company pioneered research and development in papermaking, becoming by World War I the world's largest chemical pulp mill. With improved wood fiber processing came a product long the industry's standard, kraft paper. In 1921 the company introduced wet-strength kraft paper with the ubiquitous Nibroc label (the name of the inventor, Corbin, spelled backwards).

Of equal importance to the state's economic and environmental history is the nineteenth-century logging industry's second legacy, the aroused consciousness of the urgent need to protect the north country's woodlands from further heedless exploitation. Public awareness of the wanton harvesting or destruction of hundreds of thousands of acres of timber led in 1911 to the passage of legislation which insured the region's protection for tourists and environmentalists and encouraged carefully managed forest cutting operations.

Pulp mill in Berlin. c. 1900. New Hampshire Historical Society.

In the 1980s nearly 90 percent of the state is once again under forest cover, but it took several hundred years to learn that ecological abundance must be carefully protected from economic prodigality.

If in southern New Hampshire the town of Harrisville's story reflects in microcosm the history of the state's passage from agriculture to wool manufacturing, with a little tourism as a cushion against hard times, the story of the town of Whitefield, "north of the Notch," may serve the same purpose. The last town to be chartered under the English provincial government and John Wentworth, Whitefield was granted its charter on July 4, 1774, in an agreement that included Jeremy Belknap's name. From the time of its incorporation in 1804 and until the Civil War, it was primarily an agricultural community; its only mills — grist, starch, and sawmills — were extensions of its principal occupation. In 1870 two brothers, Alson and Warren Brown, moved in from Bristol and established what was to become one of the larger mills in the state. This active mill produced shingles, clapboards, door mouldings, butter tubs, and furniture.

Whitefield soon became a "company" town, as the Brown Company built houses and a store for its local and immigrant workers on Brown Street. Later the Boston & Maine was persuaded to extend a spur line to Whitefield in return for a monetary "gift." Eventually the Brown brothers' land holdings included forty thousand acres of wooded area in nearby Jefferson and Carroll. In an all too familiar turn in the story, the Brown Lumber Company was sold in 1900, by which time the company's land had been destroyed by clear-cutting. A condensed milk factory, which later burned, kept the town from immediate economic ruin until it, like numerous former logging towns, was able to turn its other natural resource (its setting) to an economic advantage. Tourism remains Whitefield's principal industry.

From the driving of the first spike, the railroad both complicated and profited the state's economic and political life. Whether it had challenged assumptions about the future of farming, created both markets and transportation for manufactured goods, opened the North Country for logging and tourism, or spawned complex political alliances, the railroad interests exerted influence in New Hampshire. And before long a wary legislature began once again to consider means of controlling this powerful partner.

REFORM BEGINS

Even the Boston & Maine Railroad could not count on a docile electorate forever. By 1906 the voice of a citizens' group led by a lawyer from Concord, E.C. Niles, persuaded novelist Winston Churchill, who had moved to New Hampshire and become involved in state politics, to seek nomination for governor in the 1906 election. In secret even from the railroad's arch enemy William Chandler, this politically naive group mustered its forces to fight the railroad. Chandler at last had an ally in his battle against the Boston & Maine.

It was already late in the campaign, and even Chandler's own papers had chosen another candidate to support, when Churchill's supporters asked Chandler to draw up a platform for the new Lincoln Republicans, as they were called. Chandler did so with enthusiasm—no more free passes, election of the Railroad Comissioner by the people, fair evaluation of railroad property for taxation, a corrupt practices act, public disclosure of campaign funds, registration of lobbyists and disclosure of their fees, the establishment of a Tax Commission, and, perhaps most important in a one-party state, the establishment of a primary election instead of the old corrupt party caucus to nominate candidates. Two other proposals were included in the platform that are amusing in light of the state's current dependence on "sin" taxes—a stringent enforcement of antigambling laws and liquor laws.

Since the new Lincoln Republicans, more properly called progressives, were late getting into the campaign and had few experienced politicians in their number, their chances looked bleak. Churchill and the reformers campaigned tirelessly, though Chandler warned him to prepare for defeat. And by a close margin Churchill was defeated when the other candidates united against him. However, the new legislature was embued with the spirit of progressivism and passed a law prohibiting the granting of railroad passes to public officials, including legislators. The new law proved to be a straw in the wind.

Though Churchill did not campaign again, Robert Bass, a wealthy young forest conservationist and farmer from Peterborough, took up the standard for the reformers in 1910. Bass, who had proposed a bill creating a direct primary election, was already a leader of the progressive movement in the state. Bass ran successfully, and under his administration the groundswell for reform continued. The legislature curbed the power of the railroads and made strides toward putting the reins of government back in the hands of the people. Two years later the state had a Public Service Commission, a Tax Commission, and a workman's compensation program. Though the Republican party continued to dominate state politics, that party split into two camps—the progressive and the conservative—which took very different stands on many issues. It was a new phenomenon that has persisted in the state's politics.

After his term as governor Robert Bass did not abandon politics, and his concern for the forests of the White Mountains finally bore fruit, not only on the state level, but on the national level with the passage in 1911 of the Weeks Act, so important to tourism and conservation. His support for Theodore Roosevelt and the Bull Moose party instead of the Republican party's nominee, William

Howard Taft, destroyed most of his support from Republican regulars and any immediate hopes he might have had to run again. Though Bass's first foray into reform was short—he served only one term as governor—he would remain for years as a force for social progress in the state.

Despite the reforms under Bass, however, neither the political situation nor the economic situation in the state changed instantly, dramatically, or permanently. The workers in the mills were still poor, while most of the profits from the mills flowed out of the state to the mill's headquarters and stockholders in Boston. In 1920 after the First World War, the Boston & Maine remained a powerful influence in the state government as did the Amoskeag Manufacturing Company which shared several members of their boards of directors. They continued to exercise their control largely through the conservative Republicans who after the Bass reform dominated the state government.

Significantly, in 1922 during the economically and psychologically devastating strike at the Amoskeag mills, the Democrats elected Fred Brown, their first governor since the Republicans took over in 1857, and voted in the first Democratic House since 1874. During the strike the depth of the workers' disillusionment with their employers could be gauged in their recognition that their government, which had helped them not at all during the nine months of the strike, acted as an arm of the corporation, and the corporation's interests did not necessarily coincide with what they saw as their own best interests. They might be frustrated in their efforts to control the mill's management and to improve their working conditions, but they did not have to tolerate a Republican government which supported the corporation against them. It was a rude awakening.

As a matter of fact, probably the worst result of the dominance of the state government by the railroads was that it caused the government to neglect the needs of the people. While the legislature worried about the railroads, it did not worry about the poor farmers who had fallen on hard times because of competition with produce from the rich western plains arriving by the trainload over the tracks laid on the farmer's land. Nor was it concerned about the newly arrived textile worker who worked under conditions difficult and unhealthy. While William Chandler and others worried about the corruption of the state's leaders, they did not worry enough about some of the daily problems of the majority of the people of the state.

However, factory workers were fragmented by differences in religion, national origin, and language which complicated efforts to unify them politically. The farmer, on the other hand, did not trust a businessman who claimed to have the interests of the farmer at heart any more than he trusted a businessman who simply promised a small government that would leave him alone. They turned to the Grange to lobby for their interests, but the factory workers refused to vote for a platform of agrarian reform. And no strong leader or party evolved to meld these two disparate groups into a cohesive political voice.

The population continued to grow slowly, and the image of the small town in New Hampshire (now forever imprinted in our imagination as picturesque, clean, and wholesome) was very dismal, indeed. Articles such as "Doom of the Small Town" and "Decay of Rural Life in New England" reflected the unhappy vision of New Hampshire before 1940. Even the local government which controls the issues closest to the citizens — zoning and land use, town roads, sewers, schools, snow removal, and local taxes — looked bleak, and the town meeting, which we often idealize as the surest path to civic virtue, was suspected of widespread corruption. In 1906 in a popular novel called *Coniston*, Winston Churchill portrayed the rise to power of a political boss who began by controlling the town meeting of a small New Hampshire town and rose to great power in the state. Chandler challenged Churchill's accuracy in his portrayal of Jethro Bass, a fictional Ruel Durkee who was a friend of Chandler. The truth of this specific case perhaps will never be known, but during the last decades of the nineteenth and the first decades of the twentieth century social, economic, and political progress in the state was exceedingly slow.

9

The Challenge of New Growth

SINCE THE MIDDLE of the nineteenth century, the most powerful current in the state's development has been the growth of business and industry. However, a secondary current — the desire to create a happy society based on local autonomy and individual freedom in a congenial rural environment — has both challenged and enriched the desire for economic growth. In fact, it is this image of New Hampshire that has made the state attractive to many corporations as well as its visitors and its new citizens.

Robert Bass, the reformer from Peterborough, continued working in the government from 1910 until he met a young man with political ambitions and political philosophy sympathetic to his own. John G. Winant, who had been a teacher at St. Paul's School in Concord, agreed with Bass that the success of any progressive movement lay in working within the Republican party, but the two of them laid out a platform that in effect usurped the Democrats' program. Winant established himself as a leading Republican progressive voice in the state and ran for governor in 1924. With the support of Bass and Bass's executive secretary, H. Styles Bridges, he succeeded in defeating the Democratic governor on a platform calling for strong social programs including reforestation of much of the state, establishment of cooperatives for the farmers, and programs to support agriculture and improve highways. Ironically, his programs included an appeal by the state to the Interstate Commerce Commission to reject the Boston & Maine Railroad's appeal to allow them to abandon one-third of its trackage in New Hampshire. The

John Winant. New Hampshire Historical Society.

railroad, which had been so determined twenty years before to control all the lines in the state, now wanted to abandon those that it found inconvenient or unprofitable, the beginning of the decline of the railroads in the state.

In the wake of the disillusioning strike at Amoskeag, the voters elected progressive Governor Winant, a progressive House Speaker, and a progressive president of the senate, Charles W. Tobey, who was elected governor in 1929. Tobey joined the core of progressive leadership in the state for years that followed.

Opposing Winant, Bass, and company was the old-line conservative branch of the party, the leadership of which had fallen to George H. Moses, who had been a protegé of William Chandler. (Surely the old party boss and enemy of the Boston & Maine would have found it ironic that the man who had learned political strategy at his knee turned out to be an ardent supporter of big corporations and an opponent of most progressive legislation.) Moses, a great orator who served many years in the United States Senate and in 1925 became president pro tempore of the Senate, supported antistrike legislation and tariffs to protect the textile industry, and opposed woman's suffrage and the League of Nations. At the same time he made his voice heard on the national scene, Moses led the powerful conservative wing of the Republican party in the state. Among the other leaders of the Republican party was Frank Knox, publisher of the *Manchester Union*, who had originally been lured to the state by Bass and Churchill to begin a newspaper to support the Bull Moose candidacy of Theodore Roosevelt but who ran against Winant in 1924.

During his first term as governor, with Bass absent on personal business much of the time, Winant's reluctance to work with the whole progressive caucus in the state hurt the progressive's program. They barely managed to save the direct primary election law which Bass had pushed through in 1909 and which was under attack by Knox's *Manchester Union*. The progressives again lost the proposed forty-eight-hour work week, and the legislature rejected the Federal Child Labor Law. The Assembly did approve a large highway improvement bill, improved accounting for the state, substantial funds for the University of New Hampshire, and money to hire legal counsel to oppose successfully the Boston & Maine's desire to abandon much of its trackage in New Hampshire. All of the progressive's platform was not lost, but even so, they might have remained in power except that Winant and Bass squabbled over which of them would run for the senate and which for the governorship until both were replaced with conservative candidates during the primary.

However, the loss for the progressives was temporary. By 1928 they had elected Charles W. Tobey governor of the state and, of course, the collapse of the stock market and the beginning of the depression gave credence to their philosophy of liberal social legislation, though New Hampshire had actually been in an economic slump for years before the depression hit the rest of the nation. Economic conditions deteriorated, and towns, which in New Hampshire take much of the responsibility for social services, struggled to provide for the increasing number of unemployed workers. The Democrats, split by internal strife among various ethnic groups, notably the Franco-American and the Irish, still could not turn the bad economic conditions to their political advantage. The progressive Republicans remained in power in the state, and until 1936 the state continued to vote for Republican presidential candidates.

Meantime, in 1931 and in 1933 John Winant was reelected governor of the state. Winant campaigned on the traditional liberal issues of improved schools, forestry conservation, workmen's compensation, independent regulatory agencies and, that favorite cause of the progressives, the forty-eight-hour week for women and children — many of them issues that appealed to the industrial workers. The General Court, though more conservative than the governor, nevertheless passed legislation to provide some emergency relief for mothers and children, to increase aid to cities and towns for highway maintenance, to regulate banking and the sale of stocks and bonds, and to provide funds to help towns with hospital construction among other things.

However, much of the legislation aimed at bettering the conditions of industrial workers failed. The forty-eight hour bill and the workmen's compensation act failed once again, as did personal and corporate income tax, and a teachers' retirement system and an old age pension law. Although the progressive program made great strides, it scarcely made a dent in the economic problems facing the workers as Amoskeag mills closed forever, leaving Manchester destitute, while the depression ravaged the whole state. Winant had not been in office long before he realized that the state government could not cope with the woes of the depression.

In 1931 with unemployment in the state at 33 percent, Winant appeared on a newsreel describing a "New Hampshire Plan" which proposed a nation-wide four-day work week with the additional hours to be divided among additional workers to ease unemployment. After that he moved further away from President Hoover, but even so, Winant dutifully supported Hoover to the end as did the rest of the state, sending him their four electoral votes in 1931. During that same election Fred Brown, Democrat, challenged George H. Moses for the United State Senate. Brown attacked him as "the tool of the corporations" and read off lists of out-of-state businesses which contributed to Moses' campaign fund. Of course, since the progressive Republicans had allied themselves with the Democrats, they did not leap to Moses' defense, and Brown easily went to the Senate as that rare breed, a Democratic representative from New Hampshire.

These desperate economic times produced some inventive ideas by private individuals as well as by governments. In 1926, concerned that old crafts might be forgotten in face of competition from manufactured goods, Mary Hill Coolidge of Sandwich had opened a small shop in her house selling handcrafts as a way of encouraging artisans. In 1931 when Governor Winant heard of her work, he persuaded the legislature to appropriate a small sum to support her efforts. Thus began the League of New Hampshire Craftsmen which has become a prestigious outlet for local handcrafts with shops all over the state.

But such enterprises could not stem the tide of economic trouble sweeping the state. As economic conditions worsened, Winant supported Democrat Franklin Roosevelt's methods of seeking solutions to the problems on a national level. In New Hampshire he became a leading exponent of Roosevelt's New Deal. Later he served in Washington under Roosevelt as the first director of the Social Security Board and abroad as Director of the International Labor Organization and as ambassador to England, though he remained a Republican. It was his commitment to the New Deal that prevented him from allowing himself to be considered for the presidential nomination when various Republicans suggested him in 1936. Without this favorite son as candidate, the voters followed the way Winant had pointed and gave their electoral votes to Franklin Roosevelt in 1936, 1940, and 1944.

WARTIME AND WASHINGTON

During the depression and World War II, then, the voters of the state cast their support to the liberal Democrats in national elections, perhaps reviving some of their historic faith in the central government. When Winant left the governor's office in 1935, however, he was replaced by Styles Bridges who had worked from the early days with Bass and Winant in the progressive movement in the state. But unlike Bass and Winant, Bridges had grown more conservative; Winant no longer considered him part of the progressive movement in the state. In fact, in his opening speech Bridges recommended a "thorough study of public expenditures and a most vigorous application of economy"[1] which reflected his fiscally conservative approach to the problems of the depression. After his term as governor, Bridges went on to the United States Senate where he remained until 1961, helping to bring Pease Air Force Base to New Hampshire in the 1950s. He was soon joined in the Senate by his former political ally, Charles Tobey, while Frank Knox became secretary of the navy.

Three men who had worked for the progressive causes in the state took opposing positions on international issues facing the nation just before World War II. Bridges often blamed Roosevelt for leading the nation to war, but he supported most of the measures Roosevelt proposed to help the Allies in the hope they would keep us out of the war. Tobey voted against most of the same measures believing they would get us into the war. He accused Frank Knox, who had become secretary of the navy, of being a warmonger. Warmonger or not, Knox certainly predicted in a letter to the secretary of war the attack on Pearl Harbor, described how the Japanese would attack, and what precautions and countermeasures should be taken. Why this warning was ignored is a mystery. Knox also accomplished a near-miracle by building a massive armada after the debacle at Pearl Harbor destroyed almost half the United States Navy.

Both Bridges and Tobey supported the war effort after the bombing of Pearl Harbor, and both men played significant roles in the federal government during the war. Roosevelt trusted Bridges and three other senators with the secret of the atomic research, relying on him and the others to persuade the senate to allocate funds for the secret project without further explanation. Tobey, who became a member of the Banking and Currency Committee, delivered the keynote address at the conference at Bretton Woods, New Hampshire, where some of the world's most prominent economists and financiers met in July of 1944 to establish the International Monetary Fund and the World Bank.

During World War I New Hampshire's sentiments and responses mirrored the national sense of both outrage and willingness to sacrifice time, food, money, and sons to the war effort. Faced with another threat in the 1940s, New Hampshire citizens again rose to the challenges, though this time with assistance peculiar to well-developed strengths in its own industrial sector. New Hampshire's civilians produced more, worked more, earned more, saved more, and spent more than ever before. Joining the war effort at home, the state's businesses and industries under government direction were rewarded for their extraordinary efforts in the face of shortages in manpower and materials by record-breaking sales and frequent government recognition for the quality and quantity of manufactured goods.

Conserving the View

While a number of tourists and vacationers had always visited New Hampshire, after World War II the new advertising campaign combined with improved highways enticed many more visitors to the state. Vacationers, tourists, second-home and condominium owners, and retired families attracted to New Hampshire's rural and mountainous settings, recreational opportunities, and low taxes have become an increasingly important component of the state's population and an important source of its economic well-being. While such part-time residents cannot be expected to exert much pressure on the state's politics, they can certainly be expected to take an interest in taxes, land values, land use, and environmental quality. And such has been their interest and influence.

New Hampshire's land and water, its hills, mountains, lakes, and seacoast had long been attractive to outsiders as well as a source of pride to its residents. From Captain John Smith's enthusiastic reports of the natural riches he spotted from the shore and Jeremy Belknap's description of the state's air as "pure and salubrious," to weekly advertisements in national newspapers and magazines promising "a White Mountain view from your window," New Hampshire has had its ardent promoters.

The urban rich of the late 1800s were among the state's most committed visitors and were also among the first to cry foul when they noticed that the same railroad that made the trip from New York or Philadelphia or Boston to the nearest mountains and wilderness also provided access to the mountains' timber riches.

On June 4, 1896, for instance, the *Nation* published a letter from a professed "mountain-lover-in-mourning" who spoke for many when he wrote: "You may sit on your piazza and possess the mountains."[2] Like many other visitors to New Hampshire's White Mountains in the late 1800s, the visitor was appalled, however, by what he called the lumber industry's "uglification" of and environment which he believed to possess more potential value and benefit for tourism.

By the beginning of the twentieth century the state and national press began to hear more and more frequently the voice of the tourist whose White Mountain idyll was interrupted by the acrid smell of burning forests or the inconvenience of ashes drifting onto his "porch-with-a-view." And while the appreciation of the wilderness may have begun with city folks who were mildly inconvenienced or horrified on their vacation, there was at the same time a growing national view that the wilderness had moral and even spiritual value. The shift then from colonial fear of the wilderness to exploitation of its marketable resources to appreciation of its value for recreational activities and conservation was nothing less than revolutionary — and as uniquely American as one of its leading proponents, Teddy Roosevelt. The conqueror became the vacationer, second-home owner, and retiree, but not before the value of the state's mountains, lakes, and valleys achieved aesthetic and recreational dimensions.

Darby Field from Exeter is credited with being the first white man to climb the northeast's tallest peak, called Agiocochook by the Indians, and later named Mt. Washington. In the company of only two guides, since Indians believed the mountain to be the abode of invisible beings, Field ascended the summit in 1646, finding there shining stones which he mistook for diamonds. Jeremy Belknap mentions several Mt. Washington expeditions of scientific intent in his *History of New Hampshire.* Though he never reached the summit, his comments on the expeditions are a revealing blend of scientific and aesthetic interests which were to attract thousands of scientists, hikers, climbers, painters, poets, and novelists in the years following. Emphasizing the immense scale of the mountains, Belknap observed that their grandeur and sublimity made it "necessary to curb the imagination, and exercise judgment with mathematical precision; or the temptation to romance will be invincible."[3]

The White Mountains, and Mt. Washington particularly, have drawn scientists from all over the world to observe everything from its sixty-three species of tundra plant life to its extreme weather conditions, widely acknowledged to be the worst in the world. Edward Tuckerman, who in 1837 began collecting botanical specimens from the mountain, prepared the way for expeditions by other well-known botanists and geologists such as Charles Hitchcock, Sir Charles Lyell, and Louis Agassiz. In the twentieth century, year-around habitation of the summit became possible, and scientists for government and industry have been able to study everything from cosmic radiation and the physics of icing to radio transmission and the cultivation of plants in artificial environments.

Meanwhile, below the summit the battle was taking shape

among those who wanted to preserve the "wild and rugged scenes," those who saw profit in their removal, and those who continued to pursue farming. As we have seen, in the period up to the 1820s, the north country attracted hundreds of farmers, who engaged in the final attempt to push farming to its limit. One such farmer, Abel Crawford, later known as "the Patriarch of the White Mountains," left rich farmland near Lancaster to become one of the region's first innkeepers in rough woodlands near Crawford Notch. Providing first a simple stopover spot for farmers (from upper Coos County) who were travelling to seacoast markets, Abel and later his son Ethan Allen Crawford, became highly sought after mountain guides as well as innkeepers. Intrepid road and trail builders, the Crawfords in 1819 blazed the first trail to Mt. Washington's summit.

At the height of its influence and popularity the Crawford family, despite continual battles with wild animals, fire, flood, and cold, is credited with running three hotels; building and maintaining turnpikes; providing mountain lovers with the area's first history, Lucy Crawford's *The History of the White Mountains* (1846); and providing lodging and guides for everyone from Mt. Washington's first female climbers, the Misses Austin and a friend, to Daniel Webster, Ralph Waldo Emerson, Washington Irving, and Nathaniel Hawthorne. Writing with all the seriousness the mountain has always evoked, F. Allan Burt remarks: "As was usual with Mr. Crawford's parties when on the summit, they all joined in singing 'Old Hundredth' (the Doxology) before starting down."[4]

The pioneering Crawford's created a cadre of mountain lovers whose numbers swelled to the point that when in 1851 railroad service was introduced from Portland to Gorham, the region entered a "Golden Age" of hotel development. Soon a Bostonian could leave home in the morning and have supper in the White Mountains; by 1887 rail service made the trip from New York City possible in eleven hours. The appearance in 1901 of the elegant, red-roofed, turreted Mt. Washington Hotel at Bretton Woods culminated a colorful period of hotel building which included such reserves for the urbane and wealthy city-dwellers as the Fabyan House (1873), Mount Pleasant House (1876-1881), the Glen House (1884), and Twin Mountain House (1869-1870). By 1879 in Bethlehem alone there were twenty-four hotels which could handle 1,450 guests at once. Provided with the luxuries of individual train stations, telephones,

Mount Washington Hotel. Courtesy Bretton Woods Resort, Bretton Woods, New Hampshire.

post offices, elegant personal service and dining, gas lights (and later electric lights), and a variety of literary and musical entertainments, visitors also enjoyed access to Mt. Washington's summit, first by carriage road and later by cog railway. And few resort areas could boast as well of a daily newspaper published on the top of a mountain.

LEGISLATIVE ACTION

The sublime and beautiful aspects of the mountains which had attracted early explorers and decades of scientists, artists, and tourists were soon endangered, as we have seen, by the same railroads bringing the tourists to its heights. The tourist was quick to raise the battle cry.

One such voice which attracted considerable attention was that of a Philadelphia clergyman who conducted summer services in hotel parlors and on cottage porches near North Woodstock and South Littleton. Styling himself as "Missionary of the Headwaters of the Merrimack," the Reverend John E. Johnson in 1909 published a pamphlet entitled "The Boa Constrictor of the White Mountains," in which he railed against the New Hampshire Land Company, chartered, he claimed "to depopulate and deforest a section of the White Mountains."[5] Once national magazines such as the *Nation* and the *Atlantic Monthly* began to carry articles lamenting the logging company's activities, noting that the forests were dwindling and riverbeds were beginnning to dry up, and calling for a change in public policy, something of a coalition developed among nature lovers, hotel owners, and politicians interested in practical forestry.

As early as 1885 the General Court responded to public pressure by appointing a commission to investigate the state of New Hampshire forests. When the Forestry Commission's report detailed the astonishing results of private timber cutting and granted that a "new" industry, tourism, was already well-estasblished, this and future legislatures and governors began to take notice and started the movement in the state toward promoting forest management and recreational land use. For nature lovers, however, the legislature's commitment was too cautious, and in 1901 a group of state leaders formed the Society for the Protection of New Hampshire Forests to spearhead a citizen effort to preserve and protect the state's forests. Committed from its inception to the principle of public ownership and protection of land, the society has coordinated various interest groups and brought pressure to bear on the state and the federal government to set wilderness areas apart.

In 1911 the U. S. Congress passed the Weeks Act, introduced by a legislator from Massachusetts, who not coincidentally had been born on a farm near Lancaster, New Hampshire. Representing a first step toward lasting conservation of wilderness areas, the legislation was designed to protect the headwaters of navigable streams by providing grants for the purchase of abutting land. The Weeks Act proved to be a solution to the pressure being exerted on many sides — interests as seemingly diverse as those of nature lovers, hotel owners, railroad owners, practical foresters, and even the giant Amoskeag Company in Manchester, for whom a steady supply of water was essential. By enabling public ownership and protection of ultimately close to seven hundred thousand acres, which would be called the White Mountain National Forest, the Weeks Act promoted both the conservation and recreational use of land and made New Hampshire's mountains a regional attraction. It has been estimated that today the White Mountains are within a day's drive of nearly one quarter of the nation's population.

By the 1920s the state government began gradually to allocate larger sums of money for the purchase of forested land for public use, beginning a trend which produced by 1985, its fiftieth anniversary, a state park system boasting seventy-two state-run, self-supporting parks, ski areas, historic sites, and natural areas.

The Society for the Protection of New Hampshire Forests has been a sometimes silent, sometimes vocal partner with the state ever since 1901, exerting pressure and coordinating efforts as grandiose as the one in the 1920s to purchase Franconia Notch or as complex as the one in 1914 to locate one hundred and twenty-nine living descendants of twenty-one Masonian proprietors in order to purchase and protect wild lands remaining on Mount Monadnock or as seemingly insignificant as protecting twelve acres of pines near Tamworth or twenty-seven primeval white pines near Sutton. Through its membership, its cooperation with other conservation and environmental groups, and the leadership of many recent governors and legislators, the society has worked effectively to influence public awareness and sentiment, promote woodlot management, and acquire or assist in acquiring land for public protection and use. In the 1950s the SPNHF introduced the Tree Farm program to encourage careful management of privately owned wooded land. (Lands under that program now approach the acreage of the White Mountain National Forest.) In 1985, over eighty years of effort have produced a record 762,631 acres of wooded land either owned, managed, protected by easement, or secured and managed by the society in cooperation with town, state, and federal monies. The society continues to exercise the principles expressed in its founding charter—"to preserve the forests, protect the scenery . . . and cooperate in other measures of public improvement."[6] In the 1980s a new coalition of business, government, and private citizens is attempting to control longer-term and insidious effects of acid rain, polluted groundwater, and toxic wastes.

SELLING THE VIEW

The growth of the state's tourism industry has continued to both complement and parallel the hard-fought progress made by the conservationists. Vacationing in New Hampshire's "pure and salubrious air"—from grand hotels to the country's first summer camp at Squam Lake—certainly was the privilege of the well-heeled city-dweller for some years; leisure and recreational activity began to have a broader social base, particularly by the time the automobile became a force in American life. Just as the railroad had allowed manufacturing centers to become more dispersed, the car allowed workers to escape their work place. And New Hampshire encouraged its sons and daughters to come back home for "Old Home Week" (the brainchild of an earlier governor, Frank Rollins) in August for a nostalgic look at what they were missing or had forgotten. Small inns and guest houses in the central lakes region and on the seacoast began to replace the grand hotels of the White Mountains as the tourist industry became a statewide phenomenon. One study in the mid-seventies even estimated that at the peak of the tourist season the state's overnight population equalled about 90 percent of the resident population. At the same time varied interest groups from hikers to snowmobilers to all-terrain vehicle users continue to exert conflicting pressures on the recreational use of land.

Though continuing to rely on the summer visitors as the backbone of the tourism business, by the 1930s some in the state also recognized a developing market for a skiing industry. The Scandinavians who came to Berlin to build the Atlantic & St. Lawrence Railroad, which in the 1850s had opened the White Mountains to tourism, also brought with a tradition of cross-country skiing and ski jumping. As the interest in skiing spread, Dartmouth College in 1911 (the year of the Weeks Act) held its first Winter Carnival at which it introduced ski jumping and later in 1925 brought the European event of slalom racing to the United States. Still later, as ski tows and chair lifts mechanized the industry, snow-making machinery supplemented stormy weather, and automobiles made ski areas easily accessible, the state and individual investors developed a number of successful ski areas.

While it is true that manufacturing remains the state's principal economic base, the tourism and recreation industries have become important components in the state's economic growth, providing 10 to 15 percent of its annual income in the 1980s. From the White Mountains, which P. T. Barnum is reputed to have called "the second greatest show on earth,"[7] the tourism industry radiated southward to the state's thirteen hundred lakes, to the seacoast, to artistic communities near Peterborough and Plainfield, providing many a struggling rural community another lease on life — and more tax revenues.

Revenues from tourists continue to supplement the gross revenues in a state which one hundred years ago had no parks and virtually no land under public ownership and protection. It is no wonder then that a state now nearly 90 percent forested sees economic value in protecting its forests and even considers managing the species mix in woods lining public highways in order to perpetuate highly sought-after autumnal views.

PRESS AND POLITICS FACE NEW GROWTH

Practically speaking, politicians and businessmen viewed the influx of tourists to the state not only as a reason to expand tourist-related industries, but also as a source of revenue. Meals and room taxes, taxes on racetrack betting and lotteries, as well as liquor taxes provided the revenue the state needed to postpone the day when the state government might have to impose a broad-based sales or income tax. The issue of a broad-based tax became central to the political life of the state largely through the influence of the editorial policy of the only statewide newspaper, the *Manchester Union Leader*.

Frank Knox, who published the Manchester paper, had opposed Winant and the New Hampshire progressives. Knox's impact on the state continued even when he went to work for the Hearst press in Boston, for he did not give up the Manchester paper. In 1946 after Knox's death, his widow sold the paper to William Loeb, a friend of Styles Bridges. Loeb ran it much in the same spirit Isaac Hill had run the *Patriot* a hundred years before — full of flamboyance, invective, and political bias. In fact, the political slant of the *Manchester Union Leader* has pretty much the same bias that Isaac Hill had — low taxes, small government, concern for the common man — but in Isaac Hill's day these were liberal ideas; now Loeb's support for the same ideas was viewed as conservative and his unbridled language and his conspiratorial theories of politics outmoded. Perhaps the difference lies in Hill's violent opposition to religious bigotry and his support of many government projects designed to improve the quality of life in the state despite his simultaneous aim to keep the government small.

Until Loeb's death in 1981, no politician in the state could afford to be completely indifferent to him or his newspapers; since his death the paper has continued the same editorial policies under editor B. J. McQuaid. Unlike strongly political papers in other states or other cities, the *Manchester Union Leader* alone is distributed throughout the state, which makes it the voice heard most loudly in New Hampshire. And that voice cries out on page one as well as the editorial page against liberals, against government spending, and, most important, against a broad based tax — the bugabear of the conservative Republican leadership. This last issue not only saves the taxpayer money, but it also puts a lid on the expansion of the state government, a consequence of which not only Loeb, but all conservatives are well aware.

In recent years candidates for state office, particularly the gubernatorial candidates, have been pressed by the powerful *Union Leader* to take a strong stand against both an income tax and a sales tax; it gives the nod only to candidates willing to "take the pledge," as it is now commonly called. The "pledge" has turned into a two-edged sword. Without tax money governors find it difficult to accomplish much to which they can point with pride as they run for a second term, thus leaving incumbents extremely vulnerable to challengers. More important, low revenues have raised havoc with such state institutions as hospitals for the mentally and emotionally handicapped, prisons, and public assistance for the poor. And because the towns provide for most of their own services, often the town with the most services — the best schools, roads, and snow removal — attracts the most properous new resident taxpayers and so continues to grow while the poor town with few services fails to attract new and prosperous citizens, resulting in fewer services as the town gets poorer.

On the other hand low taxes as well as proximity to Boston have helped encourage rapid land development and attract an enormous number of new businesses and new citizens to the southern tier of the state, growth which the state both wanted and needed.

NEW ECONOMIC PROFILE

If on one hand the state's land and location were ultimately stubborn partners in progress for both the farmer and the traditional manufacturer, on the other hand its favorable business climate, proximity to Boston, and rural setting became distinctly cooperative factors in creating by the mid-1980s a new economic profile for New Hampshire.

Even at the height of immigration of workers for the railroads and the Amoskeag in the late 1800s, New Hampshire's population had grown very slowly, with some small, rural communities actually reaching zero population levels, fulfilling the doomsayer's prophecies about the death of isolated small towns. During the sixty years from 1880 until 1940 the state gained only about 145,000 people — startling when one realizes that in the ten years between 1970 and 1980 alone the state gained over 181,000 people. This 24.6 percent increase in population in a ten year period — among the largest in New England and the United States — began in the late 1940s. In 1880, for instance, the population grew 9 percent over the previous decade; in 1890, 8.5 percent; 1900, 9.3 percent; 1910, 4.6 percent; 1920, 2.9 percent; 1930, 5 percent; 1940, 5.6 percent; and 1950, 8.5 percent. With the dramatic growth in the population have come equally dramatic changes in the state's economy as new manpower resources and a changing economic climate have created new occasions for business growth.

Historically considered first as a rural or agrarian state and later as a mill state, renowned for its textile and shoe manufacturing, by the 1960s New Hampshire began to experience a period of major growth in nontraditional industries including a greatly increased sector of high-technology industries.

Long perceived as a rural state, farming has undergone predictable and unpredictable cycles since the mid-nineteenth century when at least 50 percent of the state's land was in agricultural use. To this day state economic planners and local and state politicians, while acknowledging the uncooperative climate and physiographic conditions which lead to forecasts of modest agricultural potential, remain dedicated to protecting some land for agricultural use. And although the actual number of farms has continued to decline in the last thirty years (from approximately ten thousand in 1950 to approximately twenty-seven hundred in 1980), other considerations suggest the stirrings of a revival of the quality of the life of those farming. While fewer acres are being farmed, while farms are shrinking in individual size and often provide second incomes, it was recognized in the mid-1970s that for the first time in years not only had agricultural production increased but more people were involved in farming and that a greater proportion of the gross state product was derived from farming. Dairying continues to hold a strong first place as the state's leading agricultural pursuit, with increasing competition from production in feed crops, fruit (especially berries), and traditional secondary crops such a maple syrup and cordwood. Of particular note in the 1970s and 1980s is the strengthening of the horticulture industry and its ingenious use of greenhouses as an adaptation which allows the farmer to beat the climate and even control winter.

As late as the 1950s New Hampshire's gross state product continued to reflect the dominance of its traditional industries — leather products, textiles, paper and wood products, minerals, and electrical and machine tools. Its industries also continued to benefit from wartime production demands and innovations in management and corporate structures. Nonetheless, steeply rising fuel and labor costs and both southern and foreign competition increasingly eroded the state's one-hundred-year-old industrial foundation.

Once again in the 1980s the state ranked as one of the most industrialized states in the nation, with a population growth more than five times that of New England, twice that of the United States, and with one of the lowest unemployment rates in the country. More and more frequently the national and regional press featured articles about the meteoric success of high-technology firms, a happy change from years of features on abandoned farms and environmental shortsightedness.

In 1982 a report from the University of New Hampshire entitled, *Industry in New Hampshire: Changes in the Manufacturing Sector, 1970-1978*, cited three significant trends in the state's recent economic development: a substantial increase in manufacturing employment (while many parts of the country witnessed a decrease); a clearly discernible pattern of concentration of new industry in the southeastern part of the state — Hillsborough, Rockingham, and Strafford counties, the "Golden Triangle" bounded by Manchester, Salem, and Nashua;

and a distinct change in the pattern of manufacturing mix throughout the state toward nontraditional and high-technology industries. Attributing the reindustrialization of the state to the combined effects of the rapid expansion of federally funded roadbuilding in the 1950s (specifically the Federal Aid to Highways Act of 1956 under President Eisenhower) culminating in the major inter- and intrastate connections, Interstate's 91, 89, 93, 95, and state highway 16; favorable tax structure; and both the availability and low cost of manpower, the report painted a rosy picture for the future.

Many of the state's new companies, like their employees, have immigrated to southeastern New Hampshire from the congested and heavily taxed environs of Massachusetts' circumferential beltway, Route 128. However, the smaller business of under fifty employees still dominates the business community, though major conglomerates account for more and more jobs in a state which in the last ten years has become the international corporate headquarters of three major corporations. Quite unlike the earlier noisy, smelly, air-polluting, high-energy consuming lumber, textile, and shoe industries, the newer industries are largely quiet, clean electronics firms as popular with town fathers and state planners as computers are with businesses and professionals. Producing products ranging from military countermeasure devices, to devices which generate, transmit, and store electrical energy, to subsurface radar devices and antennae, to components for electronic and microwave circuitry, to data display terminals, at least five of the new companies have been cited by both *Inc.* and *Fortune* magazines as among America's fastest growing private companies.

THE PRESSURES OF GROWTH

Politicians emerging from the numerous high-tech industries may find themselves in conflict with the old populist-conservative Republicans led by the *Manchester Union Leader*. When William Loeb died in 1981, his conservative coalition was already faced with new and dynamic changes in the state that would demand attention. Certainly this influx of people from outside of the state has already undermined the dominance of one party in the state. In the sixties and seventies the number of Democrats registered in the state began to approach the number of Republicans. And, indeed, the Democrats managed to hold nearly as many of the important state offices as the Republicans did in the late seventies. It was a real turnaround in the state which had been thought of as a one-party state for many years.

However, more revealing than simple party affiliation is the fact that the state continues to be dominated by a fairly conservative ideology. Whether voters are registered Republican or Democrat, they tend to identify themselves as more conservative than liberal. Clearly, the newcomers to the state have no intention of trying to transform New Hampshire into a welfare state. However, it is impossible to imagine that these new citizens will be content to remain mute in state politics, and the old guard is understandably nervous.

The *Union Leader* and most of the state's business and political leaders who prize small government, little regulation, and home rule have encouraged and applauded population and business growth. But just as community services are strained by the influx of new people, so are these principles of government. The *Union Leader* under McQuaid is still powerful after the death of Loeb and has labelled the politicians who represent these new citizens "blue suiters" and says New Hampshire legislators don't like "bankers and business-men" who might "professionalize" politics in New Hampshire. Certainly, as population increases, state governments tend to be run more by professionals than by interested citizens, and since New Hampshire's government — its huge legislature and its town meetings — demand much involvement by the citizens, it will take great determination to maintain that government in the face of the burgeoning population.

FIVE GOVERNORS

Despite the fact that the term of the governor of New Hampshire lasts only two years and he is surrounded by an Executive Council designed to curb any self-aggrandizing notions he might have, the governor is the only state-wide elected official, and his attitude is the clearest weathervane we have of the mood of the people toward the development of the state. During the period of dramatic growth from 1965 to 1985 while the state courted industrial and economic development, the state's leaders perceived that the absence of a broad-based tax encouraged industry to move to the state; at the same time, the absence of reliable and inexpensive fuel might hinder that development. Thus, the government made a concerted effort to avoid imposing broad-based taxes and to increase the state's fuel supply.

Thus the tax issue has become a touchstone in New Hampshire even more sensitive than it is in most states. Two out of the five governors were Democrats—John King and Hugh Gallen—and three were Republicans—Meldrim Thomson, Walter Peterson, and John Sununu. While Governor Meldrim Thomson, who represented the populist, conservative wing of the Republican party has been widely regarded as the major force in New Hampshire politics, the four other governors during the years 1963 to 1985 have not reflected such uncompromising conservatism, though none, not even the Democrats, have been notably liberal either. Certainly none has attempted to pass tax laws and collect enough revenue to improve or increase the state's social programs.

John King, who served from 1963 to 1969, established a new source of revenue—the sweepstakes lottery—to avoid the dreaded broad-based tax. The lottery, which has become a fixture in the tax system of the state, brought in enough revenue to keep the state solvent, and solvency seemed to have allayed any qualms the electorate might have initially felt at relying on such a source of income for the state.

Under Walter Peterson (1969-1973) the state adopted a business profits tax (which is not perceived as a deterrent to business) and a tax on income of people who work in New Hampshire but reside out of the state. But Peterson had other plans for the state. He organized a Task Force on the Future of New Hampshire—a large group of community leaders from all over the state including teachers, business people, church people, and others whose job it was to review the condition of the state and make plans for its future. Ambitious as this project was, Peterson failed to translate the vision he fashioned out of the Task Force's reports into action by the General Court.

The conservative faction in the state also perceived that executing the plans that Peterson's Task Force formulated would require money, more money than was available through the revenue sources then available. The possibility of a new, broad-based tax alarmed conservative Republicans, particularly William Loeb and the *Manchester Union Leader*, who in 1972 supported conservative Meldrim Thomson who was elected and served from 1973 to 1979. With Thomson's election the Task Force's recommendation died aborning. Thomson worked to control taxes and to promote business and manufacturing in the state, supporting among other things the building of an oil refinery in Durham and the controversial Seabrook Nuclear Power Plant which was planned to supply cheap power not only for the citizens of New Hampshire, but also for its burgeoning new businesses.

The nuclear power plant created problems from the beginning and still remains a thorn after more than ten years. While the Environmental Protection Agency and the Nuclear Regulatory Commission of the federal government ruled that the plans for the Seabrook Power Plant were safe, many people remained skeptical. By April 1977, two thousand protestors had gathered on the site and on May 1, three hundred state police officers arrested many of the demonstrators. But even without the fears for the safety of the project, the escalating cost of construction of the plant became another problem. Ironically, the Public Service Company had to put a surcharge on electric rates to pay for the bonds needed to construct the Seabrook Nuclear plant, a move so unpopular that it paved the way for Thomson's defeat by moderate Democrat Hugh Gallen in 1978.

Gallen, a newcomer to politics who had taken "the pledge" to veto any broad-based tax bill,found by the time of his third campaign that without funds he could not do the kind of things to which an incumbent can point with pride. In fact, partly because of a momentary economic downturn, a $30 million deficit loomed during his last year in office. Gallen refused to take "the pledge" a third time, promising instead only to consider what the state's needs seemed to be.

Another newcomer to politics, John Sununu, a moderate-to-conservative Republican, well-financed and supported by the new and big businesses in the state, took "the pledge" and challenged Gallen and the $30 million deficit in 1982 and won the governorship. Sununu who, like Gallen, was comparatively unknown when he came to office, soon showed a talent for political leadership in the General Court where he helped shore up the tenuous hold that moderate Republicans had on the leadership of the state senate. He also presented a balanced budget without new general taxes and increased welfare programs while he cut the budget of the University of New Hampshire, paying for these programs by modestly increasing liquor charges and taxes on business profits. Such efficiency combined with fiscal conservativism appealed to the *Manchester Union Leader* as well as the voters.

The issue of taxes has dominated the incumbencies of these five governors particularly as it became clear that the development of sources of power (needed for industrial development particularly favored by the conservatives) would probably involve higher taxes in one form or another. The more moderate governors soon discovered that the lid placed on revenues prevented them from initiating social programs that they favored, programs for which they could find only moderate support in the General Court and among the state electorate, ever wary of programs that do not grow out of their own communities.

TOWN, STATE, AND NATION

Perhaps the key factor in the state's political system has always been the emphasis placed on home rule and the suspicion of power concentrated in the hands of a few men far away. Thus the town meeting, while often attended by less than 25 percent of the eligible voters, remains a vital part of life in the state. The people are accustomed to having a direct voice in decisions about government. They expect to know and meet their leaders face-to-face and to speak their piece about taxes, services, and land use to the town fathers and to vote directly on most important issues facing their town. The people remain politically active and aware and are proud of their local autonomy.

The most outstanding feature of the state government is the huge legislature or General Court of four hundred members, paid only meager expenses and two hundred dollars every two years, which clearly results from the people's determination to keep a tight rein on political matters. Thus almost all citizens know one of the legislators (one for every 1,800 voters) who represents him or her in the state government and can speak to that representative directly on the street or in the supermarket or the coffee shop about matters of concern.

Discussing the warrant at a March town meeting. Photograph courtesy of the Argus Champion, *Newport, New Hampshire.*

Unfortunately, this unwieldy legislature is often inefficient. It is so difficult for four hundred people to decide anything together that the chairs of the legislative committees and the Speaker of the House who appoints the chairs of these committees wield an enormous amount of power. Furthermore, appealing as the ideal of an amateur legislature is, the General Court presents several problems, not the least of which is that since the legislators generally are not politically ambitious, they are not always willing to spend the time and energy necessary to know the issues and represent their constituents as vigorously as they might. Besides which between one-third and one-half of the lawmakers leave after the first term. Even so, efforts to change the structure of the General Court have been soundly defeated by the electorate who find these disadvantages offset by their perception that the General Court is the nearest thing they can get to grass-roots democracy.

The second outstanding feature of the state government is the governor's Council which passes on the governor's appointees, among other things. A holdover from the royal governor's Council, the modern Council has remained, along with the two-year term of office, as a curb on the authority of the governor. The voters, who are very aware of their representatives to the General Court, sometimes neglect to keep tabs on the members of the powerful Council whom they don't know as intimately. Again this peculiar institution reflects the state's deep-rooted desire to establish a government free from any tinge of authoritarianism, and as with all such institutions its ultimate success depends on the care with which the voters scrutinize the activities of their representatives.

Since 1952 when Governor Sherman Adams spent most of his second year in office running Eisenhower's presidential campaign, on a national level New Hampshire has been famous as the state in which the first presidential primary is held. Though small, remarkably homogenous, and inherently conservative, the state is perhaps a better proving ground than most for an office seeker. The campaigner can speak to almost every citizen in the state if he tries, and any voter, who wants to, can hear what every candidate has to say, ask him questions, and shake his hand, too, if he feels like it. Furthermore, among the participants at town meetings and the numerous past and present members of the legislature around the state, candidates easily pick volunteers experienced in political campaigning. And with their experience of the town meeting and their intimate acquaintance with their legislators, the voters of New Hampshire are not overawed by politicians seeking public office. They can enjoy or endure the whirlwind of publicity the state receives every four years while they take a clear-eyed look at the candidates and the issues and give the nation the benefit of their considered judgment based on one hundred fifty years of dealing with political whims, fooleries, and ideas.

TOWN MEETINGS AND TYCOONS

From sassafras to Seabrook the crosscurrents that have molded New Hampshire history since its beginning—public interests, private ambitions, external influences on the state, economic development and political scheming, state versus local authority, and most of all the desire to exploit the resources of the region and the impulse to conserve both the political heritage and the environment of the state clashed in a paradigmatic confrontation among international tycoons, professional politicians, and local citizens in Durham in 1974. The confrontation unified the citizens of the state as they articulated many of the values evolving out of the state's history and marshalled the institutions of government which they had so carefully preserved.

By early October of 1973, *Publick Occurrences*, a small and short-lived weekly newspaper in Durham recognized that something mysterious was going on at Durham Point when in the space of a month a real estate man had offered to buy land from every landowner that the paper contacted in a random survey. Though the buyer assured the landowners that he did not intend to turn the land into a development, his plans for the property were vague and contradictory. Six weeks later the mystery was solved. Greek entrepreneur, Aristotle Onassis, revealed that he had purchased three thousand acres of land on Durham Point, a rural-residential area of the coast that is part of the old Piscataqua region, and on it he planned to build a $600 million oil refinery. Furthermore, he was trying to buy land on the Isles of Shoals to act as a deep-water port for oil tankers. It would be the largest refinery in the world, and it was promised that more refineries would follow on the eighteen miles of coastline and the off-shore islands where New Hampshire had begun.

Fuel oil is a sensitive issue in New Hampshire which has no combustible fossil fuel within its borders. Not only do the industries in the state need a reliable source of energy but with a long, cold winter threatening, the people of the state felt particularly vulnerable when in 1973 the OPEC nations placed an embargo on crude oil. There were some who thought Onassis's company, Olympic Oil, was the answer to this delicate problem. Others saw it as a chance to unload at a substantial profit unprofitable farmland. Some saw it as broadening the tax base and providing employment. William Loeb of the *Manchester Union Leader* and Governor Meldrim Thomson, who had longed for an oil refinery in the state, were particularly delighted. Senator Thomas McIntyre approved of the idea. Others in the state, notably the great majority of citizens of Durham, were not delighted at all. There were, of course, those who resented their fellow townsmen's attempts to drive out a buyer for their land, but they were a small minority. By the end of November lines were drawn for a bloody battle which would last through the winter between the citizens of the town of Durham and Olympic Oil Company.

Arrayed against these Goliaths—House Speaker George Roberts, Jr., Loeb, Thomson, and Onassis, himself—stood many Davids, most notably Nancy Sandberg of Durham Point, a housewife who planted apple trees and who claimed that "This is the time of year when I usually sit down to read long historical novels,"[8] and Dudley W. Dudley, the freshman representative from Durham to the General Court. Nancy Sandberg soon formed a citizen's group named Save Our Shore and collected four thousand signatures from citizens living in and around Durham protesting the building of the refinery. Dudley W. Dudley, descendant of a colonial governor of New Hampshire and of Daniel Webster (the W. is for her maiden name, Webster) and married to a man descended from another colonial governor named Dudley, carried the petition to the governor and opposed the refinery in the General Assembly.

"Save Our Shore" publicized every problem the introduction of an oil refinery might bring to the area: air and water pollution, effect on fishing and tourist industries, sudden growth in population, growth of satellite industries, ecological and sociological problems of every description. They further pointed out that fuel oil was no more plentiful to New Jersey residents where refineries abound than it was in New Hampshire. In fact, the problem did not lie in a scarcity of refineries but in a scarcity of crude oil.

To counteract this hostility, the Onassis company with the help of Governor Thomson and William Loeb launched a massive public relations campaign. They assured the citizens of Durham that the refinery would provide cheap, plentiful fuel oil—no mean promise in the depths of the oil crisis—that it would be "as clean as a clinic," that it would be aesthetically pleasing. Threats that Onassis would abandon the citizens of the state to the freezing winter left the citizens of Durham unmoved. Aristotle Onassis flew in a helicopter over Durham Point, a gesture which seemed to impress Governor Thomson and, perhaps, William Loeb more than it did anyone else, and followed that with an elegant cocktail party at which none of the citizens' questions were answered to their satisfaction.

When Durham remained unconvinced, other more ominous proposals began being bruted about. The legislature might give the governor emergency powers by which he could override Durham's resistance, but that seemed an unlikely possibility since the legislature is leery of the powers the governor already has. Or the refinery might be somehow labelled a public utility and come under eminent domain by which the state could zone the land however it saw fit. Alternatively, House Speaker Roberts proposed appointing a state Energy Facility Evaluation Commission which would have final say in establishing the refinery with or without the consent of the town of Durham.

These proposals provided just the issue that Dudley Dudley needed. At once the issue shifted from ecological, aesthetic, economic, and local grounds to statewide and political concerns. If the state government in Concord could form the Energy Facility Evaluation Commission to force the town of Durham to give up a third of its seacoast land for an oil refinery, then what might the state government impose on any of the other towns in the state? What happened to home rule? Local autonomy? The town meeting? And those were the questions Nancy Sandberg and Dudley Dudley asked at every hearing and from every platform they could find between December and March.

As town meetings approached in March, Governor Thomson made an ill-advised last ditch effort to bring pressure on the Durham town meeting by proposing to every town moderator in the state that on the warrant for their town meeting they include the proposition: "Be it resolved that this town meeting go on record in favor of an oil refinery for New Hampshire that meets all environmental requirements." But the towns' voters were too canny to be fooled by those innocuous words. Overwhelmingly the towns either voted down the resolution or amended it to insure that the refinery, however safe for the environment, would be built only with the consent of the townspeople. On March 6, 1974, the Durham town meeting defeated by 1,254 to 144 the proposed rezoning of Durham Point to allow the $600 million refinery to be built in its boundaries.

When the General Assembly met a few days later, the delegates from all over the state had a strong mandate to vote against any bill which might infringe on home rule. In her summation to the General Court, Dudley Dudley epitomized the continuing commitment of the people of the state to the institutions they have defended during economic and political vicissitudes throughout the state's history. Dudley took the floor in the House.

Make no mistake that the effect of this [bill] . . . is to override the century-old tradition of home rule in the State of New Hampshire, that tradition which is the very bedrock of democracy in New Hampshire . . . that tradition which, when challenged, called the people of New Hampshire to its defense in 1974 as it did in 1776. I want to urge you to vote no on this amendment and ask you to consider your vote on this matter as a positive one—a vote for your neighbors and friends, a vote for your town, a vote for your city—and most of all for the maintenance of home rule in our whole state from Coos to the sea.[9]

10

Changes in Character

New Hampshire boomed during the 1980s. Businesses flocked from Massachusetts to New Hampshire to take advantage of the low tax rate in the state, and people followed jobs. The southern tier of the state, closest to Boston, grew the most. Businesses were generally high-tech, defense-related industries—computers, electronics, and professional business services such as software, contract research and development, management consulting, as well as insurance and advertising. Sanders Corporation, whose business was 90 percent defense-related, became the biggest employer in the state with a peak staff of 9,500 workers.

The new businesses caused a boom in commercial building. The new citizens who flocked to the state created a boom in houses and condominiums. Furthermore, with the economy of the whole country flourishing, vacation houses in New Hampshire became enormously popular. The total number of housing units in the state doubled between 1970 and 1988 and half of that increase was between 1984 and 1988. New housing starts in 1987 topped 16,000 while unemployment sank to 2.4 percent.

Towns responded to the active economy in various ways. North Conway attracted more than skiers by lining its Main Street with outlet stores. Areas like Waterville Valley exploded with vacation houses and condominiums. While its mills remained half empty, Manchester nevertheless acquired several handsome glass towers, and banks and other

198

financial institutions moved to town. In 1988, Nashua, in the heart of the industrial growth, was named by *Money Magazine* the most desirable city in the country in which to live. Downtown Portsmouth, which had fallen into disrepair, treated itself to a face lift with money generated by Pease Air Force Base and the Portsmouth Naval Ship Yard—the naval yard that has produced ships for every war since the Revolution and built the sailing ship that appears on the state flag. Local initiative preserved many historic and elegant pre–Revolutionary War houses from the demolition squads of the urban renewers, among them the house where John Paul Jones lived while he oversaw construction at the naval yard. In a period of growth for all of New England, New Hampshire grew faster than any other state in the region.

This exhilarating expansion also created anxiety in some communities about the changing environment and character of the state. Despite its long industrial past, New Hampshire has always cherished an image of itself as rural and natural. An enchanted Henry David Thoreau called New Hampshire landscape "everlasting and unfallen," and painter Thomas Cole chose the White Mountains as background for his painting *Garden of Eden*. In more modern times poets like Robert Frost, Maxine Kumin, and Donald Hall had praised its landscapes. Now trees that had grown up on farms abandoned in the nineteenth century were being cut down once again as vacation condominiums, malls, industrial parks, and housing developments sprouted up in fields and on hillsides all over the state. Development so abrupt and uncontrolled alarmed both newly arrived residents seeking to escape the city and long-time citizens of the state.

With a tradition of individual freedom and home rule, few towns had ever taken a serious interest in establishing zoning ordinances. Neighbors might grumble about the rusting car in a back yard or the trailer on the vacant lot, but most voters were reluctant to impose zoning regulations on their neighbors. Now, however, the problem was more like uncontrolled suburban sprawl with strips of fast food restaurants, shopping malls, and condominiums filling land once covered with farms or forests. In 1992 concerned planners, architects, conservationists, developers, and historians around the state wrote essays on land use in New Hampshire, which were edited by Richard Ober and collected in a book called *At What Cost? Shaping the Land We Call New Hampshire*, published by the New Hampshire Historical Society. These essays describe not only the changes in the landscape, but people's response to those changes. Voters called for town planning and zoning regulation. Some towns, like Peterborough, simply placed a moratorium on growth. Most towns quickly established agencies to organize the way in which they would expand. By 1989, 88 percent of towns had zoning regulations and 98 percent of these had subdivision regulations. Volunteer members of the new planning boards often met two or three nights a week to keep up with the flood of applicants from developers, many from outside the community or even out-of-state.

The sheer number of new people changed the environment in many places and forced some major changes in local government. The zoning regulations imposed by most towns could not recreate the kind of picturesque village many New Hampshire people treasure—village green surrounded by white spired church, mill, school, country stores, and a mixture of modest and stately homes. In the early 1970s, cluster housing was seen as a way to concentrate growth and produce something more approximating the early towns. The idea was enthusiastically supported by the Society for the Protection of New Hampshire Forests, the Land Trust Institutes, and many planners, but people did not like to build that way. When zoning became a real issue in the 1980s, towns generally adopted urban models in designing the way their towns would grow. Many of the regulations required that large houses have large, private lots, that mills and stores be separated from residences, and that stores, churches, and schools be located in an area where there was plenty of parking. Ultimately, zoning regulations could not bring back "New Hampshire everlasting and unfallen," but they might ensure that the new shopping mall didn't block the best view of the mountains.

Thus the state evolved until the late eighties. New Hampshire was prospering, its population was growing, and many economists believed the region was growing more stable. Then, to the stunned dismay of the citizens, at the end of the decade the economy of the whole region, and especially the booming economy of New Hampshire, fizzled out.

New Hampshire was not alone, of course. The nation as a whole fell into an economic slump that it had difficulty crawling out of; but all kinds of regional circumstances made the problems in New Hampshire particularly acute. The Cold War screeched to a halt, closing Pease Air Force Base in 1990 and drying up much of the market for the high-tech military products New Hampshire's industries were geared to produce. Portsmouth's population dropped from 25,900 to 20,800. For several years the same ax loomed over the head of historic Portsmouth

Naval Yard, as it has after every war since the Revolution. While that ax never fell, the ship yard shrank significantly. New Hampshire's economy suffered another serious blow in 1990 when banks inopportunely and abruptly tightened credit. The domestic and business real estate market shriveled, small businesses couldn't get loans, and bankruptcies soared. There followed a series of smaller, but still painful, local blows. Two seasons of scant snow hurt the tourist industry generally and drove several smaller ski areas out of business. The fallout from the Dairy Termination Program, in which the government propped up dairy prices by buying out dairy herds to reduce milk production, hurt local merchants dependent on the dairy industry, although northern New Hampshire farmers who participated enthusiastically in the program may have been helped by it.

Though the tourist industry barely faltered in this period, the major part of New Hampshire's economy spiraled downward as precipitously as it had risen. In 1987 New Hampshire had led the nation in rate of job growth; in 1991 it was last. Unemployment rose to 7.5 percent. New housing starts dropped to 4,000, and jobs in construction dropped from 37,800 to 16,600. Dozens and dozens of vacation condominiums fell empty. Bankruptcies rose from 608 to 3,900. Manufacturing jobs shrank by 16,000. Sanders merged with Lockheed but also cut its work force almost in half to 4,500. (It is interesting to note that in the middle of this chaos the old Amoskeag Corporation, which had operated the mills in Manchester in the nineteenth century, was rated by *Fortune Magazine* as 295th in a list of 306 of companies most admired in the United States.) Overall, New Hampshire lost 10 percent of its jobs between 1989 and 1992. Recipients of Aid to Families with Dependent Children rose from 4,800 to 14,430. The state had the fastest growth rate in the nation in numbers of families receiving food stamps and AFDC. The statistics were all dismal. In January of 1992 *The Boston Globe* ran a headline "Paradise Lost: New Hampshire's Economic Crisis."

DEFENDING THE LANDSCAPE

During the boom and bust of real estate and industry in the thickly populated southern tier of the state, another critical situation was developing in rural areas and especially in the North Country and the forests of the White Mountains.

New Hampshire's landscape and particularly its forests have from the first engendered jobs and wealth for the state, and have always proved remarkably resilient. The forests recuperated somewhat from the ravages of the royal governors who oversaw the production of masts and naval stores for the British navy in colonial days, and again from the colorful timber barons who slashed through thousands of acres of trees to produce lumber in the nineteenth century. Now the trees are largely owned by large paper companies. Unlike many great forests in the nation, the White Mountains forest, and 94 percent of all of northern New England's forests, belongs mostly to private companies.

After the devastation of the timber barons, public opinion pressured companies that owned the woods to treat the forests more responsibly. Since the paper mills were far less mobile and far more expensive than the old sawmills, the companies needed to manage their resources so that trees were always accessible, and the mills were never idle. Their method of managing the trees was simple. The paper companies owned such vast numbers of acres that they could let freshly cut areas grow back while they cut trees in other parts of the forest. Although the system might not satisfy an environmentalist, the forests remained, not untouched, but fairly stable during the thirty years from the 1930s to the 1960s. The loggers continued to cut, and their logging roads annoyed many animals and birds, but there were still enough trees to provide adventure and solitude for people to enjoy.

Beginning in the late 1970s, powerful pressures from two opposite directions began to squeeze the northern forest. The companies who owned the forest saw a way to make more profit from their land at the same time that ecologists were recognizing its biological diversity. Just as towns were attempting to preserve their identity by dramatically changing how they regulated growth, so ecologists campaigned for new protection for the ecological system of the northern forest.

Environmental laws put an end to the picturesque but destructive and wasteful log drives on the rivers of the White Mountains. The landowners replaced those drives with a network of logging roads that took trucks deep into the farther reaches of the forest to make more trees accessible to their mills. To their surprise they discovered they owned many more trees than their mills could use. Almost at the same time, technology improved and mills became more efficient. New sawmills could get lumber out of smaller softwood logs, and some mills made waferboard out of wood chips. Freed of the fear that they might run out of wood to make paper and other wood products, the companies decided it would be easier to buy timber on the open market and make some quick money by selling off their forests. The companies divided the mills from the forest land surrounding them and put much of the land on the market. The land attracted investors with no ties to the forest industries. John Hancock Financial Services, for example, bought 240,000 acres in New Hampshire, Maine, and Vermont. To these investors the question was simply, "Is it more profitable to let a tree grow another year or clear the land for another use?" That other use could be anything from building a mall or a subdivision to establishing a park, and the community that treasured the aesthetic quality and recreational opportunities of the forest had no say in the matter.

Nearly simultaneous with this revolution in the forest industry, scientists such as Edward O. Wilson began urging the protection of biological species within large ecosystems—New England's northern forest being one of those biologically diverse regions. Despite the claims of Thomas Cole and Henry David Thoreau, this forest is hardly an unspoiled Eden. The timber industry in one form or another has been busily at work in the ecosystem since 1620, and before that the Native Americans cut or burned the forest whenever they found it convenient to do so. While conservationists have been trying to protect the forest since the forming of the Society for the Protection of New Hampshire Forests in 1901, in recent years we have begun to understand the delicate interdependence of important ecosystems and the compelling case for preserving the entire habitats of all varieties of flora and fauna. These new insights conflict directly with exploitation of the land for recreation, development, and, most of all, timber, just as these uses conflict with each other.

The controversy over timbering the forests in the White Mountains might be viewed as a high-tech version of the conflict between those who would exploit the land and those who would preserve it—a conflict that has been going on since the middle of the nineteenth century. The third player in that conflict has always been the visitors who also have a stake in the character of the state. People have always been attracted to the state by agreeable summer weather, quaint inns, ski slopes, autumn leaves, hiking trails, clear lakes, Mount Washington, and famous rock formations like the Flume and The Old Man of the Mountain. A large number enjoy antiquing in the charming small towns or attending country auctions. A growing number of people come for the stock car races at Lee U.S.A. Speedway, Hudson Speedway in Hudson, and New Hampshire International Speedway in Loudon, or any of the thirteen raceways in the state—more per capita than Indiana! The five-year-old New Hampshire International Speedway near Concord with a seating capacity of 72,000 is already the hub of auto racing in the northeast. Stock car racing, a rural, blue-collar sport, is a truly homegrown New Hampshire attraction.

Tourism of all kinds has grown steadily through the boom and bust and recovery of the 1980s and 1990s. The tourist industry, which represents almost 10 percent of the gross state product, provides 55,000 jobs and about $100 million dollars in tax revenue. While it is at least partly for these 23 million visitors that New Hampshire burnishes the image of itself as a scenic and rural state, it is also true that visitors come because some people in the state have taken care of the landscape.

In recent years public concern over development and timbering and the helplessness of the community to control what happens to the land in the state has been translated into new attempts to protect undeveloped land. Private landowners have contributed over 100,000 acres of farm and forest land to local trusts or to the statewide Land Conservation Investment Program to preserve these acres from development. While it is difficult to imagine that this kind of individual initiative will protect all the woods in the White Mountains, the success of the trusts reveals once again the commitment people feel to the rural and idyllic image of the state.

SEABROOK

The ongoing problem of how to provide cheap energy to an industrial state with long winters and no fossil fuel continued to plague the state after the oil refinery proposed by Aristotle Onassis was rejected in 1974. The developing nuclear power industry offered one possible solution. The Public Service Company of New Hampshire proposed to build a nuclear power plant at Seabrook, a town on New Hampshire's seacoast near some of the earliest settlements in the state. The project was proposed in 1972 and had the immediate backing of Governor Meldrim Thomson and publisher William Loeb of the *Manchester Union Leader*. Fearing for the environment and for the safety of their towns, many people in the state opposed building the power station. They organized themselves into various groups and enlisted the support of established environmental groups as well as antinuclear activists to help them stop the building of the nuclear reactor. At first glance the battle seemed to replicate the struggle by Dudley Dudley, Nancy Sandberg, and the members of Save Our Shore against the oil refinery. In fact, one vocal member of the protest group, Guy Chichester, who headed the Clamshell Alliance opposing the power plant, had been active in Save Our Shore. But this time there was no ultimate appeal to local control.

The battle developed among several federal agencies responsible for overseeing the development of nuclear power, the New England states, investors in the project, and various "intervenors" who objected to the project on the basis of design, environmental issues, safety, regulation, nuclear power in general, and the location of the plant in particular. The battleground was officially the state board set up to oversee the project, though, of course, the battle raged in the newspapers, in the courts, in the State House and the General Court, in the State House of Massachusetts, and in the streets of Concord, at Seabrook itself, and within the federal government in Washington.

The agencies of the federal government that had the power to make the final decision about the site, the design of the plant, and the safety of the installation depended on a docile public to accept their rulings, and in this they were mistaken. The people living in towns near Seabrook had already successfully challenged the authority of government and industry in the oil refinery controversy, which probably inspired them to believe they could be effective once again. This time, too, the stakes were higher. People as well as the environment were at risk not only in New Hampshire but also in Massachusetts; and the infant nuclear power industry simply had little convincing, hard scientific data about the evolving technology and especially the safety of nuclear reactors. It was a recipe for exactly what happened—more than twenty years of controversy that became the lightning rod for the national debate over nuclear power.

Public Service of New Hampshire applied for approval of Seabrook for a site for a nuclear generator in 1972. Hearings began at a special licensing board in the state; and individuals and groups testified, expressing their misgivings about damage to the environment along the seacoast and danger to the citizens of the towns in the vicinity. Public Service of New Hampshire simply reiterated that Seabrook was the most likely place for the nuclear station. For the next few years the Society for the Protection of New Hampshire Forests, the Audubon Society, the Seacoast Anti-Pollution League, and numerous citizens groups and intervenors testified against the project before the Atomic Energy Commission, the Nuclear Regulatory Agency, the Environmental Protection Agency, and every other government forum designated to review the siting and building of the plant. They considered water and air pollution, the possible changes in the temperature of the ocean water that might endanger lobster, clams, and fish along the coast, danger to the marshlands and to the appearance of the landscape. Decisions about the design of the plant were made and rescinded. Safety rules were set and modified. Experts contradicted experts. Lawyers quarreled with lawyers. Private citizens' suspicion about expert witnesses grew. But Governor Meldrim Thomson and the *Union Leader* grew more adamant in their support of the project, and the siting of the station remained Seabrook.

Four years into the debate, construction actually began despite demonstrations on the site and the arrests of nearly two hundred people. The Seacoast Anti-Pollution League, one of the leading citizens' groups opposed to Seabrook, began to run out of money and hope. Several of the officers resigned, and a new president, Guy Chichester, was elected.

Chichester was not the respecter of legal niceties that the League represented. In 1977 he set a new tone for the protest. He shifted the emphasis from protection for the environment through legal action to political action against the political power structure. Fear of nuclear power, he saw, could be harnessed to drive a general campaign against the political power structure. Chichester, who observed the hearings for the town of Rye, New Hampshire, accused various governmental agencies of being in the pockets of the corporations they were regulating and protested the undemocratic character of the licensing hearings. He soon left the Seacoast Anti-Pollution League to become the spokesman for new sixties-style groups of antinuclear protesters under a loose umbrella organization called the Clamshell Alliance. The Clams adopted the methods of the Civil Rights movement, protesting with serious demonstrations, marches, civil disobedience, and mass arrests. On April 1, four hundred demonstrators were arrested, some of whom were sentenced to as much as six months in jail. The arrests captured the attention of the national press, and the Clamshell Alliance became far better known than the Save Our Shore group had ever been. Construction of the Seabrook Plant was temporarily suspended; and while construction was halted, the Environmental Protection Agency resolved certain environmental questions.

When the courts allowed construction to resume in July, there were ongoing protests at the construction site and ongoing arrests. In 1978, several members chained themselves to a crane and got their day in court. Robert (Rennie) Cushing, one of the Clams arrested, used the occasion as a forum in which to protest against nuclear power and the injustice of the legal system, and to testify for the sanctity of conscience and for nonviolence. He protested the innocence of the defendants, "What you have is six individuals on a crane; what you don't have, your Honor, is a crime." When his lines of questioning were denied, Cushing asked, "May I ask about justice or is there no place for that in this court room?" He was cited for contempt, and Clams disrupted the court. Despite the success of their activist stance, the Clams turned their next and most heavily attended event into a peaceful alternative energy fair. Perhaps as many as twenty thousand people showed up. Nevertheless in 1979, after the nuclear accident at Three Mile Island, the Clams produced another demonstration at Seabrook in which five hundred people were arrested. Through the eighties and nineties the Clams continued their protests, but largely without the mass arrests of the 1970s.

However, all during the seventies and early eighties Seabrook was afflicted with more problems than simply the hearings and the protesters. The worst problem of all—exacerbated by delays—was the soaring cost of the project. Because the technology was changing so rapidly, no one at first could forecast what the cost of the two proposed reactors might be. What one spokesman for the New Hampshire Public Service Commission did predict, no doubt to his everlasting regret, was that the plant would produce "electricity too cheap to meter." In fact, from the first, the costs of building the Seabrook Nuclear Power Station were exorbitant. In 1972, when the project began, the company had about $400 million in total assets, and by the summer of 1978 the estimated cost to Public Service of New Hampshire for Seabrook Station was $600 million. The General Court passed a bill forbidding Public Service to pass along costs of construction to its customers before the plant was producing power. Governor Thomson's veto of the bill became an important campaign issue and helped the Democratic candidate, Hugh Gallen, upset the Republican incumbent. In May of 1979, the General Court again passed the bill, and Governor Gallen signed it.

There were also endless delays in construction. The design of the project was modified more times than one can count. In 1983 alone the number of undocumented changes rose to 18,000. There were accusations of astonishingly shoddy workmanship. Management had had no experience with nuclear reactors and seemed not to have been able to oversee the construction adequately. Governor John Sununu, a staunch supporter of the project and a sophisticated manager himself, urged Public Service of New Hampshire to hire a few dozen senior managers experienced with building nuclear reactors and running nuclear power plants. There may or may not have been an unspoken threat to remove his support for the project if his advice went unheeded. In any case, the advice wasn't ignored. Public Service of New Hampshire revitalized its management staff with people experienced in handling nuclear power stations.

While the meter was ticking, contentious hearings went on in Massachusetts and New Hampshire through the 1980s and into the early 1990s. The frightening accident at the power plant at Three Mile Island, Pennsylvania, in 1979 and the disaster at Chernobyl in 1986 produced results that seven years of hearings had failed to produce. They caused the Nuclear Regulatory Agency and the Environmental Protection Agency to take another look at nuclear power. The agencies issued a new requirement: that every nuclear facility present a plan for an evacuation of people in the region surrounding it. The area included part or all of eleven towns in New Hampshire and three in Massachusetts, and the beaches on New Hampshire's tiny coast line that are heavily populated in the summertime.

Opponents of Seabrook saw this as a new opportunity to shut down the plant for good. Massachusetts Governor Michael Dukakis declared it impossible to evacuate the Massachusetts towns safely and refused to create a plan. In New Hampshire home rule prevailed on this issue—some town councils made evacuation plans with the police and firefighters and even went through the exercise of simulating an evacuation. Some towns refused to cooperate. Evacuation exercises, they maintained, were futile and hypocritical and led to a false sense of security. In some towns the police chief and the council were split on the issue, and heated debates within the town went on for months.

With costs soaring, utilities in Vermont and Maine put their shares up for sale. Public Service of New Hampshire borrowed money to sustain Seabrook, but construction slowed as funds dried up. One of the two original reactors was mothballed when it was half-completed. Not surprisingly, in January of 1988, when the price tag hit something over $4.5 billion, Public Service of New Hampshire, chief owner of Seabrook, went bankrupt. Everything had mitigated against the project: oil prices, interest rates, construction costs, schedule delays, and nuclear accidents, not to mention the ongoing protests, new regulations, and design and construction flaws. Public Service of New Hampshire filed for Chapter 11 bankruptcy, under which it could restructure itself and continue to do business while it negotiated with its creditors about its debts.

The financial crisis made the public more jittery than ever that power rates would continue going up and up. The fight became nastier. Public utilities from Vermont, Maine, and Connecticut joined the chorus. Articles in state and national newspapers were filled with mention of agencies old and new—such as the Campaign for Ratepayers Rights, the Rural Electrification Agency, the Vermont Public Service Department—that represented one or more interests in the controversy. Pictures of demonstrations and arrests appeared on the nightly tele vision news. Citizens of all stripes leapt into the fray citing any matter they could think of that would stop the project. The hearings became more and more unruly. Federal agencies overseeing the project had become a chief object of people's wrath. Though many intervenors limited their objections to the Seabrook Power Station in particular, others protested against all nuclear power, and some, like the Clams, protested against state and federal governments in general. One witness protested the "steamroller" of federal power that subverted local control and pressed people to submit to "totalitarian forms." Others sang songs, some read from the Book of Revelation, and yet others masqueraded as Indian sages and ranted against white man's dangerous technology. Both sides accused each other of deliberately causing delays.

Though experts continued to testify in Concord and Boston on everything from disposal of nuclear waste to safety of groundwater, after Three Mile Island and Chernobyl the sticking point became the problem of evacuation. At first Public Service of New Hampshire insisted that emergency evacuation procedures were the responsibility of the state. Then, when Massachusetts refused to outline emergency measures for its towns, the company promised to do so.

The wrangling went on until the reactor was capable of its first low-power test in 1989. The test was the occasion for a revival of the kind of massive civil disobedience that had marked the protests of the 1970s. There was loud music and antinuclear rhetoric, groups from the old Clamshell Alliance, signs, and banners in the sky. Guy Chichester appeared on National Public Radio in support of grass-roots control of energy policy. And, of course, there were numerous arrests. But the protest had a tame, mainstream ambiance. There was a schedule that almost everybody followed. Ben and Jerry's gave away free ice cream and yoghurt, and the music was as much urban rap as country. The owners of the plant, who had overcome gigantic legal, political, and regulatory obstacles, were not deterred by one more rally.

It was around this time that the state government in Concord pointed out an absurdity in the towns' noncooperation. They persuaded the Nuclear Regulatory Agency and the Environmental Protection Agency that whether the uncooperative town councils, police, and firefighters in New Hampshire and Massachusetts went through the evacuation exercises or not, they would of necessity respond to an actual emergency. Those emergency responses were simulated more or less convincingly on a computer—at least to the official satisfaction of the NRA and the EPA, which allowed Seabrook Station to begin operation.

Finally, at astronomical cost in money and discord, Seabrook I began operating in 1991. The project had cost nearly $6 billion, the construction had taken sixteen years, and the quarrels within towns, between towns, between towns and state government, towns and federal agencies, and between New Hampshire and Massachusetts continued for nearly twenty years.

Ironically, the power plant that promised to provide cheap electricity for consumers not only left a wake of political damage but also drove up the price of electricity. Consumers, especially industries that rely heavily on public power, were upset. In August of 1995 they, along with private consumers and several entrepreneurs, proposed to start new utility ventures in the state that would compete with the costly power provided by Seabrook. Whether such an unprecedented change in the structure of utilities in the state is ever implemented or not, it testifies once again to the seriousness of the hydra-headed problem of providing affordable energy for the people and industries of the state.

A Slow but Reassuring Recovery

In 1991 and 1992, the dismal headlines and statistics about the condition of New Hampshire's economy distracted many people from the opening of Seabrook. Layoffs, unemployment, bankruptcies, vacant condominiums, and general retrenchment haunted the state. Few people could have believed that by 1995 the economic slump would be largely over. Without much help from anybody, least of all from the banking industry, which had done little to stop the collapse in the first place, and with the federal government still threatening to close Portsmouth Naval Yard, New Hampshire pulled itself out of recession. Unemployment peaked in the state in 1992 at 7.5 percent. By mid-1995 it was down to 4 percent. Even in the southern tier, where military high-tech had ratcheted the economy to dizzying heights and dropped it to gloomy depths, unemployment fell to under 5 percent. Recovery was slow, but steady. Some economists saw the skyrocketing economy of the eighties as an anomaly and the recovery as a more familiar, slow and predictable pattern of economic development in the state. Perhaps the best indication of this recovery is that in 1995 *Money Magazine* placed Salem, New Hampshire, in seventh place on its list of Best Places to Live in the United States—the same list that had featured Nashua as the best place in 1988. The magazine credited small businesses with sparking the economic recovery. Nothing has filled the void left by the defense contracts, but small high-tech industries remain vigorous. Industries such as Digital Equipment and Cabletron, as well as many small manufacturers, have flourished in the state just as Amoskeag did in the nineteenth century. Some of these industries have occupied the long-vacant mills along the Merrimack, and many of them represent the cutting edge of industry of the last years of the twentieth century, just as Amoskeag was the high-tech industry of the nineteenth.

POLLSTERS, POLITICOS, AND NORTHERN NEW ENGLAND POLITICS

While the State of New Hampshire struggled through the economic slump of the eighties along with the rest of the region and much of the nation, its governors enjoyed remarkable success and popularity. Their steady commitment to fiscal restraint, rejection of a broad-based income tax, and continued promotion of the state's entrepreneurial advantages earned them national attention, and nowhere more consistently than in the glare of presidential primary politics. It certainly can be argued that the state's debates and practices and solutions in the late eighties and early nineties have mirrored the national debate about fiscal responsibility and restraint.

From 1983 to 1989 John H. Sununu, once called the "nuclear theologist" by his opponents, focused the state's attention again, as his predecessors had in the seventies, on the energy dependence required by its long winters, regardless of whether the economy experienced boom or bust. Even as Sununu promoted the value of "clean" nuclear energy, the citizens of Hillsborough (fast becoming the most populous county in the state) marshaled their energies to oppose the federal Nuclear Regulatory Agency's inclusion of Hillsborough as a site for a nuclear waste depository. By the time a grateful President George Bush invited Governor Sununu to become his White House Chief of Staff, the state's economic problems (and some of Sununu's solutions) came under closer scrutiny, and the discoveries were not encouraging. In the mid-eighties the average price of a family home had reached $140,000, and while condominium development and second-home building starts were strong, the state could not offset the federal government funding cutbacks. New Hampshire faced budget deficits and shortfalls as the economy spiraled downward. John Sununu's tenure in the White House kept New Hampshire's politics and concerns in national newspapers even as his flamboyant use of government perks caused President Bush to replace him.

In 1989 Judd Gregg of Greenfield, well-schooled in the governance of New Hampshire by his father Hugh Gregg's example, entered the gubernatorial office, strengthening the state's commitment to fiscal restraint as the region continued to be jolted by economic downturns. Gregg's broad and deep support in the state's Republican party and his success as a trusted fiscal conservative made him a natural candidate to run for the U.S. Senate when Warren Rudman after twelve years decided to leave the Senate. Though the state lost a popular governor, on the Capitol Hill of the mid-nineties Judd Gregg's voice and perspective are prominent and his leadership persuasive.

In 1991 Steve Merrill, who like Judd Gregg had been the state's Attorney General, became governor. Under him, in the wake of the 1994 mid-term national election, New Hampshire became the "most Republican" state in the nation. As governor he can be expected to continue in the fiscal footsteps of his immediate predecessors.

New Hampshire's governor, is subject to biennial reelection; but he (or she) is backed by the support and advice of the influential but little-known governor's council, the last such body in the United States. The governor thus remains the powerful voice for state policy, because the state's large and sometimes unwieldy independent citizen legislature cannot formulate so clear a message.

The structure of the state government supports the development of interest group politics. While the members of the large General Court are earnest and hardworking, they have no real office space, no staff, and in fact receive their mail in boxes attached to their legislative seats. A small in-house House Committee Research Office provides assistance but can hardly be relied on for extensive background material on issues facing the General Court. Lobbyists, one for each representative, supplement that material. Two powerful forces keep the lobbyists' influence in check: Since 1909, "sunshine laws" have required lobbyists to register with the Secretary of State and report their expenditures; and the watchdog *Union Leader* monitors their records carefully. The influence of interest groups is thus carried on in the light of public scrutiny. In the 1990s, on average, two hundred lobbying interests pay the $50 registration fee to conduct their business. By far the largest number of lobbyists press issues related to economic growth and business development, with those for banking and financial services, insurance interests, and public utilities following behind. Still, lobbyists mostly conduct their business on a part-time basis and, according to current statistics, barely 13 percent earn $20,000 or more per year for providing information in the characteristically informal legislative setting.

At least one nonpartisan political action group based in Concord is nationally prominent and takes its name from the state capital. The Concord Coalition, founded by former New Hampshire Senator Warren B. Rudman and Massachusetts Senator Paul E. Tsongas, describes itself as "a grassroots movement to eliminate the deficit and bring entitlements down to a level that's fair to all generations." The coalition, with chapters in fifty states, promises to encourage and support elected public officials who work for deficit reduction.

FIRST IN THE NATION

Every four years the nation's pollsters, politicos, and presidential aspirants turn to New Hampshire for endless breakfast, lunch, and dinner meetings, moose sightings, and parking lot handshakes in pursuit of the country's highest office. The trailing press examines the candidates' every move, but they, like the politicians, study the voters as well. New Hampshire's hold on the "first in the nation" primary meets regular challenges, as yet unsuccessful. History and precedent aside, how does a northern New England state, fortieth in population in the country, a state controlling only four electoral votes, continue to command so much attention? First of all it is small—an ideal laboratory for studying the attitudes of a high-polling populace. What sort of discontents or complaints might a politician of the 1990s expect to encounter in a state with one of the lowest unemployment rates in New England and thirtieth in the country? At least some of the reasons attach to ideas and attitudes established in the state's evolution. New Hampshire's constitution supports values of moderation, industry, and frugality, and its system of governance has always suspected central authority and leaned toward citizen politics. The people of New Hampshire like to talk about government, they like to hear about government, and they like to know who they vote for. They consider themselves savvy amateur politicians and pretty good judges of those who would be President. Aspirants must work hard for this advice, however. Large-scale, glitzy ad campaigns have an effect on the voters but are no substitute for pressing the flesh, looking a potential voter in the eye, and bracing for tough questions. Candidates' ambitions sometimes flourish here, as Jimmy Carter's did in 1976, or founder, as Gary Hart's did in 1988. News media follow almost every appearance by national politicians in New Hampshire, and officials can find themselves making policy under public questioning by citizens of the state. In the summer of 1995 a sitting President Bill Clinton and Speaker of the House of Representatives Newt Gingrich found at a senior citizen's barbecue, for instance, that when a questioner asked about party reform, not only did he expect a direct answer, but he expected several months later to see the answer implemented by more than talk.

New Hampshire imposes its own quirky style on presidential politics. In recent years, candidates have been invited to appear at one unusual political breakfast called "Politics & Eggs." At the breakfasts, held in a Bedford barn and organized and sponsored by a steering committee comprised of influential business and political leaders of the state, good humor and hard questions are the order of the day. Throughout the primary season candidates are invited to address the group, which declares itself neutral at the beginning of the season. The group's motto features a "Great Politics & Egg Seal" showing a golden egg with a crack down the side and the White House emerging from a hole in the top of the egg.

While local citizens enjoy the attention the national press and media have attached to our primary, credibility accrues to the primary because since the 1950s the sagacious voters of New Hampshire have

President Clinton and Speaker of the House Newt Gingrich
at a senior citizens' barbecue in Claremont, summer 1995.
Photograph by Geoff Hansen, © Valley News, 1995.

picked electable candidates. No candidate of either party who lost in the New Hampshire primary has succeeded in winning the presidency, while the President who was elected has always been either the Democratic or Republican candidate who won his party's top position in the New Hampshire primary. It is worth noting that in 1992, in a slight exception to this precedent, Senator Paul Tsongas of Massachusetts won the Democratic primary over Arkansas Governor Bill Clinton; however, shortly thereafter Tsongas withdrew his candidacy and Bill Clinton went on to win the nomination of his party and election to the presidency. It can certainly be argued once again that the national media attention Clinton received in that close contest with Tsongas provided the kind of exposure and opportunity for scrutiny that voters translate as "electability." New Hampshire attorney and historian Richard Upton agrees with the late historian Theodore H. White, who asserted in 1982 that the state's primary, by permitting a direct popular vote for presidential candidates, had revolutionized the process of nominating candidates and marked "a farewell to an American political system approaching its obsolescence."

STAYING THE COURSE—AT WHAT PRICE?

As New Hampshire enters the complex economic realities of the twenty-first century, how do its citizens and politicians chart a steady course through the crosscurrents that have molded its history from the beginning? How does a state deeply rooted in a self-sufficient approach to government and life plan for a world of FAX machines and Internet connections? This new world-shrinking technology allows newcomers to come share in the benefits of what Jeremy Belknap has called the state's "pure and salubrious air" and its low taxes.

What will have to change and what will have to stay the same? R. Kelly Myers, director of the University of New Hampshire Survey Center, estimates that roughly 75,000 New Hampshire residents commute to work in Massachusetts, a state with a very different political and economic culture. Yet the emigres from "Taxachusetts" vote as conservatively as the Granite State's natives, leading Myers to comment in the "New Hampshire Weekly" section of the *Boston Sunday Globe* in 1995 that the "New Hampshire political traditions and New Hampshire political culture seem to assimilate others rather than adapt to the influence of outsiders." Sometime in the mid-1970s, according to comparative U.S. Census statistics, people from outside the state finally outnumbered the natives. In 1970, 55.1 percent of the state's residents had been born here. The new percentage from the 1990 census had fallen to 45.9. Drawn by jobs, open spaces, low crime rates—the good life—new residents soon become more conservative voters.

Even as the issues reemerge in election after election, the elected officials of the state and the state's leading newspaper continue to resist changes in the tax structure. Perhaps nowhere are the results of this refusal to increase tax revenues more visible than in the matter of how the state does and does not assist in funding primary, middle school, and secondary education in the local communities and regional school systems around the state. Funding of education has long been considered a local responsibility, with the state theoretically providing "foundation aid," on which community budgets have been built. In 1986 guidelines for the distribution of foundation aid were revised to allow poorer districts to receive more aid than other tax-rich districts. Under this plan communities would receive 8 percent of their budgets in foundation aid.

For at least one school district the burden of raising money for education solely from local property taxes became intolerable, and in 1993 the Claremont, New Hampshire, School District filed a lawsuit against the governor and the state in order to highlight the problem and press for solutions. The plaintiffs in the case had originally filed a petition with the State Superior Court for injunctive relief from the state and, when the petition was dismissed "for failure to state a claim upon which relief could be granted," returned with an appeal. In their appeal, the five "property-poor" school districts, five school children, and five tax-payers (one from each of the school districts) agreed that the system by which the state financed education violated the New Hampshire Constitution on six counts. In their appeal to the Supreme Court of New Hampshire, they wrote that the state fails to spread educational opportunities equitably among its students and unconstitutionally restrains state aid to public education by capping state assistance at 8 percent. They went on to say that the state school finance system and the laws governing state aid to education deny plaintiffs equal protection. Finally they contended that heavy reliance on property taxes to finance New Hampshire public schools results in an unreasonable, disproportionate, and burdensome tax in violation of the State Constitution.

Concerning education, the New Hampshire Constitution adopted in 1784 originally stated:

> Knowledge and learning, generally diffused through a community, being essential to the preservation of a free government; and spreading the opportunities and advantages of education through the various parts of the country, being highly conducive to promote this end; it shall be the duty of the legislators and magistrates, in all future periods of this government, *to cherish* the interest of literature and the sciences, and all seminaries and public schools, *to encourage* private and public institutions, rewards, and immunities for the promotion of agriculture, arts, sciences, commerce, trades, manufacturers and natural history of the country; *to countenance and inculcate* the principles of humanity and general benevolence, public and private charity, industry and economy, honesty and punctuality, sincerity, sobriety, and all social affections, and generous sentiments, among the people. [Italics added.]

That language has been amended twice: in 1877 to prohibit money raised by taxation from being used by religious schools, and again in 1903 to prevent control of education by corporations and monopolies.

Since its adoption, questions about the state's responsibility to provide significant support for education have centered particularly on the italicized words of the document. Did the language indicate a duty or an aspiration, plaintiffs and others have asked? Deliberations on the Claremont suit failed to produce a clear victory for the plaintiffs since the State Superior Court remanded the suit back to the lower courts. More recently, when the news of the federal government's funding support and goal-setting guidelines known as Goals 2000 reached New Hampshire, Governor Merrill in 1995 left to the State Board of Education the decision whether or not to accept the $9 million offer of support to each state. Fear of federal meddling inspired the Board to respond with a definitive "no." Some say that a home school movement may become more visible in the state; others point to the state's excellent private schools, which provide alternatives and incentives to excellence. Still others continue to object to the inequities attending disparities in quality of education between property-rich and property-poor communities.

In the late 1990s, New Hampshire's elected officials, from its governor to its citizen legislature to its local officials, along with its homogeneous citizenry remain fiercely attached to the political philosophy of the state's motto, "Live Free or Die." With the tap of a key on a computer terminal keyboard or the click of a nearby "mouse," any individual or company in the United States or abroad may be invited to explore the advantages of living in New Hampshire, "The Entrepreneurial State," on "New Hampshire Access Internet." Attractive full-color screens, charts, tables, narratives, and enthusiastic bulleted lists describe and applaud the state's advantageous lifestyle and business climate. New Hampshire, says the computer screen, is a place that, with a "mix of mountains and rural charm . . . comfortable modern cities and economic stability," has something for everyone. "Its quality of life saw it recently voted the most livable and healthiest of the 50 states. Robert Frost, in the poem 'New Hampshire,' called the Granite State 'a restful state' with a 'touch of gold,'" a place with "one each of everything as in a show-case."

Perhaps we could send a message to that website from Jeremy Belknap, the state's first historian, who concludes his *History of New Hampshire* with this vision:

> Were I to form a vision of a happy society, it would be a town consisting of a due mixture of hills, valleys, streams of water: The land well fenced and cultivated, the roads and bridges in good repair; a decent inn for the refreshment of travellers,

and for public entertainments: The inhabitants mostly husband-men; their wives and daughters domestic manufacturers; a suitable proportion of handicraft workmen and two or three traders; a physician and lawyer, each of whom should have a farm for his support. A clergyman of any denomination, which should be agreeable to the majority, a man of good understanding, of a candid disposition and exemplary morals; not a metaphysical, nor a polemic, but a serious and practical preacher. A school master who should understand his business and teach his pupils to govern themselves. A social library, annually increasing, and under good regulation.

A club of sensible men, seeking mutual improvement. A decent musical society. No intriguing politician, horse jockey, gambler or sot; but all such characters treated with contempt. Such a situation may be considered as the most favourable to social happiness of any which this world can afford. (Vol. 3, p. 251)

Two hundred years after Belknap wrote, the Governor's Commission on New Hampshire in the 21st Century has encouraged citizen groups to study the strengths and weaknesses of their towns and establish goals for development into the next century. With broad participation by the citizens of the towns, the Commission hopes to coordinate the communities' specific social and economic needs with the natural resources and landscape. Though we are a long way from Jeremy Belknap's imaginings, New Hampshire still struggles to construct a vision of a happy society that harmonizes our desire for economic growth with many of his ideals.

NOTES FOR CHAPTER TEN

The New Hampshire Historical Society and the Society for the Protection of New Hampshire Forests published a major wide-ranging collection of essays, *At What Cost? Shaping the Land We Call New Hampshire: A Land Use History* (1992), edited by Richard Ober, exploring historical, artistic, economic, and environmental aspects of the use of land in New Hampshire.

The Seabrook controversy was extensively covered by the *Manchester Union Leader* from 1972 through 1991 when Seabrook I went on line. The *Boston Globe* and the *New York Times* also covered the story. Henry F. Bedford has exhaustively researched all the thousands of pages of testimony as well as the political and economic factors involved for his book *Seabrook Station: Citizen Politics and Nuclear Power*, published in 1990 by the University of Massachusetts Press, Amherst.

The *Federal Reserve Bank of Boston Regional Review* provides analytical essays on all aspects of economic developments in New England. It offers some particularly interesting insights into the boom and bust and revival of New Hampshire's economy in the 1980s and 1990s. The *New Hampshire Business Review Book of Lists 1995* (Dec. 23, 1994, vol. 16, no. 26), sponsored by the Shawmut Bank, provides useful statistics and revealing rankings of industries.

For developments in specific industries we have used J. D. Kline's *Impacts of the Dairy Buyout on the Colebrook Region* (University of New Hampshire 1988) and John R. McKernan, Jr.'s *Impact on the Maine/New Hampshire Seacoast Economy of Closing Portsmouth Naval Shipyard*, 1992. Special thanks to Dennis Delay, Alice Pearce, and Bruce Bennett, who were helpful in providing us with vital and current information.

A student of New Hampshire politics, just as the New Hampshire voter, learns much about the political waters from the print and electronic media, but must of course filter that information carefully. Ronald J. Hrebenar and Clive S. Thomas' *Interest Group Politics in the Northeastern States* (Pennsylvania State University Press, 1993) is a very useful study with regional implications. For anedotal and up-close observations on the political scene former governor Hugh Gregg's two books *The Candidates: See How They Run* (Peter Randall, 1990) and *A Tall State Revisited: A Republican Perspective* (Resources of New Hampshire, Inc., 1993) are useful sources. Historian Charles Clark's paper for the Business and Industry Association, "The Future of Tax Policy in New Hampshire," provided useful background material.

Once again Professor Richard Winters of Dartmouth College steered us to important sources of information on both the politics and economy of the state.

Bibliographic Notes

NOTES FOR CHAPTERS ONE AND TWO

Every history of New Hampshire begins with Jeremy Belknap's three-volume history of 1792 (Jeremy Belknap, *The History of New Hampshire*, Boston, 1792, reprinted in various editions). Belknap, who not only lived through, but participated in many of, the events at the time of the Revolution and after, writes an engaging, colorful, and detailed description of the political and natural history of the state to that time. Two modern histories of the colonial period — Charles E. Clark's *The Eastern Frontier: The Settlement of Northern New England: 1610-1768*, New York, 1970 and Jere Daniell, *Colonial New Hampshire A History*, New York, 1981 — are extensively researched, highly readable sources on which we have relied heavily.

For information on Portsmouth's maritime economy and timber trade, most useful sources and ones used extensively in this chapter are: Robert H. Albion, *Forest and Sea Power: The Timber Problem of the Royal Navy: 1652-1862*, Cambridge, Mass., 1926; William G. Saltonstall, *Ports of the Piscataqua*, Cambridge, 1941; Joseph J. Malone, *Pine Trees and Politics: The Naval Stores and Forest Policy in Colonial New England 1691-1775*, Seattle, 1964; Charles F. Carroll, *The Timber Economy of Puritan New England*, Providence, 1973; David E. VanDeventer, *The Emergence of Provincial New Hampshire: 1623-1741*, Baltimore, 1976; and James L. Garvin, "Portsmouth and the Piscataqua: Social History and Material Culture," *Historical New Hampshire* 26(Summer 1971): 3-48.

Other informative books and articles concerning this early period in the state's history include: Nathaniel Adams, *Annals of Portsmouth*, Portsmouth, 1825; Charles W. Brewster, *Rambles about Portsmouth*, New Hampshire, 1869; William Cronon, *Changes in the Land, Indians, Colonists, and the Ecology of New England*, New York, 1983. Olive Tardiff, *They Paved the Way*, New Hampshire, 1980.

Other general references and histories used in these chapters and throughout the book include: John D. Haskell, Jr. and T. D. Seymour Bassett, *New Hampshire A Bibliography of Its History*, Boston, 1979; R. Stuart Wallace, ed. *Historical New Hampshire* (Concord, N.H., quarterly, 1944-); United States Works Progress Administration, Federal Writers' Project, *New Hampshire: A Guide to the Granite State, 1938*; Ronald and Grace Jager, *New Hampshire An Illustrated History of the Granite State*, California, 1983; Elizabeth Forbes and Elting E. Morison, *New Hampshire A Bicentennial History*, New York, 1976; William E. Taylor, ed. *Readings in New Hampshire and New England History*, New York, 1971; and James Duane Squires, *The Granite State of the United States*, 4 vols., New York, 1956.

Chapter 1
1 Clark, 4.
2 Saltonstall, 8.
3 Saltonstall, 9.
4 Saltonstall, 9.
5 Clark, 13.
6 Daniell, *Colonial History*, 24-25.
7 Daniell, *Colonial History*, 31.
8 Belknap, vol. 3, 113-119.
9 Belknap, vol. 3, 159.
10 Balknap, vol. 3, 56.

Chapter 2
11 Daniell, *Colonial History*, 217.
12 Belknap, vol. 1, 229.
13 Belknap, vol. 1, 223n
14 Daniell, *Colonial History*,135.
15 Belknap, vol. 1, 254.
16 Belknap, vol. 1, 250.
17 Clark, 309.
18 Clark, 298.
19 Clark, 315.
20 Daniell, *Colonial History*, 214.
21 Belknap, vol. 1, 272-280 passim.
22 Belknap, vol. 1, 324.
23 Daniell, *Colonial History*, 210.
24 Upton, 7.
25 Daniell, *Colonial History*, 231.
26 Daniell, *Readings*, 44-45.

NOTES FOR CHAPTER THREE

We relied on Jere Daniell, *Experiment in Republicanism, New Hampshire Politics and the American Revolution, 1741-1794*, Cambridge, Massachusetts, 1970, for a scholarly account of this period. Belknap's *History of New Hampshire*, Charles Clark's *The Eastern Frontier*, and Jere Daniell's *Colonial New Hampshire* were still useful for chapter 3. Richard Francis Upton, *Revolutionary New Hampshire, An Account of the Social and Political Forces Underlying the Transition from Royal Province to American Commonwealth*, Hanover, New Hampshire, 1971, is a detailed account of the Revolution in the state. Leon W. Anderson, *To This Day, the 300 years of the New Hampshire Legislature*, Canaan, New Hampshire, 1981, gives an account of the history of the state from the perspective of the General Court which we used throughout this book. Lynn Warren Turner, *The Ninth State, New Hampshire's Formative Years*, Chapel Hill, 1983, also tells something about the Revolution as it affected the state.

William G. Saltonstall, *Ports of Piscataqua*, Cambridge, Massachusetts, 1941, is a general account of the development of the ports of the Piscataqua while John P. Adams, *Drowned Valley, the Piscataqua River Basin*, Hanover, 1976, is an illustrated account of that history. David E. Van Deventer, *The Emergence of Provincial New Hampshire, 1623-1741*, Baltimore, 1976, continues to be a useful source. John P. Adams, *The Piscataqua River Gundalow*, Durham, New Hampshire, 1982, and Richard Elliot Winslow, *The Piscataqua Gundalow: Workhorse for a Tidal Basin Empire* provide vivid pictures of the gundalow's contribution to the state's development.

Caleb Stark, *Memoir and Official Correspondence of General John Stark, with notices of several other officers of the Revolution also, a biography of Captain Phinehas Stevens, and of Colonel Robert Rogers*, Concord, 1860, is the source for information about John Stark and Robert Rogers.

Karen Andresen, "A Return to Legitimacy," *Historical New Hampshire* 21 (Winter 1976):155-164; Deborah Downs, "The New Hampshire Constitution of 1776: Weathervane of Conservativism," *Historical New Hampshire* 23 (Spring 1967):164-175; and John K. Gemmill, "The Problems of Power: New Hampshire Government during the Revolution," *Historical New Hampshire* 23 (Spring 1967):27-28 are interesting discussions of the problems of governing the state during the Revolution.

1 Daniell, *Experiment*, 109.
2 Anderson, 69.
3 Upton, 45.
4 Anderson, 71.
5 Stark, 14.

6 Stark, 19.
7 Stark, 60.
8 Saltonstall, 108-111.
9 Adams, 143.
10 Belknap, vol. 1, 394-395.
11 Anderson, 74.
12 Daniell, *Experiment*, 165.
13 Daniell, *Experiment*, 169.
14 Turner, 17.

NOTES FOR CHAPTER FOUR

The discussion of farming continues to draw on Jeremy Belknap's contemporary accounts of colonial farming and on the discussions of agricultural economy in Daniell, Clark, and Turner. Percy Wells Bidwell and John T. Falconer, *History of Agriculture in the Northern United States 1620-1860*, Washington, 1925; Howard S. Russell, *A Long Deep Furrow, Three Centuries of Farming in New England*, Hanover, 1982; and *The Hill Country of Northern New England, Its Social and Economic History 1790-1930*, New York, 1967 are the most comprehensive treatments of the history of farming in New Hampshire and the New England region and all three are used extensively in this chapter.

A recent work, *Changes in the Land, Indians, Colonists, and the Ecology of New England* by William Cronon (New York, 1983) addresses the issues of land use and ecology in the prespective of recent scientific and historical research and provides an indispensible point of view. In the same way, Roderick Nash's *Wilderness and the American Mind*, New Haven, 1982, gives essential background not only for an understanding of the colonist's view of the wilderness they encountered, but also for the formation of the consciousness of conservation. Claire S. Haughton, *Green Immigrants, The Plants that Transformed America*, New York, 1978, is a fascinating account of the plants introduced into American horticulture. Important new research and understanding of women's lives in the colonial period may be found in Laurel Thatcher Ulrich's *Good Wives: Image and Reality in the Lives of Women in Northern New England 1650-1750*, New York, 1980.

Additional sources for material on farming in New Hampshire may be found in: Donald Hall, *String too Short to be Saved*, Boston, 1979, and *Kicking the Leaves*, New York, 1978; Elmer Hunt Munson, *New Hampshire's Town Names and Whence They Came*, New Hampshire, 1920; *Portrait of a Hill Town*, Ronald Jager and Grace Jager, New Hampshire, 1977 (an excellent example of a local history, in this case of Washington, N.H.); and Norman W. Smith, "A Mature Frontier, the New Hampshire Economy, 1790-1850,"

Historical New Hampshire 24 (Fall 1969): 3-19. Thomas Coffin's diaries are the subject of an article by Robert H. George, "Life on a New Hampshire Farm, 1825-1835," *Historical New Hampshire* 22 (Winter 1967): 3-17. For information on railroads and their impact on the agrarian economy, E. C. Kirkland, *Men, Cities, and Transportation: A Study in New England 1820-1900*, 2 vols., Cambridge, 1948, is an excellent source.

1 Ulrich, 172.
2 Hall, *Kicking the Leaves*, 47.
3 George, HNH, 16.
4 Kirkland, 165.
5 Emerson, "Self Reliance," *Essays*, 75.

Notes for Chapter Five

Generally speaking the literature on the nineteenth century of New Hampshire's history is sparse and specialized. No one has written a comprehensive and scholarly history of the century on the order of Daniell and Clark's treatments of the colonial period. Daniell's *Experiment in Republicanism* is a vital scholarly source for chapter 5. Turner's *The Ninth State* is important and covers this period in some detail. Upton's *Revolutionary New Hampshire* and Anderson's *To This Day* also provided material for this chapter. Saltonstall's *Ports of the Piscataqua* was also useful. Charles G. Douglas III, "Judicial Review and the Separation of Powers under the New Hampshire Constitution of 1776 and 1784," *Historical New Hampshire* 21 (Winter 1976):176-191 is an interesting discussion of the problems of the two constitutions.

William A. Robinson, *Jeffersonian Democracy in New England*, New York, 1969, and Donald B. Cole, *Jacksonian Democracy in New Hampshire 1800-1851*, Cambridge, 1970, have provided serious studies of the political developments of the period.

1 Anderson, 92.
2 Turner, 56.
3 Turner, 66-67.
4 Turner, 66.
5 Turner, 72.
6 Turner, 116.
7 Robinson, 36.
8 Turner, 170.

9 Turner, 179.
10 Turner, 180.
11 Turner, 181.
12 Robinson, 53.

NOTES FOR CHAPTERS SIX
The most useful sources for political developments in the state from the Revolutionary War to the Civil War are Turner's *The Ninth State*, Robinson's *Jeffersonian Democracy in New England* and Donald Cole's *Jacksonian Democracy in New Hampshire* for the early years of the century.

Maurice Baxter, *One and Inseparable Daniel Webster and the Union*, Cambridge, Massachusetts, 1984, and Richard W. Morin, "Will to resist; The Dartmouth College Case," *Dartmouth College Alumni Magazine*, April 1969, unnumbered, are the sources for our discussion of the Dartmouth College Case.

Roy Franklin Nichols, *Franklin Pierce: Young Hickory of the Granite State*, Philadelphia, 1931, is the best biography of New Hampshire's president of the United States. Richard H. Sewell, *John P. Hale and the Politics of Abolition*, Cambridge, Massachusetts, 1965 contains interesting information on the formation of the Republican party besides giving an excellent account of the life of Hale. Philip M. Marston's article, "Amos Tuck and the Beginning in New Hampshire of the Republican Party," *Historical New Hampshire* 15(November 1960):32-37 also gives an account of the GOP's beginning.

1 Turner, 261.
2 Turner, 271.
3 Turner, 295.
4 Turner, 300.
5 Cole, 37.
6 Robinson, 141.
7 Cole, 169.
8 Cole, 49.
9 Cole, 64-65.
10 Cole, 65.
11 Cole, 75-76.
12 Cole, 117.
13 Cole, 118.
14 Cole, 124-125.
15 Cole, 128.
16 Smith, 462.
17 Sewell, 32.

18 Sewell, 55.
19 Nichols, 136.
20 Cole, 224.
21 Sewell, 73-74.
22 Nichols, 139.
23 Nichols, 521.

NOTES FOR CHAPTER SEVEN

General information on the development of the manufacturing economy in New Hampshire may be found in the general histories of the state: J. Duane Squire's history, *The Granite State of the United States*, and the WPA guide, as well as Daniell, Clark, and Norman Smith (see chapter 4) are useful sources. Thomas Dublin's two books, *Women at Work*, New York, 1979, and *Farm to Factory, Women's Letters, 1830-1860*, New York, 1981 are invaluable and lively accounts of the mill girl culture in northern New England, and many of the letters in the second book are from New Hampshire farm girls. Material for the portrait of the world-famous Amoskeag mills relies heavily on the superb social and economic histories of these mills by Tamara K. Haraven, *Amoskeag, Life and Work in an American Factory-City*, (with Randolph Langenbach), New York, 1978, and *Family Time and Industrial Time*, Cambridge, Mass., 1982. Material on the town of Harrisville may be found in John Borden Armstrong's *Factory Under the Elms: A History of Harrisville, New Hampshire, 1774-1969*, Cambridge, Mass., 1969, another fine example of the particular historical genre, local history.

1 Belknap, vol. 3, 198.
2 Clark, 226-227.

NOTES FOR CHAPTER EIGHT

Leon Burr Richardson, *William E. Chandler, Republican* tells the story of the politics of the railroads as well as the life of William Chandler. Barry A. Macey, "Charles Sanger Mellen: Architect of Transportation Monopoly," *Historical New Hampshire* 26(Winter 1971):2-29 gives an account of the career of Charles Mellen who engineered the railroad monopoly. George Pierce Baker, *The Formation of the New England Railroad System, A Study of Railroad Combinations in the Nineteenth Century*, New York, 1968, tells the history of the growth of the railroads, themselves. Edgar T. Mead, Jr., *Through Covered Bridges to Concord; a recollection of the Concord & Claremont RR (NH)*, Brattleboro, Vermont, 1970, and Edgar T. Mead, Jr., *The Up-Country Line: Boston, Concord & Montreal RR to the New Hampshire lakes and White Mountains*, Brattleboro, Vermont, 1975, are interesting anecdotal accounts of the railroads.

Fredrick W. Kilbourne, *Chronicles of the White Mountains*, Boston, 1916, is the standard work on the White Mountains. C. Francis Belcher, *Logging Railroads of the White Mountains*, Boston, Massachusetts, 1980, and Robert E. Pike, *Tall Trees, Tough Men*, New York, 1967, give vivid accounts of logging in New Hampshire. William Robinson Brown's *Our Forest Heritage: A History of Forestry and Recreation in New Hampshire*, Concord, New Hampshire, 1956, provides useful information on the relationship between conservation and recreation. Gordon B. McKinney, "The Land No One Wanted: An Economic History of Whitefield, New Hampshire," *Historical New Hampshire* 27(Winter 1972):185-209 recounts the interesting development of Whitefield.

1 Anderson, 169.
2 NHHS Newsletter, 1.
3 Brown, 6.
4 Belcher, 131.
5 Belcher, 54.
6 Belcher, 80.
7 Belcher, 128.

NOTES FOR CHAPTER NINE

Material in J. Duane Squire's, *The Granite State of the United States*, continues to be a useful source in this period. For information on the career of John G. Winant the standard and informative source is Bernard Bellush, *He Walked Alone A Biography of John Gilbert Winant*, The Hague, 1968.

Sources for political and economic developments in the twentieth century are found in the work of: Kevin Cash, *Who the Hell Is William Loeb?*, Manchester, N.H., 1975; W. H. Chittenden, A. E. Luloff, and J. P. Marcucci, *Industry in New Hampshire: Changes in the Manufacturing Sector 1970-1978*, Durham, N.H. 1982; Robert E. Craig and Richard F. Winters, "Party Politics in New Hampshire," in *New England Political Parties*, ed. Josephine F. Milburn, William Doyle, Cambridge, Mass., 1983; Philip Guyol, *Democracy Fights: A History of New Hampshire in World War II*, Hanover, N.H., 1951; Information on P.O.W. camp derives from Dr. Allen V.

Koop's, *Stark Decency: German Prisoners of War in a New England Village,* Hanover, N.H., 1988; League of Women Voters, *New Hampshire's Land,* Concord, N.H., 1975; Gordon B. McKinney, "The Politics of Protest: The Labor Reform and Greenback Parties in New Hampshire," *Historical New Hampshire* 36(Summer/ Fall 1981): 149-170; *Made in New Hampshire, A Directory of Manufacturers, Manufactured Products, Exports and Mining,* State of New Hampshire Office of Industrial Development, 1982-83 edition; recent issues of the *New Hampshire Times*; Neal R. Pierce, *The New England States: People, Politics and Power in the Six New England States,* New York, 1976, Eric P. Veblen, *The Manchester Union Leader in New Hampshire Elections,* Hanover, N.H., 1975; "A New Hampshire Statesman," *Granite Monthly* 46(1914):113-115; and *Publick Occurrences*: November 2, 23, 30, 1973; December 7, 14, 21, 1973; January 4, 11, 25, 1974; February 1, 8, 15, 22, 1974 and March 1, 1974.

The best studies of the White Mountains, its social and economic history, and material to which this chapter is indebted include: Peter B. Bulkley, "Horace Fabyan, Founder of the White Mountain Grand Hotel," *Historical New Hampshire* 30(Summer 1975), 53–77; Peter B. Bulkley, "A History of the White Mountain Tourist Industry, 1818–1899," M.A. Thesis, University of New Hampshire, 1958; F. Allen Burt, *The Story of Mount Washington,* Hanover, N.H., 1960; Frederick W. Kilbourne, *Chronicles of the White Mountains,* Boston, 1916; Peter Randall, *Mountain Washington, A Guide and Short History,* Hanover, N.H., 1974; Charles D. Smith, "The Mountain Lover Mourns, Origins of the Movement for a White Mountain National Forest 1880–1903," *The New England Quarterly* 33(March 1960) 37–56; and Paul E. Bruns, *A New Hampshire Everlasting and Unfallen,* Concord, N.H., 1969 and other annual publications of the Society for the Protection of New Hampshire Forests. For information on the history of the skiing indestry see: E. John B. Allen, "The Development of New Hampshire Skiing: 1870s–1940," *Historical New Hampshire* 36(Spring 1981): 1–37.

1 Bellush, 106-107 n.
2 Smith, 206.
3 Belknap, vol. 3, 32.
4 Burt, 29-30.
5 Belcher, 217.
6 Bruns, 8.
7 Burt, 3.
8 *Publick Occurrences,* January 11, 1974, 9.
9 Cash, 401 and corroborated by Dudley Dudley.

Index